VEGETARIAN
CLASSICS

ALSO BY JEANNE LEMLIN

Simple Vegetarian Pleasures

Main-Course Vegetarian Pleasures

Quick Vegetarian Pleasures

Vegetarian Pleasures: A Menu Cookbook

VEGETARIAN CLASSICS

 300 Essential Recipes for
Every Course and Every Meal

JEANNE LEMLIN

HarperCollins*Publishers*

HarperCollins books may be purchased for educational,
business, or sales promotional use. For information please write:
Special Markets Department, HarperCollins Publishers, Inc.,
10 East 53rd Street, New York, NY 10022.

FIRST EDITION

Designed by Joel Avirom

Library of Congress Cataloging-in-Publication Data

Lemlin, Jeanne.

Vegetarian classics: 300 essential recipes for every course and every meal / by Jeanne Lemlin.

p.   cm.

Includes index.

ISBN 0-06-019482-0

1. Vegetarian cookery.   I. Title.

TX837 .L4497   2001

641.5′636—dc21

00-053870

96 97 98 99 00 RRD 10 9 8 7 6 5 4 3 2 1

To my mother, Rita Lemlin,
with love and thanks

―――――――

Contents

ACKNOWLEDGMENTS

A book is built of many layers, from the initial idea that struggles to take shape to the final bound copy. Along the way many have helped this cookbook come into being, and I am grateful to all who, in their own ways, have lent a hand.

First and foremost, a special thanks to my editor, Susan Friedland, her assistant, Vanessa Stich, and all the staff at HarperCollins who have supported and encouraged me; and to both my agent, Susan Lescher, and my friend and colleague, Darra Goldstein, who have helped me keep on track and stay true to my vision. Thanks to the following family and friends who inspired me with food tales, discoveries, and suggestions: my mother, Rita Lemlin;

my sister Julianne Lemlin-Dufresne and her husband, Roland Dufresne; my sister Jackie Lemlin; my sisters-in-law Megumi Lemlin and Beth Curtin; my brother-in-law Pete Simigan; and friends Jane Walsh, Billie Chernicoff, Maureen Fox, Gerry Curtin, and Gail McMillan. To Pat White and Becky Couch who were just a phone call away when my computer tormented me with new challenges, thanks for being so helpful; and to the reference staff at the Berkshire Atheneum, thanks for your helpful research and good-natured attitudes.

And finally to my husband, Ed Curtin; son, Daniel; stepdaughter, Susanne, and her boyfriend, Keith Michel, thanks for being the best.

VEGETARIAN CLASSICS

INTRODUCTION

Over the past thirty years or so the United States has come of age in the culinary world. Food and cooking have finally established themselves in our culture, and this interest is strengthening. Trends develop almost as fast as seasons change, and we are continuously being enticed by new, exotic ingredients, the charms of different ethnic cuisines, and the promises of increasingly pleasurable dining experiences. This is true of meat-centered as well as vegetarian cooking. For those of us who have chosen a meatless diet, the allure of fresher and more unusual vegetables, grains and beans from far-off lands, and sensational artisan cheeses have shaped modern vegetarian cooking into a serious cuisine that has been embraced by the mainstream.

Yet for all the progress that has been made toward greater culinary sophistication for vegetarian and non-vegetarian cooking, I sometimes find myself yearning for old-time classic dishes. Many of these have become comfort foods for me, and I enjoy alternating more adventurous menus with tried-and-true favorites that have withstood the test of time. A meatless lasagna bolstered by a garlicky marinara sauce, a thick and hearty lentil soup, vegetarian enchiladas that stick to your ribs, and a vegetable pot pie are just a few exam-ples of dishes that have become staples in vegetarian kitchens over the last thirty years.

It is essential to point out that the concept of "classics" for vegetarians in the United States is not something that would have made much sense twenty-five years ago. Since vegetarian cooking began to take hold in the 1960s, we've needed a few decades for classics to develop. By classics I mean popular meatless dishes that have lingered in the vegetarian repertoire, some of them improvisations of dishes that may originally have included meat.

For example, a mushroom ragu (sauce) has become a favorite vegetarian way to make a meatless tomato sauce for pasta, but a traditional Bolognese ragu is filled with meat. Vegetarians love to use mushrooms as a meat substitute. Chili is another example of a meat-based dish by definition, but vegetarians have been making meatless bean-laden versions for decades. So we're talking about vegetarian classics and not traditional, historically accurate classics that have been in various ethnic cuisines for centuries.

To suit all tastes and moods, and to keep alive traditional favorites that longtime vegetarians, newcomers, and part-time vegetarians will enjoy, here is a collection of old-time classics, updated versions of classics, and a sprinkling of soon-to-be classics that will satisfy adventurous appetites.

A MATTER OF STYLE

As with all areas of cooking, the vegetarian approach to meal planning has gone through many transformations over the last few decades. For many years the primary focus had been to include as much protein in the diet as possible to compensate for the absence of meat that was the main source of protein in an omnivorous diet. The result

was a cuisine that was nutrient-rich but so heavy and bland that vegetarian food developed a bad reputation it is still trying to shake. Casseroles with soy beans, brown rice, and sunflower seeds might top the charts when nutritionally analyzed, but they won't keep eaters satisfied. In the culinary world when duty is substituted for pleasure, boredom and rebellion set in. The reality behind this preoccupation with protein sufficiency has turned out to be far different from what we had been led to believe. Meat traditionally has been associated with wealth and health, and the prevailing wisdom has long been that the more protein one can ingest, the better. We now know this is untrue. Recent studies have shown that we can get too much protein, and an excess of protein robs the bones of calcium and strains the kidneys.

This discovery can certainly help us relax about vegetarian cooking. My conclusion, after keeping up with all the latest health and scientific studies, is that the best approach to vegetarianism is to eat a wide variety of foods, primarily vegetables, beans, grains, and some dairy products in moderation, and to prepare meals that are truly enjoyable to you and your family. A preoccupation with nutrition is counterproductive because it often leads to fatigue and the eventual abandonment of the diet altogether. Learn what foods are nutritious, include a variety of them, and avoid junk food that is highly processed and filled with additives. If you follow these guidelines, you'll have an eating plan that is sound and not overly fussy; in other words, one that is meant for a lifetime, not just a passing phase.

With the heavy burden of nutritional perfection lifted from our shoulders we can create food that is lighter, more spontaneous, and more in keeping with our need for pleasure. Tortellini with Spinach, Garlic, and Smoked Cheese (page 215) is a far cry from Whole Wheat Spaghetti with Tofu and Tomato Sauce (not in this book, thankfully) because the former dish is not only nutritious but it has been created with flavor as the foremost concern. And that has made all the difference.

A DASH OF HISTORY

Vegetarianism has occurred at such an accelerated pace over the last thirty years or so that one could almost conclude that meat-free diets were a phenomenon begun in the 1960s. We know this isn't true, but few people realize how far back the history of vegetarianism extends.

The first solid evidence of flourishing vegetarian communities can be found around 500 B.C. The Jains of India and the followers of Buddha (also in India) and Pythagorus in Greece all concurrently preached nonviolence and vegetarianism.

Around 150 B.C. a sect of Jews known as the Essenes, who were preoccupied with cleanliness because they believed it was an indication of one's inner purity, adopted a vegetarian diet as part of their philosophy. From here on for hundreds of years key historical figures, rather than communities, brought vegetarianism to the forefront. St. Francis of Assisi (born in 1181), Leonardo da Vinci (1452), Percy Bysshe Shelley (1792), Leo Tolstoy (1828), and George Bernard Shaw (1856) were all vegetarians and were vocal about their decisions to shun meat.

In England in the 1700s there were the stirrings of vegetarian movements, but it wasn't until the 1840s that the word "vegetarian" first appeared. A formal secular vegetarian organization was established, the British Vegetarian Society, and attracted members from all over England. Not long afterward it had branches in various parts of the United Kingdom, and there were other unrelated vegetarian groups.

During this same period about forty British immigrants to the United States, led by pastor William Metcalfe of the Bible Christian

Church, started an American vegetarian society. Sylvester Graham, a health enthusiast known for his creation of the graham cracker, became their most ardent and vocal spokesman. Though not as large a movement as the one taking place in England, the United States did have numerous vegetarian societies in the 1800s and could claim some famous advocates. Bronson Alcott (Louisa May Alcott's father) and Dr. John Harvey Kellogg, a prominent Seventh-Day Adventist and the creator of Kellogg's cornflakes, both championed a meat-free diet and drew many followers.

During the first half of the twentieth century the American vegetarian movement dwindled and was virtually silent. But this was all to change with the hippies and anti-war activists in the 1960s. A dedication to "natural" living and health foods and the commitment to nonviolence extending to animals fueled the popularity of the vegetarian diet during this period. Since that modern wave of vegetarianism took hold, there have been no signs of its letting up. It is estimated that there are now more than 20 million vegetarians in the United States (including both "lacto-ovo" vegetarians who abstain from meat but eat eggs and dairy products, and

"vegans" who forgo meat and also exclude eggs and any animal by-products, such as milk, cheese, and honey), and countless others who consider themselves semivegetarians or at least enjoy eating meatless food on a regular basis.

Contemporary vegetarians choose to embrace a meatless diet for the same reasons that have existed throughout history: compassion for animals, the health benefits of a diet based solely on plants and dairy products, and the spiritual benefits of eating "purer" foods. A fourth consideration has recently been added: a concern for the ecological strain on the planet that cattle grazing and other meat-producing activities impose.

So whether you are a vegetarian, semivegetarian, or dedicated meat eater who likes to eat meatless meals a few times a week, you're part of a phenomenon that has waxed and waned throughout history. Abstaining from meat, whether consistently or occasionally, has been an option for centuries. The recipes in this book are intended to make your choice of going meatless not only easy but a source of great culinary pleasure and satisfaction. And these classics are the perfect way to begin and continue the tradition.

BALSAMIC VINEGAR: With so much attention placed on balsamic vinegar and so many choices in the market, it's good to know what the product really is and how to select a good brand. Balsamic vinegar is made from the boiled-down must of Trebbiano grapes. Balsamic vinegar falls into two categories. *Traditional artisan* versions must be aged a minimum of twelve years, are produced in the provinces of Modena and Reggio, and are certified by a consortium that they have been produced according to their strict standards. These vinegars can cost between $40 and $100 a bottle. More accessible and practical for the home cook are *commercial* balsamic vinegars. The challenge, however, is to avoid cheaply made imitations that have a mixture of raw acidity and sweetness. Look for commercial balsamic vinegars produced in Modena or Reggio that don't have caramel coloring added to them.

BARLEY: Pearl barley, readily available in supermarkets, is the best choice for soups and casseroles. It has had its tough husk, bran, and germ removed. The endosperm is what remains. (Whole barley, which is hard to find, just has its husk removed and therefore cooks very slowly.) Barley is a good source of fiber.

BULGUR: Wheat berries, the kernels of the wheat plant, are cooked and crushed to form bulgur. This precooking imparts a nutty flavor and reduces the cooking time. Bulgur is often labeled "cracked wheat," but the two are not identical. Cracked wheat is not precooked and therefore has a faintly raw taste. Bulgur comes in different colors and textures depending on the type of wheat used. Reddish brown bulgur, which is usually coarsely ground, indicates hard American winter wheat. Golden bulgur is Middle Eastern soft wheat, and it is available in different gradations from fine to coarse. For skillet preparations I usually prefer coarse reddish brown bulgur for its nubby texture. For salads, such as tabbouli, I use a coarse or medium-cut golden bulgur for its attractive color and more delicate texture. Fine, presoaked bulgur is a good choice to add to breads. Bulgur is an excellent source of protein, B vitamins, and iron.

BUTTER: Most professional cooks prefer unsalted (sweet) butter for its fresh, delicate flavor and low moisture content, which is an asset when baking. Salted butter (usually marked "lightly salted") is generally not as fresh as unsalted butter because salt extends its shelf life and can mask the altered flavor when butter isn't fresh. Many people wonder when they see unsalted butter as well as salt in a recipe. Unsalted butter is usually chosen for its superior flavor, not because the cook is trying to omit salt from the recipe.

CHEESE: A moderate use of cheese can greatly enliven vegetarian cooking, adding a touch of richness and making meals satisfying for vegetarians and non-vegetarians alike. The key is moderation, however, because cheese is high in fat. The sensible way to cook with cheese is to enjoy it in meals a couple of times a week and then choosing cheeseless, low-fat

dishes for the remaining days. In this way you will not feel deprived of this glorious food, and you can still maintain a healthful diet. Here are some notes on some of the cheeses used in this book. *Italian fontina* has a distinct nutty flavor and firm, smooth texture that can be grated easily. It is a wonderful addition to sandwiches, pizzas, and baked pasta dishes. American versions of fontina lack the rich, buttery quality of imported fontina. *Goat cheeses* (chevres) range from soft, creamy, and mild to hard, shrunken, and strong-flavored. In this book, soft, mild goat cheese is preferred for use as a spread, on pasta, and on pizza. Montrachet is one of the mildest goat cheeses from France, as is Bucheron, which has a more distinct "goaty" flavor. Many similar cheeses are produced in this country, and possibly some at local farms near you. This type of creamy goat cheese has a delightful tang to it, and is lower in fat than cream cheese and most other soft cheeses. *Gorgonzola* is one of the great cheeses of the world. This Italian blue cheese has a lovely mild, pungent flavor that makes it a superb addition to polenta, and the best choice for spreading on crackers and crusty bread. Other blue cheeses such as French Roquefort, English Stilton, and domestic versions can be substituted with good, albeit slightly different results. Before purchas-

A Guide to Ingredients

ing blue cheese, check to see that it is not over-ripe—that it doesn't have brownish outer edges or a faint scent of ammonia (similar to overripe brie). *Monterey Jack with jalapeño peppers,* also known as "pepper jack," contains a sprinkling of red and green chilies that give it some kick. The spicy edge is moderate, so the cheese adds a distinct chili pepper flavor to a dish without overpowering it with hotness. Because it nicely enhances omelets, sandwiches, casseroles, and Mexican tortilla concoctions, I almost always have this cheese on hand. *Parmigiano-Reggiano* is probably the most imitated of cheeses. Parmigiano-Reggiano is not a *type* of Parmesan cheese, it is the *only* Parmesan cheese. This hard, grainy cheese with a golden color and distinctive flavor is made only in the Emilia-Romagna region of Italy according to strict standards. There are many imitations; they can bear the name Parmesan but not Parmigiano-Reggiano. It is an expensive cheese, and I therefore use it sparingly or for special dishes. If you eat a lot of pasta and want to be thrifty, there are some good substitutes available. Do a taste test to compare and then make a note of your favorite. *Smoked cheese* comes in three varieties: smoked Gouda, smoked mozzarella, and smoked Gruyère. You can also find smoked cheddar and smoked provolone, but

they are not as prevalent. Smoked Gouda and mozzarella have the best melting qualities, while smoked Gruyère retains some of its shape when heated and doesn't melt easily. They all have a rich smokiness that imparts an outstanding flavor to sandwiches, pastas, omelets, and cheese spreads.

CHILI PASTE WITH GARLIC: A thick red paste made of ground chilies, garlic, and a little oil, this Chinese concentrate is sold in small jars in most supermarkets and specialty stores. You need only a dab to add an explosion of flavor to Asian stir-fries, marinated noodle dishes, and sauces. It lasts indefinitely when refrigerated, so it's easy to keep on hand to use at a moment's notice.

CHIPOTLE PEPPERS: These smoked, dried jalapeño peppers have become quite popular recently for the rich smoky hotness they lend to dishes. Chipotle peppers are available two ways: either *dried*, to be reconstituted in boiling water, or *canned in adobo sauce*, a piquant tomato sauce that has a deep lingering flavor. These are actually two different varieties. Although both are good, I prefer the reddish black canned chipotle to the tannish brown dried because it has a fruitier flavor. Once a can of chipotles has been opened, the unused contents can be kept in a small plastic container or jar in the refrigerator for up to a few months or frozen in small portions in individual packets. Place a few sheets of plastic wrap (each about 6 × 6 inches) side by side on a baking sheet. Put one chipotle with some sauce on each sheet. Place the baking sheet in the freezer for an hour. When the peppers are hard, wrap the plastic around the chipotles to make a packet. Place the packets in a large plastic bag and freeze them.

You should never handle chipotles or any other hot chili peppers with bare hands because the juices could get transferred to your eyes, should you touch them, and cause intense burning. Either wear rubber gloves or use a knife and fork or 2 knives to mince the chilies without touching them with your fingers.

COUSCOUS: Similar to a grain in appearance and texture, couscous is actually a pasta. It is made by mixing semolina (the hard durum wheat that pasta is made from) with water to form tiny granules. "Cooking" couscous is one of the quickest of tasks in the kitchen. You just pour boiling water or stock over the couscous, cover the pot, and let it sit for 5 minutes. *Israeli (Middle Eastern) couscous*

(sometimes called Mediterranean pearl pasta) has been appearing in specialty shops recently; it resembles large pearls of tapioca or white BB pellets. Cook it as you would orzo, that is, in boiling water until al dente, about 8 minutes. Taste a few to test for tenderness. Drain in a colander and toss with a little butter and Parmesan cheese. It is delicious and has a pleasant texture that resembles pasta (orzo) rather than the more familiar North African couscous.

EGGPLANT: Used as a meat substitute in many parts of Asia and Africa, eggplant takes on a rich, deep flavor when browned and will come to life when simmered with an aromatic sauce. In addition to the large teardrop-shaped dark purple eggplants that have been widely available in markets all over the United States for many years, we now have several other varieties to choose from, including long, thin Asian eggplants, creamy white, round eggplants, and baby "Italian" eggplants. There are subtle nuances in texture and flavor among the different varieties, but the common dark purple eggplant is ideal for the recipes in this book. Select an eggplant that is very firm to the touch and has no bruises on it. The skin should be taut and glossy. If the eggplant is very fresh, as

A Guide to Ingredients

these signs will indicate, it will not be necessary to salt the eggplant before cooking it. Salting is used to remove any bitter juices and some of the moisture. While it has been said that eggplant absorbs less oil during browning if some of the moisture is removed beforehand, I haven't found this to be true. Eggplant is like a sponge no matter what. The best way to cut back on the oil absorption is to broil rather than fry eggplant.

HOISIN SAUCE: A thick, sweet paste made from beans, sugar, and spices with a nuance of anise that is usually mixed with soy sauce, sherry, and some stock. A thin film of it can be brushed on vegetables and tofu for grilling. Once opened it will keep up to two years when refrigerated. Hoisin sauce can be found in the Asian foods section of most supermarkets, in natural foods stores, and in specialty food shops.

LENTILS: One of the oldest foods known and an excellent source of protein and iron, lentils are an easy legume to add to your repertoire. Unlike beans, they don't require any soaking or long hours of cooking. *Brown lentils* (actually greenish brown) are the most common variety and are easily found in the supermarket. They are used for traditional lentil soup and are excellent when marinated as a salad. Cook them only 20 minutes so they retain their shape. *French green (Le Puy) lentils* are smaller than common lentils and have a stronger flavor. Because they are firmer and retain their shape when cooked, they are ideal for salads. *Red lentils* (actually light orange in color) are the softest of lentils and dissolve into a puree when cooked. They have a rich, buttery flavor that is enhanced when cooked with a mixture of curry spices. Store lentils in a covered jar in a dark area of your kitchen; they will keep at least 6 months.

MISO: This highly nutritious Japanese concentrate is a naturally fermented soybean and grain puree that is replete with friendly bacteria and digestion-aiding enzymes. It comes in various colors (the darker the color, the longer the fermentation and the stronger the flavor) and strengths, and is aged anywhere from one month to three years. It is sometimes used as a spread either alone or mixed with other ingredients such as tahini, but its primary use is to make a delicious stock. It is diluted with a small amount of water before being added to soups, and so forth, to prevent clumps. Avoid boiling miso to keep its beneficial bacteria alive. Miso is filled with protein, vitamin B_{12}, and minerals. Unpasteurized miso can be found refrigerated in natural foods stores. The unpasteurized product contains the lactobacillus bacteria that aid digestion. Store it in the refrigerator and it will last indefinitely; the high concentration of salt acts as a preservative.

OATS: Oats come in various shapes, thicknesses, and sizes, but they are all just different cuts of the same whole oat kernel (the groat). All oats are unrefined and therefore contain the bran and germ. The thickest oats are referred to as *steel cut* and are also called *Scotch oats. Old-fashioned oats,* also called *rolled oats,* are whole groats that have been thinly sliced, steamed, rolled, and dried. They take considerably less time to cook than steel cut oats and are the most commonly used oats. Quick-cooking oats are cut the thinnest and flattened the most, and this accounts for how fast they cook. All oats contain high-quality protein and B vitamins, and are an excellent source of both soluble and insoluble fiber.

OLIVE OIL: There is great variation in the quality and flavor of the numerous olive oils on the market. The key to the difference lies in the number of pressings and filterings used. *Extra-virgin* olive oil is a full-bodied first pressing that has a robust, fruity flavor and dark green or gold color. It is pressed without heat and is the most expensive olive oil. *Virgin* oil is also from the first pressing, but the flavor is more subtle because of additional filtering, and the color is much lighter. Herein lies the confusion. Olive oil that is bottled in this country is not subject to the strict labeling regulations that apply to imported bottled olive oil. If the oil is made from further pressings of the remaining flesh and pits, it can still be labeled "virgin" in this country, whereas it would have to be labeled "100% olive oil" in other countries. Therefore, make sure your expensive olive oil is *bottled* in the country in which it was made—France, Italy, or Greece—and is marked "extra virgin," "virgin," or "first pressing" if you want a fruity olive oil. Save this special oil for preparations where its flavor will stand out, such as salads and marinades, rather than sautéeing. If you want a mild oil, then purchase one that is labeled "100% olive oil." "Light olive oil" is a new marketing gimmick in the United States that refers to flavorless olive oil. Since it doesn't add much to your finished dish, why not use flavorless canola oil and save money. Store olive oil in a cool, dark place but not in the refrigerator because it will solidify. Olive oil can become rancid if exposed to hot weather for too long.

OLIVES: The selection of olives, as with olive oil, should ultimately depend on your preference. Flavor varies significantly among the varieties, and it is only through tasting that you can make the best choices. Olives can be classified as green, unripe olives and ripened black olives. They can be cured through three methods: oil-cured, brine-cured, and salt-cured. (Also, to complicate matters, some olives are cured in brine and packed in oil.) The most popular black olives are Greek, brine-cured *Kalamata,* which have a purplish tone and a salty, rich flavor; French *Niçoise,* which are tiny, sweet, and packed in oil; and brownish black Italian *Gaeta,* which have an earthy flavor. Green olives are harvested just before they ripen. Their meat is generally firmer, and their flavor is tangier than black olives. The most popular are *Picholine* from France, which are mild, crisp, and large; green *Sicilian,* which are cracked and usually marinated with hot pepper flakes to contrast nicely with their tartness; and *Cerignola* from Italy, which are very large, pale green in color, and barely salty.

To pit olives, handle them the way you would a clove of garlic. Lay the flat side of a sharp knife on the olive, and with your hand clenched into a fist, firmly thump the knife. The flesh (of the olive, not your hand) will crack, and you can then remove the pit.

PINE NUTS: These seeds can come from about twelve different species of pine trees. Italy and Spain produce the majority of pine nuts used in cooking. It is always more economical to purchase pine nuts in bulk at natural foods stores and specialty markets rather than in tiny jars or packages. Store pine nuts in a plastic bag or plastic container in the freezer to keep them fresh and available at a moment's notice. Because they contain delicate oils, they are apt to become rancid if forgotten in a room-temperature cabinet. Toasting pine nuts accentuates their flavor. You can toast them in a dry skillet over medium heat by shaking the pan continuously until the nuts become golden, or bake them in a shallow pan at 350 degrees for about 5 minutes. In either case, watch them carefully because they burn easily.

RICE: There are essentially two major categories of rice: brown rice and white rice. Brown rice has had only its hull removed. It therefore remains the most nutritious of rices, containing fiber, B vitamins, minerals, and protein. Brown rice has a nuttier flavor and chewier texture than white rice, and takes about twice as long to cook. White rice has had the bran layer and germ removed and has been polished. It then has almost no

Vegetarian Classics

nutritive value and so must be enriched. *Converted* rice is considerably more nutritious than common enriched white rice because it is partially cooked to force the nutrients into the core of each kernel; the bran and germ are then removed to create white rice. The length of the grain is another factor in defining rice. The longer the grain, the fluffier the rice. One of the shortest, starchiest rices is *Arborio,* which is ideal for making risottos where you want the finished dish to have a glutinous consistency. *Basmati* and *Jasmine* rice are aromatic long-grain rices that have a nutty flavor and subtle perfume. Basmati, which is grown in India, Pakistan, and now also in the United States (and called *Texmati*), can be either white or brown. When cooked, its grains remain light and separate, and so it is the favored rice for pilafs and other rice dishes served at special feasts in India. Jasmine rice from Thailand and also the United States is a little starchier than basmati but tender and velvety smooth in texture. The general rule for cooking rice is to bring the cooking liquid to a boil, add the rinsed-off rice, cover the pot, and reduce the heat to a low simmer. I always add a speck of oil to the liquid to prevent the contents from foaming up while cooking. Never stir or disturb the rice while it cooks. Both brown and white rice take about 2 cups of liquid per cup of rice, but brown rice will need about 40 minutes to absorb the liquid and become tender, whereas white rice will be cooked in 18 to 20 minutes. Let both types of rice sit undisturbed, off the heat, for 5 minutes before serving them. This will help the moist rice settle and become fluffier.

SEMOLINA: This roughly milled flour made from the yellow endosperm of durum wheat is available in fine, medium, and coarse textures. The finest grind (semolina flour) is used to make pasta, bread, and pizza crust, whereas the coarser texture is just right for pudding. Semolina provides strength and elasticity to pasta dough and a crispy texture and distinctive flavor to pizza crusts. Semolina is available at specialty food shops, including Italian markets, and some natural foods stores.

SESAME OIL: This dark, strong-flavored Asian oil is made from toasted sesame seeds. It is not the same as cold-pressed sesame oil (sold in natural foods stores), which is a light golden color and has a milder flavor. Toasting the sesame seeds before pressing out the oil makes the taste very pronounced, so only a small amount is needed to flavor a dish. Asian sesame oil is not used for sautéeing or stir-frying but instead is added to the sauce or drizzled on the finished dish at the last minute. If kept in a cool, dark cupboard, it will keep at least a year.

SOBA: These Japanese noodles made from buckwheat flour have an assertive flavor and are best served in Asian-style salads or soups with soy sauce and sesame oil as flavor enhancers. Soba is a good source of protein, B vitamins, and iron. These noodles must not be overcooked, or they will break into small pieces rather than remain in long chewy strands. It is much more economical to purchase soba in bulk rather than in small (8-ounce) packages. Many natural foods stores and large upscale produce markets sell soba loose—that is, by the pound—so take advantage of this option when you can.

TAMARI SOY SAUCE: This sauce is aged in wooden vats for at least two years to develop a full-bodied flavor and color. Commercial soy sauce is not aged, has caramel coloring added, and is treated with a preservative. Stored in the refrigerator, tamari lasts indefinitely. In addition to using it in Asian dishes, I like to use it in all types of soups and sauces for added flavor. Tamari

can be purchased in health food stores and specialty food markets. Some soy sauce is labeled "shoyu" tamari, or just "shoyu." This means that it is made from wheat as well as soybeans, but its flavor is almost identical to regular tamari. Commercial soy sauce may be substituted for tamari, but you'll need to use more to compensate for tamari's deeper flavor.

TEMPEH: When ground soybeans are mixed with a rhizopus culture, formed into a cake, and then allowed to ferment, tempeh is created. This Indonesian staple, like most soybean products, is packed with nutrients—complete protein, iron, and vitamin B_{12}—and is low in fat. Tempeh is usually cut into cubes and either steamed, sautéed, or fried, and then can be seasoned in numerous ways. When finely chopped, sautéed, and then mixed with mayonnaise and chilled, it makes a delicious sandwich filling reminiscent of chicken salad. Fresh tempeh often has black spots on it; that is natural and not a sign of spoilage. When tempeh is spoiled, it is somewhat slimy, may have an ammonia smell, and have blue, pink, yellow, or green mold. Check the expiration date on the package when you buy it. Tempeh freezes very well with no change in texture or flavor, so it is a good idea to keep a package or

Vegetarian Classics

two in the freezer. Tempeh can be found in natural foods stores and in many supermarkets in the dairy section.

TOFU: Also called bean curd, tofu is a type of soybean "cheese" made through a process similar to cottage cheese making. Soybeans are cooked and mashed, and then their liquid (soy milk) is pressed out and mixed with a coagulant to separate the curds from the whey. The curds are formed into cakes called tofu. It is an excellent source of complete protein and iron, and a good source of calcium when the added coagulant is calcium sulfate. Tofu is low in fat and easy to digest. It can be purchased in three styles: extra-firm, which is my favorite because it has a firm, chewy texture when sautéed or roasted; firm; and soft (or silken), which many people prefer for pureed salad dressings and sauces. I always keep extra-firm on hand; it is a great all-purpose tofu that holds its shape when fried but also becomes creamy when placed in a blender. When you purchase tofu, check the expiration date on the container. Once the package is opened, store the remaining tofu in water in a covered container in the refrigerator. Change the water every day until you finish the tofu. It should keep a few days this way. When spoiled, tofu becomes slimy and smells sour. You can freeze tofu by draining it and wrapping it in plastic wrap. The texture will change and become crumbly, so it won't be suitable for stir-fried dishes that call for cubed tofu.

TOMATILLOS: Often referred to as Mexican green tomatoes (and sometimes Chinese lantern plants because of the papery covering that encloses them), tomatillos are actually members of the same family as the Cape gooseberry and Mexican ground cherry. They are almost always cooked to soften them and can be either boiled or roasted in the oven. To purchase them, look for fruits that are hard and whose papery husks are tight fitting—a sign of maturity and freshness. Tomatillos keep very well stored loosely in the vegetable bin in the refrigerator, about two to three weeks. Always remove the husks and then wash the fruit thoroughly to eliminate the sticky residue that coats it.

TOMATOES (CANNED): Unless you live in a hot climate, you probably don't have year-round access to beautifully ripened tomatoes. For cooking we are fortunate to be able to purchase canned tomatoes that have been picked at their peak. More often than not the best canned tomatoes are imported plum varieties.

A Guide to Ingredients

Experiment with different brands because there is definitely a difference in quality among them. *Ready-cut diced tomatoes* are a relatively new offering in supermarkets and are available in 14-ounce and 28-ounce cans. They are more expensive than canned whole tomatoes but well worth the extra cost because of their convenience. *Crushed tomatoes* and *tomato puree* are often spoken of as identical, but they are, in fact, slightly different. Canned crushed tomatoes have more texture than tomato puree, which is almost silky smooth. I prefer to use crushed tomatoes, but tomato puree can usually be substituted without causing a dramatic change in the finished recipe.

TOMATO PASTE: We all are familiar with a situation that arises when a can of tomato paste is opened: only a small portion of this potent concentrate is needed, and the remainder gets forgotten in the refrigerator and collects mold. Here's how to avoid that predicament: freeze portions of the leftover tomato paste in little packets. Cut 4 × 4-inch squares of plastic wrap and lay them on a baking sheet. Using a measuring spoon, scoop out 1 tablespoon of tomato paste (level off the top with a knife) and place it in a mound on a square of plastic. Repeat with the remaining tomato paste. (There are about 10 tablespoons of paste in a 6-ounce can.) Place the baking sheet in the freezer and freeze until the tomato paste is hard, about 1 hour. Remove from the freezer and fold each square of plastic to cover the tomato paste. Place these frozen tomato paste packets in a small zippered freezer bag and return them to the freezer. When you need tomato paste in the future, just remove one or more packets; they will keep for four to six months in the freezer.

UDON: These thick Japanese wheat noodles have a mild flavor and are delightful served in a broth and sprinkled with scallions, as is traditional in Japan. They have an appealing chewy texture that should be preserved by not overcooking the noodles. Linguine can be substituted if udon are not available.

WASABI: This green Japanese horseradish is available in powdered form and is traditionally mixed with an equal part of water to create a paste. It should then sit for 10 minutes or so to develop its flavor. I especially like to mix wasabi paste with a little mayonnaise to use as a spread on vegetable-based sandwiches, such as cucumber or open-faced vegetable melts. Wasabi can be found in natural foods stores and gourmet food shops. Wasabi slowly loses its potency once it is opened, so it is a good idea to purchase it in small individual packets if you use it infrequently.

WHEAT BERRIES: The wheat berry is the edible portion of a shaft of wheat. Resembling a seed in appearance, it contains the bran, germ, and endosperm of the wheat plant. Whole wheat flour comes from ground wheat berries. When just the starchy endosperm is used, white flour results. Wheat berries are high in protein and B vitamins, and can add a delightful nubbiness to breads and grain salads. They must be soaked overnight if added to bread dough and should be cooked for about 1 hour if used in salads. Wheat berries can be purchased at natural foods stores and should be stored in the refrigerator to prevent rancidity.

THE BASICS

Need the perfect pie crust or want to whip up a batch of pesto from bunches of fresh basil that you've just harvested from your garden? Well, here's the chapter that contains recipes for items that can usually be store-bought but taste so much better when homemade. You might be in the habit of purchasing roasted red peppers from the grocery store, but then fresh scarlet red peppers are marked down at the market and you just can't resist buying them. What is the best and easiest way to roast them? Check this chapter to find out. Whether you make these items to use in recipes in this book or in impromptu cooking that is a result of inspiration or necessity, you'll find that the quality of these basic preparations is first-rate and will enhance every dish.

VEGETABLE STOCK

Although I think it is unrealistic to expect today's busy cooks to make their own stock, I do want to include a basic recipe for an all-purpose vegetable stock should you have an opportunity to use some leftover vegetables from the garden or decide some leisurely Sunday afternoon to indulge in the sensuous ritual of simmering a pot of vegetables and herbs to extract a homespun stock.

MAKES 7 CUPS

1 tablespoon olive oil

6 garlic cloves, chopped

2 onions, roughly chopped

1 bunch scallions, roughly chopped

3 celery ribs, roughly chopped

3 unpeeled carrots, roughly chopped

6 mushrooms, chopped

½ bunch parsley with stems, roughly chopped

2 bay leaves

2 tablespoons tamari soy sauce

10 cups water

Dash nutmeg

Freshly ground pepper to taste

1. Heat the oil in a large stockpot over medium heat. Add the garlic, onions, and scallions, and sauté 10 minutes, stirring often. **2.** Mix in all the remaining ingredients and bring the stock to a boil. Lower the heat to a gentle simmer and cook 1 hour, stirring occasionally. Strain the stock through a large strainer or a colander set over a large bowl. With the back of a large spoon, press out as much liquid as possible from the vegetables. Discard the vegetables. Let the stock cool to room temperature. Refrigerate the stock up to 1 week or freeze up to 3 months.

BREAD CRUMBS

There are basically three different types of bread crumbs, and it is important that you use the correct type called for in a recipe. *Dry bread crumbs* refer to fine, almost powdery crumbs. These are usually store-bought bread crumbs sold in tubelike containers, although you can make your own by using hard toasted bread and processing it until extremely fine. *Fresh bread crumbs* refer to fresh or day-old bread torn into pieces and processed in a blender or food processor. These crumbs are soft and coarsely textured, about the size of lentils or peas. *Toasted fresh bread crumbs* are made from slices of toasted bread or from fresh bread crumbs that are baked until golden. These crumbs are crisper than those made from fresh bread crumbs but not as dry or powdery as dry bread crumbs. You can also "toast" fresh bread crumbs (for tossing with pasta or vegetables) by sautéeing them in olive oil or butter until crisp or golden.

CLASSIC PESTO

I think you'll agree that this version of pesto is far superior to any other. The addition of a little soft butter enhances its flavor and texture, making it sensational as a spread on lightly toasted French bread slices as well as a sauce for pasta or an addition to soups. Be certain to stir in the cheese and butter by hand rather than put them in a blender or processor because this will ensure a smoother-textured pesto. Follow the tips below for freezing this pesto, and you'll thank yourself come winter when a dose of this summer-drenched delicacy is just what you need for curing cold weather blues.

MAKES 1⅓ CUPS

**2 cups moderately well packed fresh basil
leaves, well washed and spun dry**

½ cup olive oil (preferably mild-flavored)

4 medium-size garlic cloves, chopped

2 tablespoons pine nuts (optional)

½ cup grated Parmesan cheese

2 tablespoons unsalted butter, very soft

Combine the basil, oil, garlic, and pine nuts (if you are using them) in a blender (preferably) or food processor and process until it is a smooth puree. Scrape the pesto into a container and stir in the cheese. Use a fork to stir in the soft butter. Chill until ready to use. When using as a sauce for pasta, thin with a few tablespoons of boiling pasta water before using. This pesto will keep about 1 month if covered with a thin film of olive oil and refrigerated.

TIP: To prepare pesto for freezing, don't mix in the cheese or butter. Freeze the basil, olive oil, garlic, and pine nut puree in a tightly covered container (such as a plastic deli container) for up to 6 months. When ready to use, thoroughly defrost the pesto and then stir in the cheese and butter.

Taking Care of Basil

Many of us have had the experience of buying a gorgeous bunch of fresh basil, refrigerating it overnight, and waking up to find a limp bunch of blackened leaves. This is a common experience because fresh basil is highly perishable and *hates* the cold. If you washed the basil before refrigerating it, you probably couldn't even recognize it the next morning because dampness exacerbates the blackening. So how do we keep basil fresh-looking for at least a few days? (Longer than that is really asking too much.) Here are a few tips:

• An ideal temperature for storing cut basil is about 55 degrees—a *cool*, not cold, room. Many greengrocers have such a cooler. Lacking that, you should keep the basil in a plastic bag to maintain some moisture and place it near a windowsill or in a cool corner of your kitchen.

• Basil dislikes heat, and a hot day will cause it to go limp. If your room is very hot, occasionally place the basil in the refrigerator for an hour or so (set a timer), then remove it and keep it at room temperature. This will allow it to cool down a bit.

• If roots are still attached to the basil, immerse the roots in a glass of water and cover the leaves with a plastic bag to trap in moisture. This will extend the life of the basil, but you will still have to keep it cool, not hot or cold.

• Never wash basil until you are ready to use it because the added moisture encourages decay. Spin it dry as you would salad greens.

• Don't cut basil until you are about to use it because it blackens very quickly once cut.

Bright Green Pesto

Here's a trick for preventing pesto from darkening: beat 1 teaspoon of plain yogurt into a full batch of pesto. The acid will keep the basil bright green. You won't be able to see or taste the yogurt, but it will do the trick nonetheless.

WINTER PESTO

If you have run out of batches of frozen summer pesto or can't get hold of a healthy bunch of fresh basil to make Classic Pesto (page 19), relax. This pesto will produce startingly similar and delicious results using ingredients available in winter.

MAKES 2 CUPS

> 2½ cups tightly packed triple-washed fresh spinach, stems removed
>
> ½ cup chopped fresh parsley
>
> 1 tablespoon dried basil
>
> 3 garlic cloves, chopped
>
> ¼ teaspoon salt
>
> ¼ cup walnuts (optional)
>
> ⅔ cup olive oil
>
> ½ cup grated Parmesan cheese
>
> 2 tablespoons unsalted butter, very soft

1. Combine the spinach, parsley, basil, garlic, salt, walnuts, and oil in a blender (preferably) or food processor and process until it is a smooth puree. Turn off the machine and scrape down the sides as necessary. **2.** Pour the pesto into a container with a tight-fitting lid and stir in the cheese and butter by hand until well blended. If the pesto is to be used as a sauce for pasta, stir in a few tablespoons of boiling pasta water to thin it out before using. This pesto will keep for a few weeks if covered with a tablespoon of olive oil and refrigerated.

TIPS: Omit the butter and cheese when freezing. To use, defrost thoroughly and then stir in the cheese and butter.

For a delicious variation you can omit the spinach and use a total of 3 cups chopped parsley leaves.

SUN-DRIED TOMATO PESTO

Classic Genoese pesto has fresh basil as its key ingredient, but in recent years American cooks have developed some pleasant variations on this aromatic sauce. Pesto means "pounded," and the pasty texture that results from the traditional use of a mortar and pestle is captured here (as in Classic Pesto, page 19) using a blender or food processor.

This dynamic red pesto is especially good on pasta, bruschetta, and pizza, and as a spread on grilled vegetable sandwiches.

MAKES 1 CUP
(ENOUGH FOR 1 POUND PASTA)

½ cup packed loose sun-dried tomatoes (about 18)

2 garlic cloves, chopped

½ cup chopped fresh parsley

¼ cup chopped fresh basil, or 2 teaspoons dried

½ teaspoon salt (see Tip)

Freshly ground pepper to taste

⅓ cup olive oil

2 tablespoons pine nuts

¼ cup grated Parmesan cheese

1. Place the tomatoes in a vegetable steamer in a saucepan with about 1 inch of water. Cook, covered, over medium heat for 10 minutes. Remove the steamer from the pot and let the tomatoes cool 10 minutes. (Alternatively, you can place the tomatoes in a small bowl and cover them with boiling water. Cover the bowl with a plate and let sit 10 minutes. Drain and cool the tomatoes.)
2. In a food processor or blender combine the tomatoes, garlic, parsley, basil, salt, and pepper, and process until finely ground. Slowly pour in the oil and process until smooth. Scrape the pesto into a bowl and stir in the pine nuts and cheese. If you are using the pesto on pasta, stir in ½ cup boiling pasta water to thin it out.

TIPS: Loose sun-dried tomatoes are less expensive and store longer in the refrigerator than those packed in oil or water in a jar. If you have only the jar variety, use ⅓ cup packed and omit step 1.

If you are making this pesto for bruschetta or as a pizza sauce, use just a few dashes of salt, or enough to taste. I like to process the pine nuts with the other ingredients when making this pesto for these two purposes.

ROASTED RED PEPPER AND WALNUT PESTO

Red peppers and walnuts enhance each other, giving this pesto a rich, complex undertone. It is wonderful on stubby pasta such as farfalle (bow ties), penne, and rotini, and fabulous when spread in a thin layer on focaccia sandwiches stuffed with Portobello mushrooms.

MAKES ¾ CUP
(ENOUGH FOR 1 POUND PASTA)

1 (7-ounce) jar roasted red peppers, well drained

½ cup walnuts

3 garlic cloves, minced

¼ cup olive oil

½ teaspoon salt (use only ¼ teaspoon if not for pasta)

Freshly ground pepper to taste

⅓ cup grated Parmesan cheese

Gather the peppers between your hands and gently squeeze out all the moisture you can. Place the peppers and all the remaining ingredients except the cheese in the container of a food processor and process until very smooth. Scrape the pesto into a bowl and stir in the cheese by hand.

TIPS: This pesto can be flavored with herbs to give it a new dimension. Try a few sprigs of basil, rosemary, parsley, or chives.

To serve this pesto on pasta, stir in ¼ cup boiling pasta water to thin it out.

FLAKY PIE CRUST

(Savory or Sweet)

Creating a flaky, tender pastry is not a matter of alchemy but instead requires following a few essential rules: Always use cold butter so it remains in bits when it is blended with the flour. Don't overwork the dough. Add a tiny bit of an acidic ingredient such as lemon juice or vinegar to tenderize the gluten. And make sure the pastry is cold when it goes in the oven to help the formation of flakes.

MAKES ONE 9- OR 10-INCH CRUST

Water

1¼ cups unbleached flour

¼ teaspoon salt (for a savory crust) *or*
    2 teaspoons sugar (for a sweet crust)

6 tablespoons chilled unsalted butter

2 tablespoons canola oil

1½ teaspoons lemon juice or apple cider vinegar

1. Fill a glass halfway with water and drop in an ice cube. Set aside. **2.** In a large bowl combine the flour and salt or sugar. Cut the butter into bits and drop them in the flour. Toss to evenly coat them. With your fingertips, a pastry cutter, or 2 knives, rub the butter into the flour until they are flattened and the size of dimes. You don't want the pieces to be too small, or they will melt too quickly in the crust and not create flakes. **3.** In a small bowl or glass combine 3 tablespoons of the ice water, the oil, and lemon juice or vinegar. Drizzle this over the flour mixture and stir with a fork to distribute it. Gather the dough into a ball and knead 3 or 4 times to make it pliable. (If the dough is very dry and crumbly, add a few more teaspoons of ice water.) Gather into a ball again, then flatten into a disk. Wrap in plastic wrap and chill for at least 20 minutes, or up to 48 hours. **4.** To roll out the dough, let it come to a cool tempera-

Roasting Peppers

——

There are essentially two methods of roasting peppers in the indoor kitchen (as opposed to the outdoor grill): over a gas flame or under an electric broiler.

To roast a pepper over a gas flame on your stove, use tongs to hold the pepper and place it directly over the flame so that it makes contact with it. Keep rotating the pepper until it gets charred (blackened) all over. This will take about 10 minutes.

To roast a pepper under an electric broiler, remove the core of the pepper and cut the pepper in half vertically. Discard all the seeds and fibrous interior. Place the pepper halves, cut side down, on a baking sheet. Broil on the top rack of the oven so the pepper pieces come as close to the broiler as possible. When the skins are blackened all over, remove from the oven. (You can help the skins get evenly charred by flattening the peppers with a spatula halfway through broiling them.)

Whether you have roasted over a flame or under the broiler, place the charred peppers in a bowl and cover with a plate to trap the heat. Let sit 10 minutes. The steam will cause the skins to loosen. When cool enough to handle, peel the blackened skin off the peppers and discard it. (Discard the core and seeds if you have roasted the whole pepper over a flame.) You can now use the roasted peppers in your recipe or pat the pieces dry, seal them in a zippered freezer bag, and freeze up to 2 months.

ture. It will be too firm and crumbly if rolled when it is too cold. It must be cool but not at room temperature because the butter bits must remain firm and not melt into the dough. Lightly flour the work surface, rolling pin, and the surface of the dough. Roll the dough into a circle about 2 inches larger than the pie plate. Keep turning the dough as you roll it to keep it a perfect circle. Lightly flour underneath and on top if it sticks. Pinch together any areas that break. **5.** Place the rolling pin in the center of the dough and fold half of the pastry over it. Unfold the dough onto the tart pan or pie plate. Press it into the edges and trim any excess. Place the tart pan or pie plate in a plastic bag or cover with foil. Chill for at least 30 minutes or up to 24 hours before baking. You can also freeze the crust if it is thoroughly wrapped.

Vegetarian Classics

SPRUCED-UP STORE-BOUGHT TOMATO SAUCE

Although the contribution a homemade tomato sauce makes to a finished dish cannot be overstated, even the most serious cooks can find themselves so pressed for time that they must use a purchased sauce. When that happens to me, I doctor the commercial sauce to deepen its flavor and add a fresh touch. The results are surprisingly good. Below are the additions I make to a 28- or 32-ounce jar or can of sauce. Feel free to improvise.

MAKES 3¼ CUPS

> 1 (28- or 32-ounce) can or jar store-bought tomato sauce
>
> 3 tablespoons dry red wine
>
> 2 garlic cloves, put through a press (preferably) or minced
>
> 1 teaspoon dried oregano
>
> ½ cup minced fresh parsley
>
> Generous seasoning freshly ground pepper

Combine all the ingredients and mix well. Store any unused portion in the refrigerator.

TIP: For an all-purpose sauce with a flavor that is familiar, favored by kids, and well suited to being altered, I have found that Hunt's Four Cheese Tomato Sauce works well. It is sold in a can, not a jar, and is inexpensive.

EASY MARINARA SAUCE

With the right balance of flavorings you can create a delectable, fresh-tasting tomato sauce without having to simmer it for hours, and using tomato puree eliminates the need for a food processor or blender. This garlic-infused sauce is outstanding on pizzas, pastas, and lasagnas.

MAKES ABOUT 3 CUPS

> ¼ cup olive oil
>
> 4 garlic cloves, put through a press or minced
>
> 1 (28-ounce) can tomato puree
>
> 3 tablespoons dry red wine
>
> 1 teaspoon sugar or honey
>
> 2 teaspoons dried oregano
>
> 1 teaspoon dried basil
>
> ¼ teaspoon salt
>
> Generous seasoning freshly ground pepper

Add the oil to a large stockpot (which helps to avoid splattering) and warm it over medium-low heat. Add the garlic and cook 30–60 seconds, or just until it sizzles a bit but doesn't become at all colored. Stir in all the remaining ingredients and raise the heat to medium. Simmer the sauce for 20 minutes, stirring often.

PERFECT BROWN RICE

When properly cooked, brown rice is a delicious nutty-flavored rice that can be far superior to white rice in many dishes. Brown rice often has a bad name because of incorrectly cooked versions that are gummy and heavy. Brown rice should always be light in texture.

Here's how to do it: *Never* stir brown rice while it is cooking. Do not overcook the rice by using too much water because the starch will escape from the grains, making the rice gummy. Use long-grain brown rice for extra lightness. Use the proper size pan in proportion to the amount of rice cooked. Add a little oil and salt to prevent foam from rising during cooking. Regulate the heat so that it is at a perfect simmer (if the rice cooks too slowly it will get overcooked; if it cooks at too high a temperature, it will cook too fast and be undercooked when all the water has been absorbed). To ensure a fluffy texture when making fried rice dishes or cold rice salads, always begin with *cold* cooked rice.

**MAKES 2½ TO 3 CUPS RICE
SERVES 4 AS A SIDE DISH**

1 cup long-grain brown rice

2 cups water or vegetable stock, store-bought or homemade (page 18)

½ teaspon salt

1 teaspoon canola oil

1. Place the rice in a strainer and rinse under cold running water. Place in a 1½-quart saucepan. Add all the remaining ingredients.
2. Cover the pan and bring the mixture to a boil. Lower the heat to a simmer and cook undisturbed for 40–45 minutes, or until all the liquid has been absorbed. Use a knife to make a separation in the rice to ensure that there is no liquid left. Remove the rice from the heat and let sit, covered, for at least 5 minutes, or up to 20 minutes before serving. Serve at once or scoop the rice into a covered baking dish and keep warm in a 325-degree oven.

TIP: To reheat cold rice, sprinkle a few tablespoons of water on it for moisture. Heat over low heat in a skillet or cover and heat in a 350-degree oven. Stir as little as possible.

GREEN SALSA

This classic Mexican salsa based on tomatillos instead of red tomatoes (see tomatillos on page 15) has a delightful piquancy and citruslike flavor that is best appreciated when served within 24 hours of being made. It can be used in place of or in combination with red salsa for enchiladas, tacos, and other foods, and is especially good with egg dishes.

Makes 1⅔ cups

> 12 ounces tomatillos (about 18 small-golf-ball size, or 10 medium)
>
> 1 very small onion, chopped
>
> 1 garlic clove, chopped
>
> 2 jalapeño peppers, seeded and chopped (wear rubber gloves)
>
> 1 tablespoon lime juice
>
> ¼ teaspoon sugar
>
> ¼ teaspoon salt
>
> 2 tablespoons minced cilantro

1. Remove the husks from the tomatillos, then rinse under cold running water to clean off any sticky residue. Place in a medium-size saucepan and cover with water. Bring to a boil, lower the heat to a lively simmer, and cook 10 minutes, or until softened. Drain thoroughly and let cool. **2.** Place the onion, garlic, jalapeños, and lime juice in the container of a food processor and pulse a few times until coarsely chopped. Add the tomatillos and process until finely chopped but not completely smooth. Scrape the mixture into a bowl. **3.** Stir in the sugar, salt, and cilantro. Serve at room temperature.

Tip: Chilled green salsa becomes somewhat firm and gelatinous, so bring to room temperature before using.

COOKING BEANS FROM SCRATCH

I always used to cook beans from scratch, but I didn't eat beans that often. Since I have increased my bean consumption and now use them in all types of cooking, including appetizers, salads, soups, and entrees, I find it much more convenient to purchase canned beans. The key is to try different brands and avoid those that overcook the beans. Canned organic beans sold at health food stores are usually cooked just right. Always rinse canned beans in a strainer before adding them to any dish; that packing liquid is meant to be discarded.

If you have time to cook beans from scratch, all the better. It is considerably cheaper to purchase dried beans, and you'll have control over how much they are cooked. If you have a large batch of beans, you can freeze leftovers for use at another time.

Spread the beans on a baking sheet and pick through them to remove any stones or little clumps of dirt. There are two methods for soaking them. The first method involves soaking the beans overnight in plenty of water. The next morning, drain away the soaking water and replace it with enough fresh water to cover the beans by about 2 inches. Bring the beans to a boil and then simmer, uncovered, until tender, 1 to 1½ hours depending on the size of the beans. To avoid breaking or splitting the beans, keep the heat at a simmer rather than a rolling boil.

The second method is the quick-soak approach. After picking through the beans, place them in a large pot and cover with water by 2 inches. Bring to a boil, lower the heat to a simmer, and cook 2 minutes. Turn off the heat, cover the pot, and soak the beans for 1 hour. Drain the soaking liquid from the beans and replace with enough fresh water to cover by 2 inches. Cook the beans, uncovered, as described in the first method.

Both methods of soaking work well. Make your choice depending on your schedule.

APPETIZERS

An appetizer should awaken the palate and satisfy predinner hunger without diminishing one's appetite for dinner. Spreads, dips, and little nibbles are what I rely on to accomplish this, and the ease with which they can be put together adds to their appeal. Almost all these recipes match well with either Garlic Pita Chips (page 39) or Basic Crostini (page 39). The homemade versions of these two accompaniments are quite special and will enhance your spreads and dips; if you are pressed for time, however, you can purchase good-quality crackers or toasts and still serve a superlative starter.

The general rule regarding appetizers for a menu is to select one made of ingredients that are *not* in your entree. For example, if you are serving a pasta or casserole that contains beans, then choose a spread with a cheese base. Likewise, if your entree contains cheese or is on the rich side, select an appetizer that is dairy-free, such as White Bean and Roasted Red Pepper Spread (page 31). You want the ingredients in your various courses to be compatible but not duplicated.

CLASSIC HUMMUS

Hummus has been a staple appetizer and vegetarian sandwich filling for decades, with good reason. When properly made with a lavish amount of tahini, this Middle Eastern spread is exquisite. It is an ideal appetizer when surrounded by hot pita bread triangles and is equally dynamic when used as a sandwich spread topped with sliced cucumber and sprouts, or slathered on bagels. Hummus can now be purchased in supermarkets, but the commercial varieties can't hold a candle to this heady rendition.

MAKES 2½ CUPS

> 1 (19-ounce) can (2 cups) chickpeas, rinsed well in a strainer, or 2 cups freshly cooked chickpeas (page 27)
>
> 3 garlic cloves, minced
>
> ½ cup fresh lemon juice (about 3 lemons)
>
> 1 cup tahini (stirred well before measuring)
>
> ½ teaspoon salt
>
> ½–1 cup water
>
> Paprika for garnish

Place the chickpeas and garlic in a food processor and process a few seconds, until the chickpeas are ground. Stop the machine and add the lemon juice, tahini, salt, and ½ cup water. Process until the mixture is very creamy, at least 2 minutes. Check the consistency. For a sandwich spread it should be slightly firmer than for a dip. Add a bit more water if necessary and process until very smooth.

TIPS: Well-made hummus has a creamy, almost silken consistency. To achieve this, process it until there are no bits of bean visible and it is absolutely smooth.

If well sealed, this hummus can be stored in the refrigerator for up to 1 week.

ROASTED RED PEPPER HUMMUS

This popular variation of hummus includes two compatible flavors—roasted red peppers and cumin—while maintaining a Middle Eastern theme. Its rosy hue makes it particularly attractive when sprinkled with fresh parsley and surrounded by small bowls of mixed olives. Make this hummus at least a few hours before you intend to serve it so the flavors have time to meld.

MAKES 2½ CUPS

> ⅔ cup diced roasted red peppers (homemade, page 24, or store-bought), patted very dry
>
> 3 garlic cloves, minced
>
> 1 (19-ounce) can (2 cups) chickpeas, rinsed well in a strainer
>
> ½ cup fresh lemon juice
>
> ⅔ cup tahini, stirred well before measuring
>
> ½ teaspoon ground cumin
>
> ½ teaspoon salt
>
> ⅓–⅔ cup water
>
> Minced fresh parsley for garnish

Combine the red peppers and garlic in a food processor and process until liquefied. Stop the machine and add the chickpeas, lemon juice, tahini, cumin, salt, and a ⅓ cup water. Process

Vegetarian Classics

until very smooth and creamy, at least 2 minutes. Check the consistency; if the hummus is too thick, beat in a little more water. Top with fresh parsley.

TIP: Store, covered, in the refrigerator for up to 1 week.

WHITE BEAN AND ROASTED RED PEPPER SPREAD

This Mediterranean-style bean spread resembles hummus in texture but has a lighter consistency. Sure to be a hit at any party, it is especially good when spread on Basic Crostini (page 39) and accompanied by a glass of wine.

MAKES ABOUT 1½ CUPS

- 1 (15-ounce) can white beans (such as Great Northern, cannelini, or navy), rinsed thoroughly and drained, or 1½ cups freshly cooked white beans (see page 27)
- ¼ cup diced roasted red peppers, patted very dry (homemade, page 24, or store-bought)
- 2 medium garlic cloves, minced
- 2 tablespoons fruity olive oil
- ¼ teaspoon good-quality paprika

Salt to taste

2 tablespoons minced fresh basil, or ½ teaspoon dried

1. Combine all the ingredients except the basil in a food processor and process until very smooth and creamy, at least 3 minutes. **2.** Scrape the mixture into a bowl and stir in the basil. Cover and chill at least 1 hour. Bring almost to room temperature before serving.

TIPS: This spread can be made up to 2 days in advance.

For a dynamic variation substitute ¾ teaspoon ground cumin for the basil.

The Noble Bean

Although most vegetarians will readily acknowledge the culinary and nutritional value of beans, who would expect that beans occupied such a place of honor in ancient Rome that four prominent Roman families took their names from four common legumes of that time? Cicero comes from the chickpea (ceci); Lentulus from the lentil; Piso from the pea; and Fabius from the fava bean. In case you're wondering whether legumes could have been named after the families rather than the other way around, please note that those beans predated the famous Roman families by a few thousand years.

Appetizers

WHITE BEAN SPREAD WITH LEMON AND MINT

Here is another white bean spread that makes a memorable prelude to a meal. The fabulous flavor combination here of garlic, lemon, and mint will transport you to the Mideast. Hot pita bread or Garlic Pita Chips (page 39) are the perfect accompaniments.

MAKES ABOUT 1½ CUPS

> 1 (15-ounce) can white beans (such as navy, Great Northern, or cannelini), rinsed and well drained
>
> 3 tablespoons lemon juice
>
> 3 tablespoons olive oil
>
> 2 garlic cloves, minced
>
> ¼ teaspoon salt
>
> Freshly ground pepper to taste
>
> 2 tablespoons chopped fresh mint
>
> 2 tablespoons chopped fresh parsley

1. In the container of a food processor combine the beans, lemon juice, oil, garlic, salt, and pepper, and process until smooth, a least 1 minute. **2.** Stop the processor and add the mint and parsley. Process just until the herbs are minced and blended. Scrape the mixture into a serving bowl; it will be a little soupy but will get firmer upon chilling. Cover with plastic wrap and chill at least 1 hour or overnight. Bring almost to room temperature before serving.

TIP: The fresh mint available at the market is usually spearmint. When I have been unable to obtain it and my garden was not in bloom, I opened a spearmint tea bag and used the dried mint within with surprisingly good results. Sounds crazy but it works.

PORTOBELLO MUSHROOM PÂTÉ

Vegetarians have long used mushrooms to make a pâté. This luxurious garlic-infused spread has a pebbly texture and resembles black caviar. Serve it on chewy toast points or crisp Basic Crostini (page 39) with a dab of sour cream and a leaf of parsley for contrast.

MAKES ABOUT 1 CUP

> 4 medium-large Portobello mushrooms (with caps 4 to 5 inches in diameter)
>
> 1 tablespoon unsalted butter
>
> 4 garlic cloves, put through a press or minced
>
> 1 teaspoon fresh thyme, or ¼ teaspoon dried
>
> Salt to taste
>
> Freshly ground pepper to taste
>
> Sour cream for garnish (optional)
>
> Italian flat-leaf parsley leaves for garnish (optional)

1. Remove and discard the stems of the mushrooms. Wipe the mushroom caps clean with a damp paper towel. Use a spoon to scrape off some of the bottom gills of the mushrooms; this will reduce moisture in the spread. Cut the mushroom caps into quarters and place in a food processor. Pulse a few times until the mushrooms are evenly ground and resemble coarse bread crumbs. Do not overprocess them. It is better to process them in 2 batches if the bowl of the processor seems too crowded. 2. Heat the butter in a medium-size skillet over medium heat. Add the garlic and cook 1 minute. Do not let it get brown. Stir in the mushrooms and thyme, and sauté about 5 minutes, or until the juices have evaporated and the mushrooms are cooked through. Season with salt and pepper. 3. Scrape the mixture into a bowl and let cool to room temperature. Serve on toast points or crostini with a garnish of sour cream and parsley, if desired.

TIP: This treatment also works with common button mushrooms, but the flavor is less earthy. You can include the stems with common mushrooms, but they are inedible on Portobellos.

ROASTED EGGPLANT CAVIAR

"Poor man's caviar" is the nickname Russians have given this eggplant spread because it was often made by those unable to afford the high cost of caviar made from fish roe. Vegetarians have adopted it for another reason, namely that its deep, rich flavor is utterly satisfying. Serve this with coarse pumpernickel bread, hot pita bread triangles, or Basic Crostini (page 39).

SERVES 6

> Olive oil for greasing plus 2 tablespoons
>
> 1 medium-large (1½–2 pounds) eggplant, halved lengthwise
>
> 2 tomatoes, cored, cut horizontally in half, and seeded
>
> 1 green pepper, cored and halved lengthwise
>
> 2 onions, quartered
>
> 4 garlic cloves, minced
>
> ½ teaspoon salt
>
> ½ teaspoon sugar
>
> Liberal seasoning freshly ground pepper

1. Preheat the oven to 400 degrees. 2. Oil a baking sheet that has sides or a large roasting pan. Place the eggplant, tomatoes, green pepper, and onions, cut-side down, on the pan. Bake 45 minutes. Let cool about 15 minutes,

then peel the skin from the pepper and tomatoes with your fingers. Remove whatever slips off easily; it doesn't have to be perfect. **3.** Scrape the eggplant out of its skin and place in a large bowl. Discard the skin. Add the pepper, tomatoes, and onions. Use 2 knives in a crisscross fashion to finely chop all the vegetables. **4.** Heat the 2 tablespoons oil in a medium-size skillet. Add the garlic and sauté 1–2 minutes. Stir in the vegetables, salt, sugar, and pepper, and cook until thick and the mixture begins to stick to the pan, about 15 minutes. **5.** Puree half the mixture in a food processor, then place in a bowl. Stir in the remaining mixture. Chill several hours before serving.

T I P : Achieving the right texture is important with this spread. There should be a thick puree with tiny pieces of vegetables, not chunks, throughout.

SMOKED CHEESE AND SUN-DRIED TOMATO SPREAD

Cheese spreads have been popular in the United States and England for decades. This updated version uses smoked cheese to add a shadowy richness and sun-dried tomatoes to lend a rosy color. It is sensational on Basic Crostini (page 39) and crackers, as well as slathered on bagels.

MAKES 1¼ CUPS

> 5 loose sun-dried tomatoes
>
> 8 ounces Neufchâtel (**light cream cheese**), at room temperature
>
> ½ cup grated smoked Gouda

1. Place the tomatoes in a small bowl and cover with boiling water. Let sit 30 minutes. Remove them with your hands and squeeze out all their liquid. **2.** Place the tomatoes in a food processor and process until pureed. Add the cream cheese and smoked cheese, and process until very smooth and fluffy, at least 3 minutes. Scrape the mixture into a bowl. This spread will keep, covered and refrigerated, up to 5 days.

T I P : If you have sun-dried tomatoes packed in oil, you don't need to soak them. Just pat them dry with a paper towel before processing.

CREAMY RICOTTA BASIL SPREAD

Pairing ricotta cheese with cream cheese gives this pesto-flavored spread a seductive, silken consistency that makes it especially wonderful when mounded on crisp toasts such as Basic Crostini (page 39).

MAKES 1¼ CUPS

1 cup ricotta cheese, preferably whole milk

¼ cup cream cheese, preferably
    Neufchâtel (light cream cheese)

1 garlic clove, minced

2 tablespoons grated Parmesan cheese

Dash salt

3 tablespoons minced fresh basil, plus a
    little extra for garnish

1. Combine all the ingredients except the basil in a food processor and process until smooth. **2.** Scrape into a bowl and stir in the basil by hand. Cover and chill at least 1 hour for the flavors to meld. Serve with some basil sprinkled on top.

T I P S : If you don't have any fresh basil, substitute ¾ teaspoon dried and 2 tablespoons minced fresh parsley.

This spread will keep up to 3 days if well wrapped and refrigerated.

SPICY BLACK BEAN DIP

This updated black bean dip includes chipotle peppers and lime juice rather than the traditional salsa. Chipotle peppers (smoked jalapeños) and black beans are a match made in heaven. The peppers impart an irresistible smoky flavor to this dip while adding just enough heat to give it a spicy but not over-whelming edge. Corn chips or Garlic Pita Chips (page 39) are ideal to scoop it up. If you are serving this at a party, the recipe can be easily doubled or tripled.

MAKES ABOUT 1½ CUPS

1 (15-ounce) can black beans, rinsed in a
    strainer and drained very well, or 1½
    cups freshly cooked black beans (page
    27)

2 tablespoons lime juice

3 tablespoons olive oil

1 chipotle pepper in adobo sauce, or dried
    chipotle soaked in boiling water 30
    minutes (see page 8)

1 very small garlic clove, minced

1 tablespoon sour cream for garnish
    (optional)

Minced fresh parsley for garnish

1. Combine all the ingredients except the sour cream and parsley in a food processor and process until fluffy. **2.** Scrape the dip into a serving bowl. Place the sour cream in the center if you are using it and sprinkle the dip with some minced parsley.

T I P : I highly recommend using chipotle peppers in adobo sauce because they have such a rich flavor. If you can't find them, you can add a few drops of liquid smoke seasoning to give the dip that delicious smoky character.

CLASSIC TZATZIKI

This Greek yogurt and cucumber dip has been a summer favorite in the United States since the 1970s. The tangy yogurt base contrasts perfectly with the minced cool cucumbers and herbs, making it especially refreshing. The yogurt becomes thick and creamy if you let it drip in a strainer. You do have to plan ahead because it should drip for 24 hours, but it is not a difficult task. Serve tzatziki with warm pita triangles or as a dip with raw vegetables.

MAKES ABOUT 1½ CUPS

> 2 cups low-fat or whole milk yogurt (**not nonfat**)
>
> 1 cucumber, peeled, seeded, and grated
>
> 1 garlic clove, put through a press or minced
>
> 1½ teaspoons minced fresh dill
>
> 1 tablespoon minced fresh parsley
>
> 1 tablespoon olive oil
>
> ¼ teaspoon salt
>
> Generous seasoning freshly ground pepper

1. Line a strainer with a single layer of cheesecloth, letting the cloth hang over the sides. Spoon the yogurt into the strainer and place it over a medium-large bowl to allow the drippings (whey) to collect. Cover the strainer with plastic wrap and place it and the bowl in the refrigerator for 24 hours. (You should pour out the liquid at least once during this time because a lot will accumulate and you don't want the bottom of the strainer to sit in it.) **2.** Place the grated cucumber in a cotton kitchen towel and gather into a ball. Squeeze out all the juices. Drop the ball of grated cucumber onto a cutting board and mince it with a large knife. **3.** Put the yogurt in a medium-size bowl and discard the accumulated liquid. Mix in the cucumber and all the remaining ingredients. Chill at least 2 hours so the flavors can mingle.

TIP: Wash your cheesecloth with soap and water, rinse thoroughly, let dry, and save to reuse.

CLASSIC GUACAMOLE

When visiting the Yucatán, on several occasions I had guacamole that had been whipped smooth into a silken consistency. It has now become my favorite way to prepare this dip because I enjoy the texture so much.

SERVES 4

> 2 ripe Haas (dark pebbly-skinned) avocados
>
> 4 teaspoons fresh lime juice
>
> 2 tablespoons minced red or white onion
>
> ¼ cup minced tomato
>
> ¼ teaspoon salt

1. To open the avocado slice it lengthwise around the pit. Twist both halves to separate them and discard the pit. Slip the end of a teaspoon handle between the skin and flesh of the avocado and slide it all around to separate the avocado half from its skin. **2.** Place the avocado halves and lime juice in a food processor and process until smooth and fluffy. Scrape the mixture into a bowl. Stir in the remaining ingredients. Serve immediately or cover and chill up to 24 hours, then bring to room temperature before serving.

T I P : Minced cilantro and jalapeños can be used to add flavor.

GARLIC AND OIL DIPPING SAUCE FOR TUSCAN-STYLE BREAD

This simple yet dynamic dipping sauce derives its intoxicating flavor from the gentle warming of the oil just to the point where the aromatic flavors are released. Choose a fruity extra-virgin olive oil as the building block for this sauce, and you will be greatly rewarded.

The ideal bread to dip is a chewy Tuscan-style loaf that has large holes and a rustic, thick crust.

MAKES ⅓ CUP, ENOUGH FOR 4 PEOPLE

⅓ cup fruity, extra-virgin olive oil

1 large garlic clove, put through a press or minced

⅛ teaspoon crushed red pepper flakes

1 long strip orange peel, 3 × 1 inch

Tuscan-style bread pieces for dipping

1. Place the oil, garlic, and red pepper flakes in a small saucepan. Heat just until the garlic begins to sizzle. You don't want it to get at all colored. Immediately drop in the orange peel. **2.** Pour the mixture into a shallow medium-size bowl. Let sit at least 20 minutes. Discard the orange peel. Serve surrounded by pieces of bread. (I like to cut the bread into triangles.)

T I P : Good olive oil is the key to the success of this dipping sauce. It is better to have a light-flavored oil than one that is strong and bitter, a problem with some inferior oils.

CLASSIC FRESH SALSA

Whether it is called Pico de Gallo or Salsa Fresca, this all-purpose salsa should be made just before serving so the flavors remain subtle and fresh. Serve it with Garlic Pita Chips (page 39) or corn chips, or alongside quesadillas (see The Sandwich Board chapter, page 136).

MAKES ABOUT 2 CUPS

2 large ripe tomatoes or 5 ripe plum tomatoes, seeded and finely diced

¼ cup minced red onion

¼ cup finely chopped cilantro

1 jalapeño pepper, or more to taste, seeded and minced (wear gloves)

1 garlic clove, put through a press or minced

2 tablespoons lime juice

¼ teaspoon salt

Combine all the ingredients in a medium-size bowl. Serve immediately.

TIP: You can make a delightful fruit salsa by substituting diced mango, peaches, or oranges for all or some of the tomatoes.

COOKED TOMATO-CHIPOTLE SALSA

This is one of the best salsas I've ever had. The ingredients are simmered to make a thick, richly textured sauce. The chipotle pepper (smoked jalapeño) adds a smoky dimension without overpowering the other flavors. Serve with corn chips to scoop it up.

MAKES 2 CUPS

1 tablespoon olive oil

1 small onion, minced

2 garlic cloves, minced

½ green bell pepper, minced

1 (14-ounce) can diced tomatoes

1 tablespoon tomato paste

½ chipotle pepper in adobo sauce, minced (see page 8)

1 teaspoon sugar

Salt to taste

1 tablespoon minced fresh cilantro

2 tablespoons lime juice

1. Warm the oil in a medium-size saucepan over medium heat. Add the onion, garlic, and green pepper, and sauté 10 minutes. **2.** Mix in the tomatoes with their juice, tomato paste, chipotle, sugar, and salt, and simmer 20 minutes, or until the green pepper is soft. **3.** Pour the salsa into a food processor and pulse 8 times, or until it is finely minced but not pureed. Scrape into a bowl and let cool. Stir in the cilantro and lime juice. Serve at room temperature.

TIPS: You can cover the salsa and refrigerate it up to 1 week. Be sure to serve it at room temperature, not cold.

If you cannot find chipotle peppers, you can substitute 1 or 2 minced and seeded jalapeños with good results.

BASIC CROSTINI

These simple toasts are an ideal carrier for so many spreads and toppings that I think no appetizer repertoire is complete without a reliable recipe for them. Choose a rather light and airy French bread or some grinder (submarine) rolls for the most tender toasts; a firm sourdough bread will create rock-hard crostini. Also, moderate oven heat and slow cooking work better than broiling, which will brown the toasts before they have a chance to dry out thoroughly.

MAKES ABOUT 40 TOASTS

> 1 baguette (1 pound) French bread or 4 grinder (submarine) rolls
>
> ½ cup olive oil

1. Preheat the oven to 350 degrees. Thinly slice the bread with a serrated knife into ¼-inch-thick slices. **2.** Place the oil in a small bowl. Using a pastry brush very lightly coat both sides of the bread slices with the oil. Place in 1 layer on the baking sheet. You'll have to do this in 2 batches or use 2 sheets. Bake 5 minutes, turn the toasts over, and bake 5–7 minutes more, or until golden all over. Let cool completely before storing in plastic bags.

TIP: These toasts store very well in the refrigerator (up to 2 weeks) or in the freezer (up to 1 month).

GARLIC PITA CHIPS

These pita chips are far superior to any available commercial chips and are well worth the effort to make them. They are tasty enough to be eaten alone or will enhance any dip.

MAKES 64 CHIPS

> 4 tablespoons olive oil
>
> 2 garlic cloves, put through a press (preferably) or minced
>
> 4 (6-inch) pita breads

1. Combine the oil and garlic in a small bowl and let sit 30 minutes. **2.** Preheat the oven to 300 degrees. **3.** Cut 1 pita bread in half to make 2 pockets. Use kitchen shears to snip the outer edge of 1 pocket to separate it into 2 single layers. Repeat with the other pocket. Using a pastry brush lightly coat the rough side of each piece with the garlic oil, scooping up bits of garlic when you do this. With a sharp knife cut each piece into 4 triangles. Place on a baking sheet, rough side up. Repeat with the remaining pita breads. You'll have to use a couple of baking sheets **4.** Bake 12–15 minutes, or until golden and cooked all the way through. Cool completely before storing in plastic bags.

TIPS: The secret to these chips and any other "toasts" is for them to dry out and become hard before they get brown, thus the low 300-degree oven temperature. Because pita breads vary in thickness the cooking time is approximate. Make sure the chips are thoroughly cooked before removing them from the oven. They should be golden all over (not deep brown) and dried throughout.

Pita chips can be stored in the refrigerator up to 1 month if sealed in a plastic bag.

MARINATED OLIVES

You can transform an assortment of your favorite olives into outstanding nibbles by steeping them in this potent marinade. After all the olives have been eaten, you'll want to sop up the luscious pool of juices remaining with some crusty bread.

4 cups assorted olives (such as Niçoise, Kalamata, and green Picholine)

¼ cup olive oil

1 teaspoon grated orange zest (from about ⅓ of an orange)

2 garlic cloves, pressed or minced

A few dashes cayenne pepper

2 teaspoons minced fresh rosemary, or 1 teaspoon dried, crumbled

Combine all the ingredients in a glass or ceramic bowl and marinate at least 1 hour at room temperature or up to 1 week in the refrigerator. Bring to room temperature before serving.

On Olives

Olives cannot be eaten right off the tree; they are intolerably bitter. To become edible they must be processed to remove the harsh-tasting component "oleuropein." Since Roman times this has been done by soaking the fruit in a lye solution and then thoroughly rinsing it. Olives are cured (fermented) by being pickled in brine, aged in oil, or packed in dry salt. (Greek Kalamata olives retain their characteristic strong taste because they are cured without having their oleuropein removed.) Olives can be picked green (unripe) or allowed to ripen before being picked, in which case they will have blackened. Both green and black olives are cured to set their flavors and preserve them. The California (Mission) olive is a different story, however. These black olives, usually sold in cans, have a very mild flavor because they have not been cured in brine or dry salt. They are soaked in a ferrous gluconate solution to set their color, treated with lye, and then immediately canned without fermentation.

EDAMAME

(Fresh Soybeans in the Pod)

Edamame (pronounced ed-a-MAH-may) have become popular as a snack food served at bars in New York Japanese restaurants. These small soybean pods (a different variety from the soybean used to make tofu) are boiled for a short time, salted, and then served in large bowls so diners can split them open and pop the inner beans into their mouths. They are as addictive as peanuts but not nearly as fattening. Frozen edamame are found in natural foods stores and gourmet grocers. They are a snap to cook and great fun to eat. The beans have a buttery flavor and are addictive. Although most Americans enjoy edamame as a simple snack, my Japanese sister-in-law, Megumi Lemlin, tells me that in northern Japan edamame are removed from the pods, mashed with sugar, and enclosed in a ball of sticky rice to make a sweet.

SERVES 4

1 (12-ounce) bag frozen edamame
Salt to taste

Bring a medium-size saucepan filled with lightly salted water to a boil. Drop in the edamame and let the water return to a boil. Cook about 5 minutes. Drain, place in a large bowl, and let cool to warm or room temperature. Sprinkle with salt and serve. Each person can split the pods open and pop the beans into his or her mouth. Discard the pods.

TIP: On a rare occasion you will be able to find fresh, unfrozen edamame. The exterior of the pod has a lot of fuzz that must be removed before cooking. Sprinkle on a few tablespoons of coarse salt and, with your hands, vigorously rub it onto the pod. When you cook the edamame, you won't have to salt the water, but you will have to cook them about 4 minutes more than frozen ones.

HEARTY SOUPS

To my mind a steaming pot of homemade soup is the ultimate comfort food. Whether it's served in a cup (a rarity in my house) to introduce a meal or presented in a large bowl as a main course with bread and salad (a combination that is my winter staple), soup is one of the most satisfying foods to prepare and serve. No other dish benefits so much from being made in advance, so soup can be the busy person's dream dinner. Fans of soup making know how gratifying it can be to reach for a previously made pot of soup and merely heat it up after a hectic day, weekend, or week. Dinner is ready in a flash, and it's a perfect opportunity to eat a lot of another favorite food—bread.

Incorporate the art of making soup in your meal planning with these wonderful tried-and-true favorites of soup lovers.

THE ART OF MAKING SOUP

Several factors contribute to the successful transformation of a potful of mixed ingredients into a harmonious, richly flavored pot of soup. Here are some pointers:

■ For a soup to have a deep and complex flavor, you must begin with a full-bodied stock if the soup calls for stock, rather than water, as its base. (Some soups, such as Classic Lentil Soup, begin with water, and a flavorful base is created as the soup cooks.) A recipe is included for Vegetable Stock (page 18) if you want to make it from scratch, but there are some delicious ready-made stocks, stock cubes, and powders on the market. The key is to sample the stock on its own. If it is tasty enough to drink unembellished, then it will be a good building block for your soup. I purchase a dry soup stock base from the natural foods store in my town; it's called Morga Vegetable Broth. This imported soup powder is expensive, but a little goes a long way; you can use only the amount you need, so you never waste any.

■ Most soups begin with a base of sautéed onions and often garlic as a first step to building up flavors. This step is essential because the sautéeing and browning of vegetables creates more flavor than if they were just added to boiling stock. During the browning process the sugars in the vegetables caramelize and develop a rich taste. Take time with this step to help the onions start the caramelizing process.

■ Be precise with cutting the vegetables that go into the soup. Large chunks are not very appetizing, and they lead to uneven cooking. If the soup is not going to be pureed, and therefore each vegetable will show, cut them small and uniformly.

■ Make your soup early in the day or the day before so the flavors can intensify and meld. Soup is one food that benefits from being a "leftover."

CLASSIC LENTIL SOUP

When vegetarianism gained momentum in the 1960s, lentil soup became a staple. Its rich flavor, high-protein content, and ease of preparation make it an ideal "meal" for those seeking an alternative to traditional meat-centered fare. Still a favorite among vegetarians and non-vegetarians alike, lentil soup deserves a place on the list of the world's greatest soups.

For best results it is a good idea to make this soup early in the day so the flavors can develop to their fullest.

SERVES 4–6 AS A MAIN COURSE

¼ cup olive oil

3 large onions, finely diced

4 large garlic cloves, minced

10 cups water

1¼ cups lentils, picked over and rinsed

1 green bell pepper, finely diced

4 carrots, finely diced

2 celery ribs, thinly sliced

⅓ cup tomato paste mixed with ½ cup water

2 tablespoons tamari soy sauce

1 teaspoon salt

Freshly ground pepper to taste

1 tablespoon red wine vinegar

2 tablespoons unsalted buter

1. Pour the oil in a large stockpot and heat over medium-high heat. Add the onions and garlic, and sauté until the onions begin to brown, about 10 minutes. **2.** Stir in all the remaining ingredients except the vinegar and butter. Bring to a boil, lower the heat to a simmer, and cook, stirring frequently, for 45 minutes. When done, the soup will be thick and the vegetables tender. Stir in the vinegar and butter just before serving.

Lentil Lore

―――

"Lens" is the Latin word for lentil, and the shape of this legume explains the choice of that name for a double-convex piece of glass. Lentils are a food staple in the Middle East and are the oldest cultivated legume, dating back to 7000 B.C.

CURRIED RED LENTIL SOUP

Lentil soup made with common brown lentils has been a vegetarian classic for decades. Actually, so has soup made with red lentils, though it has a far smaller audience. If you are not familiar with this legume, do try it. Red lentils (they are actually orange) are unsurpassed for their nutty, buttery flavor. Unlike most brown lentil soups in which the lentils retain their shapes, red lentils dissolve to create a thick, smooth soup that is concentrated in flavor and robust in texture. This soup is my idea of comfort food.

SERVES 4 AS A MAIN COURSE

> 1½ cups red lentils, picked over for stones and rinsed in a strainer
>
> 6 cups water
>
> 1 tablespoon canola oil
>
> ¾ teaspoon salt
>
> 2 medium-size boiling potatoes (such as red-skinned), peeled and cut into ½-inch dice
>
> 3 tablespoons unsalted butter
>
> 1 medium onion, finely diced
>
> 1 teaspoon minced gingerroot
>
> 2 garlic cloves, minced
>
> 1 teaspoon turmeric
>
> 2 teaspoons ground cumin
>
> 1½ teaspoons ground coriander
>
> ⅛ teaspoon cayenne pepper
>
> ¾ cup finely diced canned tomatoes
>
> 2 tablespoons lemon juice (about ½ lemon)
>
> **Minced cilantro for garnish (optional)**

1. Combine the lentils, water, oil, and salt in a 3-quart saucepan and bring to a boil over medium-high heat, stirring often. With a large spoon skim off any foam that rises to the surface and discard it. Lower the heat and cook 20 minutes, stirring often. **2.** Stir in the diced

Vegetarian Classics

potatoes. **3.** Melt the butter in a medium-size skillet over medium heat. Add the onion, ginger, and garlic, and cook 2 minutes. Sprinkle on the turmeric, cumin, coriander, and cayenne, and brown these spices 2 minutes, stirring constantly. Mix in the diced tomatoes and cook 1 minute more. **4.** Scrape the mixture into the soup and stir well. Cook the soup 20 minutes more, or until the potatoes are tender. Stir frequently from this point on to prevent the soup from sticking. When done, the soup should be somewhat smooth and the consistency of thick cream. If it is thick and pasty, thin with a little water. Mix in the lemon juice. Serve with a sprinkling of cilantro, if desired.

TIP: This soup will become solidified when chilled. Reheat gently over low heat, stirring frequently. Add a little water to thin it, then wait until it is piping hot before adding any more water because the soup will become thinner as it heats.

CORN AND RED PEPPER CHOWDER

The creamy white soup base that defines chowder (except for the sacrilegious tomato-based Manhattan clam chowder!) was discovered in New England to be the ideal match for corn's natural starchiness and sweetness. Vegetarians eagerly adopted this classic.

Because I inevitably make this savory chowder during the winter, I use frozen corn with great results. If you plan to cook this during the summer and fresh corn is available, by all means use it. You'll need to cut the corn off about 8 ears to yield 4 cups.

SERVES 4 AS A MAIN COURSE

2 tablespoons unsalted butter

1 tablespoon olive oil

2 medium onions, finely diced

2 garlic cloves, minced

4 cups vegetable stock, store-bought or homemade (page 18)

2 large potatoes, peeled and finely diced (about 2½ cups)

2 medium-size red bell peppers, finely diced

1 celery rib, very thinly sliced

1 bay leaf

2 tablespoons finely chopped fresh basil, or ½ teaspoon dried

¾ teaspoon salt

1 tablespoon sugar

Freshly ground pepper to taste

4 cups frozen or fresh corn kernels

6 scallions, very thinly sliced

½ cup milk

½ cup heavy cream

1. Combine the butter and oil in a large stock-pot and place over medium heat. Add the onions and garlic, and sauté until the onions are tender but not brown, about 10 minutes. 2. Stir in the stock and bring to a boil. Add the potatoes, red peppers, celery, bay leaf, basil, salt, sugar, and pepper, and bring to a boil. Lower the heat to a lively simmer, partially cover the pan, and cook until the potatoes are tender, about 15 minutes. Stir in the corn and scallions, and cook 2 minutes more if using frozen corn, 8 minutes more if using fresh corn. Remove the bay leaf. 3. Remove 3 cups of the soup and puree in a blender. Return to the pot. Stir in the milk and cream, and heat a minute or so before serving.

T i p : To remove fresh corn from its cob, stand the cob upright on its wide end and slice off the kernels from top to bottom. Rotate the corn and repeat.

VEGETABLE CHOWDER

This is a classy variation of chowder—creamy yet light, and so pretty to look at. Delicate threads of dill float on an ivory surface with a colorful mélange of tasty vegetables beneath. Accompany this chowder with some crusty French bread for a good match. As with most soups, some resting time after completing this chowder will intensify all the flavors.

SERVES 4 AS A MAIN COURSE

2 leeks

2 tablespoons olive oil

4 garlic cloves, minced

8 ounces mushrooms, quartered and thinly sliced

5 cups vegetable stock, store-bought or homemade (page 18)

1 red bell pepper, cut into ¼-inch dice

3 medium boiling potatoes (such as red-skinned), peeled and cut into ½-inch dice

1 medium sweet potato, peeled and cut into ½-inch dice

1 cup frozen corn

3 cups milk

½ cup heavy cream

¾ teaspoon salt

Generous seasoning freshly ground pepper

2 tablespoons minced fresh dill, or 1½ tea-spoons dried

1. To clean the leeks slice off their root ends and the tough green leaves except about 2 inches above the white base. Slice the leeks in half lengthwise. Wash the leeks under cold running water, flipping through their leaves to dislodge any hidden dirt. Pat the leeks dry. Thinly slice the leeks, discarding any dark green pieces and saving only white and pale green ones. 2. Heat the oil in a large stockpot over medium heat. Add the leeks and garlic, and sauté 5 min-

utes, stirring often. Mix in the mushrooms and sauté the mixture until the mushrooms are juicy and begin to brown, about 7 minutes. **3.** Stir in the stock, red pepper, potatoes, and sweet potato, and bring the soup to a boil. Lower the heat to a lively simmer and cook 30 minutes. **4.** Add the corn, milk, cream, salt, and pepper, and heat to almost a boil. Remove 3 cups of the soup and puree in a blender or food processor. Return it to the pot and stir in the dill.

TIP: Onions can be substituted for the leeks, but leeks add a distinct sweetness, so do try to use them if possible.

KALE SOUP

Having grown up in New Bedford, Mass-achusetts, which has a vibrant Portuguese community, I knew when I became a vegetarian that a meatless version of their ubiquitous kale soup was essential. One of my favorite soups, it is at once robust and comforting. If you are not familiar with kale, this is a great way to be introduced to this fabulous leafy vegetable whose leaves are sturdier than spinach and whose flavor is more delicate than its relative, the cabbage.

SERVES 6 AS A MAIN COURSE

½ cup olive oil

3 large onions, finely diced

4 garlic cloves, minced

2 bay leaves

10 cups vegetable stock, store-bought
   or homemade (page 18)

1 (16-ounce) can ready-cut diced tomatoes

1 (15-ounce) can kidney beans, drained
   and rinsed well, or 1½ cups freshly
   cooked beans (page 27)

1 pound kale, leaves torn from stems and
   finely chopped (10 cups leaves)

3 medium-size red-skinned potatoes,
   unpeeled and cut into ½-inch dice

2 teaspoons good-quality (sweet) paprika

Dash cayenne pepper

1 teaspoon salt

Liberal seasoning freshly ground pepper

1. Heat the oil in a large stockpot over medium heat. Stir in the onions and garlic, and sauté until the onions are golden and tender, about 10 minutes. **2.** Raise the heat to high, stir in all the remaining ingredients, and bring the soup to a boil. Lower the heat to a lively simmer and cook about 30 minutes, or until the potatoes are tender and the soup has thickened. **3.** Discard the bay leaves. Remove about 2 cups of the soup and puree in a blender or food processor. Return it to the soup and stir to blend. This soup's flavor will intensify with time, so don't hesitate to make it a few days in advance.

TIP: If you cannot get fresh kale, substitute 1 package of frozen chopped kale.

CLASSIC BARLEY MUSHROOM SOUP

Because barley is an easy staple to keep in the kitchen and mushrooms are so often on my shopping list, this is a soup I can make quickly and with little fuss. The generous portion of mushrooms helps create a rich broth that defines this delicious soup.

SERVES 4 AS A MAIN COURSE

3 tablespoons olive oil

2 medium onions, finely diced

4 garlic cloves, minced

1 pound mushrooms, coarsely chopped into small pieces (see Tip)

10 cups vegetable stock, store-bought or homemade (page 18)

1 celery rib, very thinly sliced

2 carrots, finely chopped

½ cup barley, rinsed in a strainer

2 tablespoons tamari soy sauce

1 teaspoon fresh thyme, or ½ teaspoon dried

½ teaspoon salt

Generous seasoning freshly ground pepper

2 tablespoons minced fresh parsley

1. Heat the oil in a large stockpot over medium heat. Stir in the onions and garlic, and cook until tender and golden, about 10 minutes. Add the mushrooms and sauté, stirring often, until they release their juices and begin to brown, about 10 minutes. **2.** Stir in all the remaining ingredients except the parsley and bring to a boil. Cover the pot, lower the heat to a lively simmer, and cook 45–60 minutes, or until the barley is very tender. Stir in the parsley just before serving.

TIPS: Got some Madeira on hand? A splash adds depth and richness to this soup.

You can use all common mushrooms or 8 ounces common mushrooms and 8 ounces mixed exotic mushrooms.

This soup can be made up to 2 days in advance.

ARMENIAN BARLEY YOGURT SOUP

Here is a barley soup that is very different from the more prevalent one with mushrooms, and it is sensational. I love Middle Eastern flavors, and here they are a captivating backdrop for this soup that is equally delicious hot or cold. For a tantalizing supper or summer menu, serve with some hot pita bread, Classic Hummus (page 29), and a salad with crumbled feta cheese.

2 tablespoons unsalted butter

1 tablespoon olive oil

1 large onion, minced

2 garlic cloves, minced

6 cups vegetable stock, store-bought or
    homemade (page 18)

½ cup barley, rinsed in a strainer

1 large egg

2 cups plain yogurt

½ cup finely chopped fresh parsley

3 tablespoons finely chopped fresh mint,
    or 1 tablespoon dried

2 scallions, very thinly sliced

¼ teaspoon salt

1. Heat the butter and oil in a 3-quart saucepan over medium heat. Add the onion and sauté until golden and soft (but not at all brown), about 5 minutes. Stir in the stock and barley, and bring to a boil. Lower the heat to a lively simmer, partially cover the pan, and cook 40 minutes, or until tender. Stir occasionally. **2.** Meanwhile, beat the egg in a medium-size bowl. Beat in the yogurt, parsley, mint, scallions, and salt. When the barley is tender, stir in the yogurt mixture. Immediately remove the pot from the heat and stir the soup a few minutes. You don't want to boil the soup at this point, or the yogurt will curdle. Serve immediately or at a later time. If you chill the soup and want to reheat it, do so over low heat without boiling it.

TIP: This soup is also delicious cold and can be a wonderful luncheon offering in the summer, perhaps accompanied by a tomato salad and some corn on the cob.

BUTTERNUT SQUASH AND CIDER SOUP

A nuance of apple and curry enlivens this heartwarming soup, making it an ideal choice for a fall or winter first course or as a light meal in itself. I prefer to puree it in a food processor rather than a blender so that it retains some texture.

SERVES 4 AS A MAIN COURSE

3 tablespoons olive oil

2 large leeks, thinly sliced (including 2
    inches of light green top)

3 garlic cloves, minced

1½ teaspoons curry powder

3 cups water

3 cups apple cider

3 pounds (1 large) butternut squash,
    peeled, cored, and cut into 1-inch
    cubes (about 7 cups)

⅓ cup white rice, preferably converted,
    basmati, or jasmine

1 teaspoon salt

Minced parsley or chives for garnish

1. Heat the oil in a large stockpot over medium heat. Add the leeks and garlic, and sauté until the leeks are tender, about 8 minutes. Sprinkle on the curry powder, toss, and cook 1 minute. 2. Pour in the water and cider, then stir in the butternut squash, rice, and salt. 3. Cover the pot and bring the soup to a boil. Lower the heat to a simmer and cook until the squash is very soft, about 20 minutes. Let cool a few minutes, then puree the soup in batches in a food processor and place in a smaller pot, if desired. Check the consistency. If necessary, thin with a little water and cider until creamy like heavy cream. Serve garnished with parsley or chives, if desired.

CURRIED BUTTERNUT SQUASH SOUP WITH COCONUT MILK

This rendition of butternut squash soup is silky and wonderfully aromatic. Coconut milk combines with curry and ginger to create a sensational base that highlights the natural sweetness of the squash. Serve this as a first course to a special meal or as a main course along with a salad and some crusty French bread.

SERVES 4 AS A MAIN COURSE

2 tablespoons olive oil

2 onions, finely diced

3 garlic cloves, minced

1 tablespoon minced gingerroot

1 tablespoon curry powder

4 cups water

7–8 cups diced butternut squash
    (1 large 3-pound squash)

2 teaspoons sugar

1¼ teaspoons salt

1 (14-ounce) can coconut milk

2 tablespoons lemon juice

1. Warm the oil in a large stockpot over medium heat. Stir in the onions, garlic, and gingerroot, and cook 5 minutes. Sprinkle on the curry powder and cook 1 minute, tossing continuously. 2. Pour in the water and bring to a boil. Mix in the squash, sugar, and salt, and lower the heat to a lively simmer. Cook 30 minutes, or until the squash is very tender. Pour in the coconut milk and simmer 5 minutes. Stir in the lemon juice 3. Puree the soup in batches in a blender and return to a smaller pot, if desired. Reheat the soup before serving, if necessary.

TIP: Be certain to get coconut milk that is unsweetened. Sweetened versions, usually called coconut cream, are used for piña coladas and desserts, not soups.

THICK CORN AND VEGETABLE SOUP WITH HERB DUMPLINGS

This is a variation of one of my all-time favorite soups from my first cookbook, *Vegetarian Pleasures: A Menu Cookbook*. The addition of a few cloves gives the broth a lively edge, while the dumplings transform the soup into a rich, satisfying meal. Don't be put off by the lengthy list of ingredients; this soup is not difficult to prepare, and the result is extraordinary.

SERVES 6–8

¼ cup olive oil

2 tablespoons butter

2 medium onions, diced

4 garlic cloves, minced

2 bay leaves

4 cloves

Dash cayenne pepper

12 cups vegetable stock, store-bought
   or homemade (page 18)

1 teaspoon salt

Generous seasoning freshly ground pepper

1 (28-ounce) can ready-cut diced tomatoes

15-ounce can pinto or small white beans,
   rinsed well and drained, or 1½ cups
   freshly cooked beans (page 27)

2 medium carrots, halved lengthwise
   and thinly sliced

2 medium potatoes, cut into ½-inch dice

1 cup diced (½-inch) butternut squash
   (see Tip)

1 cup finely chopped fresh parsley, divided

2 cups frozen corn

Herb Dumplings:

1 cup unbleached flour

2 tablespoons cornmeal

2 teaspoons baking powder

1 teaspoon sugar

½ teaspoon salt

2 tablespoons minced fresh parsley

½ teaspoon freshly minced dill,
   or 1 teaspoon dried

1 tablespoon chilled butter

⅔ cup cold milk

1. Heat the oil and butter in a large stockpot over medium heat. Add the onions and garlic, and sauté until tender, about 10 minutes. Stir in the cloves, bay leaves, cayenne, vegetable stock, salt, pepper, and tomatoes, and bring to a boil. **2.** Add the beans, carrots, potatoes, butternut squash, and half the parsley, and return to a boil. Lower the heat and cook at a lively simmer for 30 minutes, or until the vegetables are tender. Stir the soup often. Mix in the corn and the remaining ½ cup parsley, and cook 5 minutes. Discard the bay leaves. (The soup can be prepared to this point up to 3 days in advance and refrigerated. Reheat before proceeding with the next step.) **3.** To make the dumplings: combine the flour, cornmeal, baking powder, sugar, salt, parsley, and dill in a medium-size bowl. Cut the butter into bits and drop into the mixture. Rub the butter into the flour with your fingertips until small crumbs form. Stir in the milk just until evenly moistened; do not overmix. Cover and chill until ready to use, up to 8 hours. **4.** To cook the dumplings, keep the soup at a lively simmer. Hold 1 tablespoon in each hand, scoop out about ⅛ of the batter, and using the spoons, quickly shape into a ball. Place the dumpling in the soup and repeat with the remaining batter. Cover the pot and cook at a lively simmer, not a violent boil, for 15 minutes. Do not uncover the pot during this time. When done, the dumplings will be fat and puffy. Serve the soup with one dumpling in each bowl.

TIP: The remainder of the butternut squash can be used in Penne with Garlicky Butternut Squash (page 210).

CHICKPEA SOUP WITH GARLIC CROSTINI

This hearty and delectable soup, which is creamy in texture and has garlic crostini floating on top, is from the central Italian region of Umbria. It is so delicious that I inevitably eat a sizable portion before serving time because I can't stop sampling it. Using canned chickpeas makes this preparation remarkably quick without sacrificing any flavor, but you can instead begin with freshly cooked chickpeas. Rather than sprinkling Parmesan cheese on the soup, it is traditional to drizzle some extra-virgin olive oil on each serving. A brilliant tradition, I might add.

SERVES 4 AS A MAIN COURSE

> ¼ cup olive oil
>
> 2 onions, diced
>
> 4 garlic cloves, minced
>
> 1 carrot, finely diced
>
> 1 celery rib, thinly sliced
>
> ½ teaspoon crushed red pepper flakes (less for a mild version)
>
> 1 cup tomato puree
>
> 3 (14-ounce) cans chickpeas, rinsed well, or 5 cups freshly cooked chickpeas (page 27)
>
> 6 cups water
>
> ½ teaspoon salt
>
> *Crostini:*
>
> 8 thin slices French bread
>
> 1 tablespoon olive oil
>
> 1 garlic clove, cut in half lengthwise
>
> Extra-virgin olive oil for drizzling
>
> Minced fresh basil, parsley, or rosemary for garnish

1. Heat the oil in a large stockpot over medium heat. Add the onion, garlic, carrot, celery, and red pepper flakes, and sauté 10 minutes. 2. Stir in all the remaining soup ingredients and bring to a boil. Lower the heat to a simmer and cook 30 minutes. Let cool slightly. 3. Remove 1 cup of the soup and set aside. Puree the remaining soup in batches in a blender; you can pour it into a smaller pot at this point. Stir in the reserved cup of soup. 4. To make the crostini: preheat the oven to 300 degrees. Lightly brush the bread slices with the oil. Place on a baking sheet and bake 10 minutes. Turn over and bake 5 minutes more, or until crisp and firm. Let cool slightly, then rub the garlic cloves all over the surface of the bread. Let the bread cool. 5. Serve the soup with a drizzle of oil on each serving, a sprinkling of one of the herbs, and a crostini to float on top.

CLASSIC VEGETARIAN SPLIT PEA SOUP

For a high-protein, low-fat, and economical meal in one bowl you can't beat split pea soup, nor are you likely to find a more flavorful soup made with so little effort. This version will please all palates.

SERVES 4 AS A MAIN COURSE

2 cups (1 pound) green split peas

10 cups water

2 bay leaves

1 tablespoon olive oil

2 large onions, finely diced

4 garlic cloves, minced

2 carrots, finely diced

2 celery ribs, finely diced

1 teaspoon good-quality paprika

3 tablespoons tamari soy sauce

Generous seasoning freshly ground pepper

3 tablespoons unsalted butter

1. In a large stockpot combine the peas, water, bay leaves, and oil. Bring to a boil, stirring the mixture often so the peas don't stick to the bottom of the pot. Reduce the heat to a lively simmer and cover the pot. Cook, stirring occasionally, for 1 hour. 2. Remove the cover and stir in all the remaining ingredients except the butter. Cook, uncovered, for 30 minutes, or until the vegetables are very tender and the peas have dissolved. When finished, the soup should be rather smooth with the consistency of heavy cream. If it is too thick, thin it with some water. Remove the bay leaves. Swirl in the butter before serving.

TIP: Be attentive to the consistency of this soup because if it is too thick, it will be pasty, and if too thin, it will be watery. It is best to err a little on the thin side because split pea soup gets thicker as it cools.

VEGETARIAN CHILI

The addition of bulgur to chili is the magical touch that gives it a texture reminiscent of traditional non-vegetarian versions. An assortment of toppings can be offered for guests to add at will, such as minced red onion, sour cream, minced cilantro, and corn chips. And for the perfect accompaniment? Corn bread, of course. Try Classic Corn Bread (page 97) or Corn Bread with Chilies and Cheese (page 98).

SERVES 4–6 AS A MAIN COURSE

¼ cup olive oil

3 medium onions, finely diced

6 garlic cloves, minced

1 green bell pepper, very finely diced

1½ tablespoons chili powder

1 tablespoon ground cumin

½ teaspoon good-quality paprika

2 teaspoons dried oregano

⅛ teaspoon cayenne pepper

2 bay leaves

½ cup bulgur, preferably coarse-cut

1 (28-ounce) can crushed tomatoes or tomato puree

3 (15-ounce) cans kidney beans, rinsed well in a strainer, or 4½ cups freshly cooked kidney beans (page 27)

2 tablespoons tamari soy sauce

5 cups water

¾ teaspoon salt

Generous seasoning freshly ground pepper

1 tablespoon butter

1. Heat the oil in a large stockpot over medium heat. Stir in the onions, garlic, and green pepper, and sauté 10 minutes, stirring frequently. Mix in the chili powder, cumin, paprika, oregano, cayenne, bay leaves, and bulgur. Cook, stirring constantly, at least 2 minutes to toast the spices. **2.** Add the tomatoes, beans, tamari, water, salt, and pepper. Bring the chili to a boil, then lower the heat and cook at a lively simmer for 30 minutes. Be certain to stir often because the ingredients will settle to the bottom and begin to stick. Just before serving stir in the butter.

TIP: To feed a crowd you can easily multiply the recipe. You can prepare this chili up to 4 days in advance.

SOUTHWESTERN BLACK BEAN SOUP

Here's another favorite bean-based soup for which there are countless versions. Chipotle peppers (smoked jalapeños) lend a smoky overtone to this hearty rendition, but if you cannot get hold of chipotles, you'll still have delicious results with plain jalapeño peppers.

1 pound dried black beans

½ cup olive oil

8 garlic cloves, minced

2 large onions, diced

1 green bell pepper, cut into small dice

1 chipotle pepper in adobo sauce,
    minced (see page 8), or 1 small
    jalapeño pepper, minced (wear gloves)

2 tablespons ground cumin

1 tablespoon dried oregano

10 cups vegetable stock, store-bought
    or homemade (page 18)

1 cup tomato sauce, store-bought
    or Easy Marinara Sauce (page 25)

1½ teaspoons salt

⅓ cup lime juice (from 1 large lime)

Sour cream for garnish (optional)

Lime slices for garnish

1. Soak the beans for 8 to 24 hours in enough water to cover by 3 inches or, alternatively, cook the beans in a large stockpot in about 5 inches of water for 2 minutes. Remove from the heat and let the beans soak 1 hour. Drain in a colander. **2.** Heat the oil in the same large stockpot. Mix in the garlic, onions, and green pepper, and sauté 10 minutes, stirring often. Add the chipotle pepper and sprinkle on the cumin. Cook the mixture 1 minute, stirring continuously. **3.** Mix in the beans, oregano, vegetable stock, and tomato sauce, and bring to

a boil. Lower the heat to a lively simmer and cook the soup 1½ hours, stirring occasionally. The beans should be very tender at this point. **4.** Remove about 4 cups soup and puree in a blender or food processor. Return to the soup and stir in the salt and lime juice. Serve in bowls with a small spoonful of sour cream, if desired, and a lime slice on top.

TIP: This soup can be made up to 4 days in advance. For a fresh citrus flavor add the lime juice just before serving.

GINGER-MISO SOUP WITH NOODLES

Miso soup, the immensely popular dish that is eaten in every household and restaurant in Japan, made its way into American kitchens in the 1970s. This invigorating soup is the perfect remedy for the winter chills. The long, chewy noodles in a mild ginger-laced broth are meant to be slurped, Japanese-style. Japanese udon, white wheat noodles, are mild in flavor in contrast to soba, the assertively flavored buckwheat noodles. Udon have a unique texture that holds up well in broth; however, linguine could be substituted, if necessary.

SERVES 4 AS A MAIN COURSE

8 ounces udon (Japanese wheat noodles)
   or linguine

¼ cup tamari soy sauce

½ cup roughly sliced gingerroot
   (with skin on)

4 ounces firm tofu, cut into
   ½-inch cubes

2 scallions, very thinly sliced

¼ cup white (sweet) miso
   (see page 10)

1 tablespoon Asian sesame oil

1. Bring 3 quarts water to a boil for the udon. Cook the udon about 6 minutes, or until tender but not mushy. If the starch from the noodles looks as if it is about to boil over, lower the heat slightly. Drain the udon in a colander, rinse under cold running water, drain again, and then set aside. **2.** In the same pot bring 6 cups water, tamari, and gingerroot to a boil. Lower the heat and simmer 10 minutes. Remove the ginger with a slotted spoon and discard. Stir in the tofu and half the scallions. Lower the heat to very low. **3.** Place the miso in a small bowl. Remove about ½ cup broth and stir it into the miso to dilute it and prevent lumping. Pour the mixture into the broth. Stir in the sesame oil and udon. Let the udon heat through, about 1 minute. Do not let the soup boil after the miso is added; it would destroy some of its nutritive value. **4.** Use tongs to remove the noodles and place them in individual serving bowls. Ladle the broth over the noodles. Garnish each serving with the remaining scallions.

TIP: Although my preference is for a light miso in this recipe, other misos will work if you enjoy a stronger flavor.

SWEET POTATO AND VEGETABLE SOUP

I am extremely fond of sweet potatoes, and here they lend a lustrous color and dynamic flavor to this thick, aromatic soup. As with most soups, this one benefits from being made at least a few hours in advance.

SERVES 4–6

¼ cup olive oil

2 onions, finely diced

4 garlic cloves, minced

1 (28-ounce) can ready-cut diced tomatoes

6 cups vegetable stock, store-bought or
   homemade (page 18)

2 large sweet potatoes (preferably dark
   orange), peeled and cut into ½-inch dice

1 (15-ounce) can small white beans (navy
   or Great Northern), rinsed well and
   drained

2 cups diced fresh or frozen green beans

1 teaspoon salt

Generous seasoning freshly ground pepper

A few dashes cayenne pepper

1 tablespoon minced fresh basil, or ½ teaspoon dried

4 cups frozen corn

Vegetarian Classics

1. Heat the oil in a large stockpot over medium heat. Add the onions and garlic, and sauté until tender and golden, about 10 minutes. **2.** Mix in the tomatoes and stock, and bring to a boil. Stir in all the remaining ingredients except the corn. Return the soup to a boil, lower to a lively simmer, and cook until the sweet potatoes are tender, about 30 minutes. Stir in the corn and heat through, about 2 minutes. Serve at once or reheat when needed.

CURRIED CHICKPEA AND POTATO STEW

This classic Indian stew is generously laced with fresh ginger, making its broth a potent balm for a wintry day. Like most soups, this one improves with age, so don't hesitate to make it up to 3 days in advance.

SERVES 4 AS A MAIN COURSE

> 3 tablespoons unsalted butter, divided
>
> 2 medium-size onions, finely diced
>
> 4 garlic cloves, minced
>
> 2 tablespoons minced gingerroot
>
> 1 tablespoon ground coriander
>
> ½ teaspoon turmeric
>
> ½ teaspoon ground cumin
>
> ¼ teaspoon ground cardamom
>
> A few dashes cayenne pepper, or more to taste

> 1 cup canned tomato puree
>
> 6 cups water
>
> ¾ teaspoon salt
>
> 3 boiling (waxy) potatoes, peeled and cut into ½-inch dice
>
> 1 (15-ounce) can chickpeas, rinsed and well drained
>
> 1 (10-ounce) package triple-washed fresh spinach, stems discarded and leaves torn
>
> 1 tablespoon minced cilantro (optional)
>
> Juice of ½ lemon

1. Melt 2 tablespoons butter in a large stockpot over medium heat. Add the onions and sauté until golden, about 10 minutes. Mix in the garlic and ginger, and cook gently for 3 minutes. **2.** Sprinkle in all the spices and "toast" them, stirring continuously for 1 minute. **3.** Mix in the tomato puree, water, and salt, and bring to a boil. Add the potatoes and chickpeas, and simmer the stew for 30 minutes, or until the potatoes are tender. Scrape the bottom of the pot to loosen any spices that may have adhered to it. As the stew begins to thicken, you will have to stir it more frequently to prevent it from sticking. (You can make the stew up to 2 days in advance. In that case, stop after this step. Just before serving, reheat it and proceed with the next step.) **4.** Stir in the spinach, cilantro, and remaining tablespoon of butter. Cook 5 minutes, or until the spinach is just wilted. Add the lemon juice and serve.

INDONESIAN-STYLE CURRIED VEGETABLE SOUP WITH COCONUT MILK

This is a variation of a fantastic stew in my first cookbook, and it won second place in an international cooking contest. The richly infused broth is redolent of fragrant coconut milk and spicy curry with just a hint of lemon. The palette of yellow, green, and red makes this meal-in-a-bowl especially pretty to look at and suitable for a special meal.

SERVES 4–6

2 tablespoons canola oil

2 medium onions, finely diced

4 garlic cloves, minced

2 teaspoons minced gingerroot

2 cups (6 ounces) thinly sliced mushrooms

2 teaspoons ground coriander

1 teaspoon ground cumin

1 teaspoon turmeric

⅛ teaspoon cayenne pepper

4 cups vegetable stock, store-bought or homemade (page 18)

1 (14-ounce) can coconut milk

1 teaspoon salt

2 large boiling (waxy) potatoes, peeled and cut into ½-inch dice

1½ cups green beans, cut into 1-inch lengths

¼ cup very finely diced (¼ inch) red bell pepper

½ cup fine egg noodles or 1-inch pieces broken vermicelli

Juice of 1 lemon

1. Warm the oil in a large stockpot over medium heat. Add the onions, garlic, and gingerroot, and sauté, stirring often, for 10 minutes, or until the onions are soft and golden.

2. Add the mushrooms and sauté 5 minutes. Sprinkle on the coriander, cumin, turmeric, and cayenne, and cook 2 minutes, stirring often.

3. Pour in the vegetable stock, coconut milk, and salt, and bring to a boil. Add the potatoes and cook 10 minutes, stirring occasionally.

4. Mix in the green beans, red bell pepper, and noodles, and cook at a lively simmer for 10 minutes, or until the vegetables and noodles are tender. Stir in the lemon juice just before serving.

TIP: Be certain to get coconut milk that is unsweetened. Sweetened versions, usually called coconut cream, are used for piña coladas and desserts, not soups.

CHILLED SUMMER BORSCHT

I am a great fan of cooked fresh beets, but canned beets work beautifully in this splendid pureed soup. Since no cooking is necessary in the creation of this borscht, it becomes an ideal soup for a sweltering summer day—and takes just 5 minutes of work. The final presentation is stunning: a snowy mound of sour cream sits atop a blazing scarlet soup with some minced chives to cap it off.

SERVES 4 GENEROUSLY

3 (16-ounce) cans beets, drained and liquid reserved

1 cup reserved beet liquid

1½ cups V-8 juice

1 small- to medium-size onion, minced

A few dashes Tabasco

2 tablespoons lemon juice

Salt to taste

Freshly ground pepper to taste

½ cup sour cream (approximately)

Minced fresh chives for garnish

1. Place the beets, reserved liquid, V-8 juice, onion, Tabasco, and lemon juice in a blender in batches, and blend until pureed. If the soup is too thick, add a bit more beet liquid or some water. Pour into a large bowl and chill until ice cold, at least 2 hours. **2.** Taste the soup for salt and pepper. Serve the soup in bowls with a spoonful of sour cream on top and some minced chives for garnish.

CLASSIC GAZPACHO

There are few dishes more refreshing in the hot summer months than the cold Spanish soup gazpacho. Rather than pureeing the whole batch of soup, I prefer to mince some of the vegetables by hand so they retain some texture and contrast. This technique, along with using summer vegetables at their prime, produces an exquisite gazpacho.

SERVES 6

3 large, ripe tomatoes, cored

2 cucumbers, peeled, halved lengthwise, and seeded

1 small onion, diced

2 garlic cloves, minced

1 jalapeño pepper, seeded and chopped (wear gloves), or a few dashes Tabasco

1 large green bell pepper, cored and very finely diced

2 tablespoons minced fresh parsley

⅓ cup red wine vinegar

⅓ cup olive oil

½ cup tomato vegetable stock, tomato juice, or water

Salt to taste

Freshly ground pepper to taste

Croutons for garnish (see Tip)

1. Roughly chop the tomatoes and place in a food processor or blender along with 1½ cucumbers, onion, garlic, and jalapeño pepper. Puree until almost smooth but not liquefied. Pour into a large serving bowl. **2.** Very finely dice the remaining ½ cucumber by hand. Stir it into the soup along with the green pepper, parsley, vinegar, oil, stock, salt, and pepper. (If you are using Tabasco instead of a jalapeño pepper, don't forget to add it.) Chill at least 2 hours before serving. Serve garnished with croutons.

Tip: To make croutons, remove the crusts from a few slices of bread. Lightly toast them in a toaster. Rub both sides with some garlic halves. Using a pastry brush lightly coat each side of bread with olive oil. Cut the bread into ½-inch cubes and place them on a baking sheet. Bake in a 350-degree oven until crisp, about 10 minutes. Turn off the oven and leave the door ajar. The croutons can dry out more while the oven cools. Let them come to room temperature before using to garnish the soup.

COLD YOGURT AND CUCUMBER SOUP

This classic Turkish soup is one of my all-time favorite summer treats. The marriage of flavors is superb, juxtaposing the tang of yogurt with the fresh taste of dill and the coolness of cucumbers. Minced hard-boiled egg and walnuts make this version especially substantial. It is equally delightful served as a first course to a summer meal or as a meal in itself accompanied by some pita bread and Classic Hummus (page 29).

SERVES 4 AS A MAIN COURSE

> 1 hard-boiled egg, cooled and very finely minced
>
> 3 cups plain yogurt
>
> ½ cup water
>
> 2 cucumbers, peeled, cut lengthwise, seeded, and finely diced
>
> 2 tablespoons minced fresh dill, or 1 tablespoon dried dill
>
> 1 tablespoon minced fresh parsley
>
> ½ cup walnuts, finely chopped
>
> 2 garlic cloves, pressed or minced
>
> 3 tablespoons olive oil
>
> 1 tablespoon red wine vinegar
>
> ½ teaspoon salt
>
> Freshly ground pepper to taste
>
> Dill or parsley sprigs for garnish

In a large bowl whisk together all the ingredients except the dill or parsley. Cover and chill at least 1 hour or up to 3 days before serving. Serve in bowls with a dill or parsley sprig on top.

DINNER SALADS AND SALAD DRESSINGS

Nearly everyone knows how to put together a salad; it's as fundamental as making a sandwich. However, creating a memorable salad that can artfully introduce a meal (or follow the main course, as is customary in Europe) is another story. I think many of the best salads are ones that offer an element of surprise: some toasted pecans and dried cranberries sprinkled on a bed of mixed greens; thin sheets of delightfully nutty Parmigiano-Reggiano accenting a lettuce and radicchio mixture; or perhaps a dressing, such as Dark Sesame Vinaigrette (page 72), is chosen to enliven a simple spinach salad.

Whatever salad you choose from this chapter, always use the freshest greens you can find and handle with care as you clean them to avoid bruising (see Washing and Spinning Leafy Greens, page 63). When you are planning a menu, see that the salad is a good match for the entree. If you have a rich main course or one with cheese in it, avoid cheese in your salad so that the menu is balanced. And, lastly, avoid overdressing your leafy greens. If you pour on less dressing than you think you will need, toss the salad to completely coat it, then sample it. You can always add more dressing if necessary. It's hard to remedy an overdressed salad.

With these tips in mind you can transform the salad offering from something taken for granted to a classy course that will enhance your menu.

MIXED GREENS WITH DRIED CRANBERRIES AND TOASTED PECANS

It's hard to beat this salad for flavor and panache. Although it's wonderful all year long, it is a particularly good choice for holiday dinners. Be certain to toast the pecans to bring out their richness.

SERVES 4

> ½ **cup pecans**
>
> 4 **cups romaine lettuce torn into small pieces, washed, and spun dry**
>
> 4 **cups mesclun (mixed baby greens), washed and spun dry**
>
> ½ **cup slivered red onion**
>
> ⅓ **cup (approximately) Balsamic Vinaigrette (page 72) or Lemon-Soy Dressing (page 71)**
>
> 4 **tablespoons dried cranberries**

1. Preheat the oven to 350 degrees. Toast the pecans in a shallow pan until they begin to get fragrant, about 5–7 minutes. Let cool completely. **2.** Combine the lettuce, mesclun, and onion in a salad bowl. Just before serving pour on the dressing and toss well. Check to see if you need to add more dressing; you don't want to make the greens too wet. Serve on individual salad plates with the pecans and cranberries sprinkled on each portion.

TOSSED MESCLUN SALAD

Here is my favorite all-purpose salad that seems to go with everything and please all palates. It has an appealing balance of tenderness and crunch, and a charming display of color. It's really no more work to purchase and use a variety of greens when you make a salad, and the results are always more interesting than when you depend on one lettuce.

SERVES 4

> 4 **cups mesclun (mixed baby greens)**
>
> 2 **cups romaine lettuce torn into small pieces, washed, and spun dry**
>
> 2 **cups Boston lettuce torn into small pieces, washed, and spun dry**
>
> ½ **cucumber, peeled, halved, and thinly sliced**
>
> ½ **yellow or red bell pepper, cut into very thin slivers**
>
> 2 **scallions, very thinly sliced**
>
> ⅓ **cup (approximately) Lemon-Soy Dressing (page 71) or Classic Vinaigrette (page 70)**

Combine all the ingredients except the dressing in a large salad bowl. Just before serving toss with the dressing. Taste and add more if necessary, but be careful not to overdress the salad. Serve at once on 4 salad plates.

Vegetarian Classics

LEAFY GREENS AND RADICCHIO WITH SHAVED PARMESAN CHEESE

Paper-thin sheets of nutty Parmesan cheese help create a superlative salad that will set an elegant tone to a special meal.

SERVES 4

> 5 cups torn-up green lettuce, well washed and spun dry
>
> 2 cups arugula, leaves torn in half
>
> 1 cup finely torn radicchio
>
> 2 scallions, very thinly sliced
>
> 1 small chunk (about 4 ounces) Parmigiano-Reggiano
>
> ⅓ cup (approximately) Classic Vinaigrette (page 70) or Lemon-Soy Dressing (page 71)

1. In a large salad bowl combine the lettuce, arugula, radicchio, and scallions. **2.** Use a vegetable peeler to shave off 12 slices Parmigiano-Reggiano. **3.** Toss the salad with the dressing just before serving. Taste to see if you need a bit more dressing. Divide among 4 salad plates. Place 3 sheets of cheese on each serving. Serve at once.

ROMAINE WITH APPLES, WALNUTS, AND BLUE CHEESE

In addition to being delightfully crunchy, this salad sports a lively contrast in flavors with tart apples, assertive blue cheese, and the rich nuttiness of walnuts.

SERVES 4

Washing and Spinning Leafy Greens

Some leafy greens harbor a lot of grit and sand. Regardless of how dirty your greens are, you should thoroughly wash all leafy vegetables before using them in your recipe. The best way to clean and dry salad greens is in a salad spinner. Here's how: The salad spinner is comprised of a bowl, a basket, and a cover. Place the bowl in the sink, fill it with plenty of cold water, and dunk in your torn-up greens. Use your hands to lift the greens up and down a bit to dislodge any hidden sand. With your hands pick up the greens and place them in the basket. Dump out the sandy water, refill the bowl with fresh cold water, and dunk the greens again. Repeat these steps until there is no residue of sand in the water. Place the clean greens in the basket and spin until very dry. You want to avoid rinsing the greens in the basket instead of soaking them because they need copious amounts of water to be thoroughly rid of sand.

3 tablespoons coarsely chopped walnuts

6 cups romaine lettuce torn into bite-size
   pieces, washed, and spun dry

2 cups arugula, large leaves torn in half

½ cup Lemon-Soy Dressing (page 71) or
   Classic Vinaigrette (page 70)

1 red-skinned apple, such as Empire,
   Macoun, or Cortland, cut into 12 slices

¼ cup crumbled blue cheese

1. Preheat the oven to 350 degrees. Toast the walnuts in a shallow pan until they get fragrant, about 5–7 minutes. Let cool completely. **2.** Combine the lettuce and arugula in a salad bowl. Pour on about ¾ of the dressing and toss. Add a little more dressing if needed. **3.** Divide the salad among 4 salad plates, surround with the apple slices, and sprinkle on the blue cheese and walnuts. Serve immediately.

TIP: To prevent the apple slices from turning brown, cut the apple just before placing it on the salad. If you want to cut the apple up to 30 minutes in advance, sprinkle the slices with a little lemon juice to prevent them from discoloring.

CHOPPED SALAD WITH AVOCADO AND CHICKPEAS

A chopped salad differs from what we call a tossed salad because it contains fewer greens and more "additions," such as avocado, hard-boiled egg, beans, and so forth, and everything is cut into bite-size pieces. It lends itself to improvisation, but be attentive to compatible flavors because it is not meant to be a mishmash but rather like a carefully crafted poem. This particular rendition is outstanding and a good choice for a special meal.

SERVES 4

4 cups romaine lettuce in small pieces,
   washed and spun dry

2 cups torn watercress or arugula

2 scallions, very thinly sliced

12 black olives, Niçoise or your favorite kind

½ cup cooked chickpeas, well rinsed if
   canned

⅓ cup Classic Vinaigrette (page 70) or
   Lemon-Soy Dressing (page 71)

1 avocado, cut into 1-inch dice

1 hard-boiled egg, minced

1. Combine the lettuce, watercress, scallions, and olives in a large bowl. **2.** In a small bowl combine the chickpeas with about 1 tablespoon of the dressing. **3.** Just before serving add the avocado and marinated chickpeas to the greens. Pour on the dressing and toss. Serve on individual salad plates garnished with minced hard-boiled egg.

TIPS: You can combine the lettuce, watercress, and scallions a few hours in advance and keep chilled, but don't cut up the avocado until serving time because it will darken.

This salad serves 4 as a first course, but it also makes a fabulous lunch or light dinner in itself; in that case it will serve 2.

SPINACH SALAD WITH ORANGES, FETA CHEESE, AND OLIVES

This salad is a feast for the eyes as well as the palate with its contrasting colors and its play on flavors from sweet oranges to salty feta cheese and spicy, garlicky dressing. Try to find flat-leaf spinach sold in bunches; it is more tender than the crinkle-leaf variety sold in bags.

SERVES 4

1 navel orange

¼ cup (approximately) **Citrus Vinaigrette (page 71)** or **Lemon-Soy Dressing (page 71)**

8 cups torn spinach leaves, well washed and spun dry

2 scallions, very thinly sliced

⅓ cup finely crumbled feta cheese

16 black olives, such as Niçoise or your favorite kind

1. Peel the orange and separate the sections. Remove any coarse membranes, then cut each section in half and place in a small bowl. Toss with a teaspoon or so of dressing, just enough to coat them lightly. **2.** Place the spinach and scallions in a large salad bowl. Just before serving toss with approximately ¼ cup dressing, just enough to coat the leaves. **3.** Divide the spinach onto 4 salad plates. Sprinkle on the oranges, feta cheese, and olives. Serve immediately.

SPINACH SALAD WITH GRAPEFRUIT AND AVOCADO

This is a good choice for the winter months when grapefruit is at its prime.

SERVES 4

1 pink grapefruit

1 ripe avocado (preferably a dark, pebbly-skinned Haas), sliced

⅓ cup **Classic Vinaigrette (page 70)**

8 cups flat-leaf spinach, torn into small pieces

¼ cup thin slivers red onion

Dinner Salads and Salad Dressings

1. Cut off the top and bottom ends of the grapefruit and stand it upright. With a sharp knife slice off the peel, cutting from top to bottom. Slice between the membranes to remove the individual sections. 2. Prepare the avocado and place in a bowl. Pour on 1 tablespoon of the vinaigrette and toss very gently to coat and to prevent it from darkening. 3. Just before serving, toss the spinach and red onion with most of the dressing; add more if needed. Place the spinach on 4 serving plates. Top with the avocado and grapefruit sections.

ROASTED ASPARAGUS WITH GARLIC OIL, LEMON, AND PARMESAN CHEESE

In my view there is no better way to prepare asparagus than this method. I like to serve these as a salad course, but they are equally good when presented as a side dish alongside a special spring dinner. Be certain to use a high-quality chunk of Parmesan cheese, such as Parmigiano-Reggiano, because its incomparable nutty flavor will enhance these delectable asparagus.

SERVES 4

3 tablespoons fruity olive oil

2 garlic cloves, sliced

1½ pounds thin (but preferably not pencil-thin) asparagus, bottom of stalks peeled (see Tip)

4 teaspoons fresh lemon juice

Salt to taste

Freshly ground pepper to taste

¼ cup freshly grated Parmigiano-Reggiano cheese

1. Combine the oil and garlic in a small bowl and let sit at least 1 hour. Remove the garlic and discard. 2. Preheat the oven to 425 degrees. Place the asparagus on a baking sheet in 1 layer. Drizzle on half the garlic oil, and then roll the asparagus with your fingers until they are completely coated. 3. Bake 8–10 minutes for thin asparagus or 10–12 minutes for thicker ones. Give the pan a shake halfway through the cooking time so the asparagus cook evenly. When done they should be tender and only slightly crisp. 4. Divide the asparagus among 4 small plates. Drizzle each portion with the remaining garlic oil, the lemon juice, salt, pepper, and cheese. Serve warm, not piping hot.

TIP: It is preferable to use a paring knife rather than a vegetable peeler to peel the bottoms of the asparagus. A knife allows you to remove a deeper layer, which is needed to make the asparagus tender.

CLASSIC SUMMER TOMATO SALAD

This salad is simplicity itself, yet so pretty and elegant. Its success depends on using perfectly ripe summer tomatoes—the more uniform in size, the better. The colors are stunning when you use a mixture of red and yellow tomatoes, but all red tomatoes are also fine.

SERVES 4

> 2–3 large, ripe, red tomatoes, cored and sliced ½ inch thick
>
> 2 large yellow tomatoes, cored and sliced ½ inch thick
>
> 10 large fresh basil leaves
>
> ½ cup (approximately) Classic Vinaigrette (page 70)

1. Alternate the slices of red and yellow tomatoes on 4 salad plates. **2.** Stack the basil leaves on top of each other to make a neat pile. Starting from the long side, tightly roll the bundle up to make a log. Using a sharp knife, cut thin slices from the top to the bottom. Shreds (chiffonade) will form. Use your fingers to separate them. **3.** Drizzle the vinaigrette over the tomatoes and scatter the basil on top. Serve at once.

TIP: To avoid having the basil turn dark, cut the shreds just before serving the salad.

BEET SALAD WITH GOAT CHEESE AND WALNUTS

If such new varieties of beets as golden and striped are available to you, combine them with their ruby red cousins to create a striking presentation.

SERVES 4

> 6 medium beets, tops removed, leaving ¼ inch of stems
>
> 2 tablespoons lemon juice
>
> 1 garlic clove, pressed or minced
>
> ¼ teaspoon salt
>
> Generous seasoning freshly ground pepper
>
> 5 tablespoons olive oil
>
> 4 cups mixed greens, such as romaine, Boston, and green leaf lettuces, or mesclun
>
> 2 cups arugula, torn into small pieces
>
> 1 scallion, very thinly sliced
>
> ½ cup chilled crumbled goat cheese, such as Montrachet
>
> ¼ cup chopped walnuts, toasted

1. Scrub the beets very well. Fill a 3-quart saucepan halfway with water and bring to a boil. Cook the beets until tender when pierced with a sharp knife, about 45–60 minutes. Drain well and let cool. Slip the skins off the beets.

Dice the beets and place in a bowl. **2.** To make the dressing: whisk together the lemon juice, garlic, salt, pepper, and oil. Pour a few tablespoons of the dressing on the beets and toss. **3.** Just before serving, combine the greens, arugula, and scallion in a large bowl. Pour on most of the remaining dressing and toss. Add more if needed. **4.** Place the greens on 4 salad plates. Spoon on a mound of beets. Sprinkle with the goat cheese and walnuts. Serve immediately.

TIPS: The beets can be cooked and dressed up to 24 hours in advance, but wait until serving time to toss the greens.

As a delightful alternative you can substitute baby spinach leaves for the mixed greens.

PROVENÇAL GREEN BEAN SALAD

The sun-drenched flavors of southern France illuminate this salad, making it the perfect choice for a summer buffet or picnic. Don't hesitate to double or triple this colorful side dish because it will require almost no extra work. It looks particularly striking when presented on an oval platter that has a subtle background so its brilliant colors can stand out.

SERVES 4 AS A SIDE DISH

1 pound green beans, tips removed

1 red bell pepper

1 yellow bell pepper

¼ cup Classic Vinaigrette (page 70) or Lemon-Soy Dressing (page 71)

Salt to taste

Generous seasoning freshly ground black pepper

¼ cup shredded fresh basil

1. Fill a 4–6-quart pot halfway with water and bring to a boil. Drop in the green beans and cook until tender yet still slightly crisp, no more than 5 minutes. Taste one to be certain; you want them perfect. Drain the green beans and then immediately immerse them in a large bowl or pot of very cold water. Let sit 1 minute, drain, then fill again with cold water. Let the beans sit until completely cold, about 5 minutes. Drain again and then dry the beans on a kitchen towel to remove all moisture. Place the beans in a large bowl. **2.** To roast the peppers: preheat the broiler and make sure the oven rack is as high as it can go. Cut each pepper in half vertically. Remove the stem, seeds, and white fibrous part. Place the peppers skin side up on a baking sheet and broil until the skin is almost all black. About halfway through the cooking time it's a good idea to press down and flatten the peppers with a spatula so they will broil evenly. It takes about 10 minutes to char the peppers. **3.** Remove the peppers from the baking sheet and place in a medium-size bowl. Cover tightly with a plate and let them steam to loosen their skins, about 10 minutes. **4.** Peel off the pepper skins with your fingertips and discard. Cut the peppers into strips about 3 inches by ½ inch. Mix into the green beans with all the remaining ingredients. Let marinate at least 30 minutes before serving, or cover and refrigerate up to 48 hours. Serve at room temperature.

BROCCOLI AND ROASTED RED PEPPER SALAD

This attractive companion dish sits nicely alongside sandwiches, pizza, omelets, and tarts. It is also an ideal dish to serve at a summer cookout.

SERVES 4 AS A SIDE DISH

> **5–6 cups small broccoli florets (from 1 large bunch broccoli)**
>
> **2 tablespoons pine nuts**
>
> **½ cup 2-inch-long roasted red pepper strips (about 1 red pepper) or one-half 7-ounce jar**
>
> **¼ cup Classic Vinaigrette (page 70)**
>
> **Salt to taste**
>
> **Freshly ground black pepper to taste**

1. Fill a 4–6-quart pot with water and bring to a boil over high heat. Drop in the broccoli florets and blanch 2 minutes, or until tender but still quite crunchy. Immediately drain the water and fill the pot with very cold water. Drain and fill again. Let the broccoli sit in the cold water for at least 5 minutes so the broccoli gets completely cold. Drain thoroughly in a colander. **2.** Place a cotton kitchen towel on the counter. Gather up some broccoli and with your hands gently squeeze out any moisture clinging to it. Place the broccoli on the towel and continue with the remaining broccoli. Pat the broccoli with the towel and let air-dry 10 minutes or so. **3.** Place the pine nuts in a small saucepan or skillet and swirl them around over medium heat until lightly golden. Be very careful; they burn easily. Immediately pour them onto a plate and let cool. **4.** Place the broccoli in an attractive bowl and mix in the red peppers. Pour on the dressing and season with salt and pepper. Toss well. Sprinkle on the pine nuts and let marinate at least 30 minutes but no longer than a few hours before serving. Serve at room temperature.

TIPS: Use the florets with only about ½ inch of stem attached for the most attractive look. Discard the rest of the stems or peel and use in a stir-fry.

Broccoli holds a lot of water, so be certain to dry it thoroughly before placing it in the bowl or the dish will become watery.

You don't want this salad to sit more than 2 hours because the acid in the dressing will slowly diminish the bright green color of the broccoli.

INDONESIAN TOFU, BEAN SPROUT, AND CUCUMBER SALAD WITH SPICY PEANUT SAUCE

This salad offers a delightful interplay of crunchy textures and chewy tofu, and it all comes together under a drizzle of creamy peanut sauce. Although this delectable salad has a decidedly Asian character, it can be a special prelude to all types of meals including many main-course soups, casseroles, and even pizzas. You just don't want to pair it with a distinctly ethnic dish such as enchiladas or lasagna because the flavors and tones will clash.

SERVES 4

1 recipe Roasted Tofu (page 189)

Peanut Sauce:

¼ cup natural-style peanut butter

2 tablespoons tamari soy sauce

1 tablespoon lime or lemon juice

2 tablespoons firmly packed brown sugar

1 garlic clove, put through a press or minced

¼ teaspoon crushed red pepper flakes

3 tablespoons water

The Salad:

2 cups mung bean sprouts, rinsed well in a strainer (see Tip)

1 small cucumber, peeled and sliced ¼ inch thick

1 scallion, very thinly sliced

1. Prepare the Roasted Tofu, cutting it into triangles as directed. Chill thoroughly. **2.** To make the sauce: combine all the sauce ingredients in a small bowl and beat vigorously with a fork or small whisk until very smooth. **3.** To assemble the salad: spread ¼ of the bean sprouts on each of 4 salad plates. Place 6 cucumber slices and 6 pieces of tofu alternately on each serving (you will probably have some left over). Drizzle some sauce over each portion and sprinkle with the scallions. Serve within 30 minutes.

TIP: Mung bean sprouts are the large, white, crunchy sprouts traditionally served in Chinese dishes. You can find them fresh in the produce section of many supermarkets.

CLASSIC VINAIGRETTE

This all-purpose dressing has exactly the right balance of flavors to make it ideal for leafy salads and pasta salads, and as a marinade for vegetables. You can vary the flavor with fresh herbs or choose a flavored vinegar to match your dish.

MAKES ABOUT 1 CUP

3 tablespoons red wine vinegar

1 teaspoon Dijon-style mustard

2 cloves garlic, put through a press or
minced

¾ cup olive oil

¼ teaspoon salt

Generous seasoning freshly ground pepper

Place all the ingredients in a jar with a tight-fitting lid and shake vigorously.

TIP: This dressing will keep for a few weeks if refrigerated. Bring to room temperature before using and shake again.

LEMON-SOY DRESSING

The flavors of lemon and soy sauce complement each other to make a rich-tasting dressing with depth. You can use this as an all-purpose dressing for leafy salads or marinaded vegetables.

MAKES ABOUT ¾ CUP

1 large garlic clove, put through a press or
minced

2 tablespoons lemon juice

1 tablespoon red wine vinegar

1½ teaspoons tamari soy sauce

⅛ teaspoon salt

Generous seasoning freshly ground pepper

½ cup mild-flavored olive oil

Place all the ingredients in a jar with a tight-fitting lid and shake vigorously.

TIP: Combining the garlic, flavorings, and other ingredients with the vinegar for a minute or so before adding the oil allows the ingredients to break down and the salt to melt in the acid. This will yield a more flavorful dressing.

CITRUS VINAIGRETTE

This tangy dressing gives a lively edge to marinated vegetables such as asparagus, green beans, and beets, and is also a good choice for a spinach salad.

MAKES 1 CUP

2 tablespoons fresh lemon juice

¼ cup fresh lime juice

3 tablespoons frozen orange juice concentrate

1½ teaspoons red wine vinegar

1 garlic clove, put through a press or
minced

¼ teaspoon sugar

½ teaspoon salt

Freshly ground pepper to taste

½ cup olive oil

Place all the ingredients in a jar with a tight-fitting lid and shake vigorously. Let stand 30 minutes before using to blend the flavors.

BALSAMIC VINAIGRETTE

MAKES ⅔ CUP

3 tablespoons balsamic vinegar

2 teaspoons Dijon-style mustard

1 garlic clove, minced

½ teaspoon salt

Freshly ground pepper to taste

½ cup olive oil

Place all the ingredients in a jar with a tight-fitting lid and shake vigorously. This dressing can be stored in the refrigerator for up to 2 weeks.

DARK SESAME VINAIGRETTE

This dressing really livens up spinach salads and cold blanched vegetables such as green beans and broccoli.

MAKES ¾ CUP

2½ tablespoons red wine vinegar

½ teaspoon tamari soy sauce

1 garlic clove, pressed (preferably) or minced

¼ teaspoon salt

Generous seasoning freshly ground pepper

1½ tablespoons Asian sesame oil

½ cup canola oil

Place all the ingredients in a jar with a screw-top lid and shake vigorously. This dressing will keep 1 week if refrigerated.

SUN-DRIED TOMATO VINAIGRETTE

This garlicky dressing has a slight tang to it and would be a good choice to enliven spinach salads and even tubular pasta and tortellini salads.

MAKES ½ CUP

3 sun-dried tomatoes

1 large garlic clove, finely chopped

⅓ cup olive oil

3 tablespoons red wine vinegar

¼ teaspoon salt

Generous seasoning freshly ground pepper

1. Place the tomatoes in a small bowl and pour boiling water over them. Let sit 30 minutes, or until very soft. Remove and pat dry with a paper towel. (If your dried tomatoes are packed in oil, omit soaking them.) Chop into small pieces. 2. Place the tomatoes with all the remaining ingredients in a blender and blend until the tomatoes are pureed and the dressing is smooth. This dressing will keep up to 2 weeks if refrigerated.

BUTTERMILK DRESSING

This piquant dressing goes especially well with crunchy salads such as those made with romaine lettuce, carrots, peppers, and so forth, and is also delightful as a topping on blanched green beans or asparagus.

MAKES ABOUT 1 CUP

> ½ cup mayonnaise
>
> ½ cup buttermilk
>
> 2 tablespoons lime juice
>
> 1 garlic clove, put through a press or minced
>
> 1 tablespoon minced scallion (white part only)
>
> A few dashes salt
>
> Freshly ground pepper to taste

Place the mayonnaise in a small bowl and whisk a few times until smooth. Slowly whisk in the buttermilk and then the remaining ingredients. Cover and let chill at least 30 minutes before using.

TIP: Whisking mayonnaise until it is smooth before adding something to it prevents it from lumping

MISO-GINGER SALAD DRESSING

Here's a classic dressing that became popular in the 1970s with the discovery of the amazing nutritional properties of the soybean. Miso, fermented soybean paste, is prized for its concentration of enzymes and other digestion-aiding properties. Combined with ginger and sesame oil it produces a tantalizing dressing that is superb on crunchy-style salads such as those containing carrot, cucumber, and green pepper.

MAKES 1½ CUPS

> 3 tablespoons rice (white) miso (see Tip)
>
> 1 teaspoon minced fresh ginger
>
> 1 medium-size garlic clove, chopped
>
> 2 tablespoons apple cider or red wine vinegar
>
> 1½ tablespoons Asian sesame oil
>
> ¾ cup canola oil
>
> ⅓ cup plus 1 tablespoon water

1. Place the miso, ginger, garlic, vinegar, and sesame oil in a blender or food processor and process until smooth. With the motor running, very slowly drizzle in the canola oil, stopping after a few tablespoons have been absorbed before adding more. When the dressing has emulsified, very slowly add the water. Process 10 seconds or so, or just until blended. When

Dinner Salads and Salad Dressings

done, the dressing should be thick and very creamy. **2.** Put the dressing in a bowl and chill until ready to use. It will keep up to 1 week.

TIP: White (rice-based) miso is actually a dark tan color. For more about miso see page 10.

CREAMY TAHINI DRESSING

This rich sesame sauce with tangy lemon-garlic overtones is wonderful on crunchy salads made with a sturdy lettuce such as romaine, and it can also enliven cucumber salad mixtures that have been stuffed into pitas.

MAKES 1 CUP

> ½ cup tahini (untoasted sesame seed butter) (see Tip)
>
> 1 large garlic clove, put through a press or minced
>
> ¼ cup lemon juice
>
> ¼ teaspoon salt
>
> 4–6 tablespoons water

Place the tahini, garlic, lemon juice, and salt in a bowl and whisk until smooth. Add 4 table-spoons water and whisk until incorporated. Check the consistency; it should be like thick heavy cream. Whisk in a bit more water if necessary. Let sit at least 20 minutes to blend the flavors or chill up to 5 days and bring to room temperature before using.

TIP: A fresh jar or can of tahini will have a layer of oil on top. Vigorously stir the oil into the tahini with a fork before measuring it.

CREAMY TOFU SALAD DRESSING

Tofu salad dressing has been a staple dressing in natural foods restaurants since the early 1980s. I love the transformation that tofu undergoes when it is pureed. It becomes velvety smooth and can be used on salads with baby greens but is ideal for salads that have a lot of crunch to them.

MAKES 1½ CUPS

> 8 ounces extra-firm or soft tofu, patted dry
>
> 2 tablespoons lemon juice
>
> ¼ cup olive oil
>
> 4 tablespoons water (use a little less for soft tofu)
>
> 1 tablespoon tamari soy sauce
>
> 2 garlic cloves, finely chopped

Place all the ingredients in a blender or food processor and puree until very smooth. Store in the refrigerator up to 4 days.

TIP: This mixture also makes a delicious dip for crudités. Use half the amount of water and then check the consistency to see if you need more. You want it to be thicker than a salad dressing.

Vegetarian Classics

MAIN-COURSE SALADS

When warm weather approaches, one of the culinary changes I look forward to is preparing and eating main-course salads. Whether it's a bowl of cold Szechuan noodles or a platter of garlicky marinated chickpeas with fiery red tomatoes and tender spinach, I love to make these easy one-dish meals that are fresh, healthful, and jam-packed with flavor. Cooking in advance is my way of ensuring a relaxed meal in the summer, and these salads actually benefit from being created early in the day or the day before. Many salads in this chapter are ideal for showing off summer produce at its peak. All you need to complete the meal is some crusty bread, perhaps some olives or other nibbles, and maybe a selection of special cheeses. (See also Roasted Tofu Salad on page 197.)

CLASSIC COLD NOODLES WITH PEANUT SAUCE

The discovery of Asian noodles with peanut sauce in the early 1980s was a revelation to me, and it is still one of my favorite salads. It is packed with flavor, filled with protein, and can be the ideal picnic food for vegetarians and non-vegetarians alike. The addition of crunchy vegetables provides a welcome textural contrast.

SERVES 4 AS A MAIN COURSE

  1 pound spaghettini (thin spaghetti)

  2 tablespoons Asian sesame oil

The Sauce:

  ⅔ cup natural-style peanut butter, chunky or smooth

  ⅓ cup tamari soy sauce

¼ cup sherry

2 tablespoons water

1 tablespoon red wine vinegar

3 tablespoons firmly packed light brown
   sugar

3 tablespoons Asian sesame oil

3 garlic cloves, minced

1 tablespoon minced fresh ginger

½ teaspoon crushed red pepper flakes

2 carrots, very finely chopped but
   not minced

1 cucumber, peeled, halved lengthwise,
   seeded, and diced

4 scallions, very thinly sliced

1. Bring a large stockpot of water to a boil. Add the spaghettini and cook until al dente, that is, tender yet still slightly firm. Drain in a colander and run under cold water. Drain again and shake the colander to remove all moisture. Place the noodles in a very large bowl and add the 2 tablespoons sesame oil. Toss the noodles with tongs to thoroughly coat them. **2.** To make the sauce, whisk together all the sauce ingredients except the vegetables in a large bowl. Pour the sauce on the noodles and toss to coat. Sprinkle on the carrots, cucumbers, and half the scallions. Toss again. Let the noodles sit at room temperature for 30 minutes to blend the flavors. Just before serving, sprinkle on the remaining scallions.

TIP: If you plan to make these noodles up to 8 hours in advance, pour on about ⅔ of the sauce, let them marinate for as long as you wish, and then pour on the remaining sauce just before serving.

SZECHUAN NOODLES WITH GREEN BEANS AND CASHEWS

Unlike creamy peanut noodles where the peanut butter in the sauce is evident, just a touch of peanut butter is added here to give the sauce some body. The final dish remains light, spicy, and richly infused with flavor.

SERVES 4 AS A MAIN COURSE

The Sauce:

   ¼ cup tamari soy sauce

   ¼ cup Asian sesame oil

   2 tablespoons natural-style peanut butter

   1 tablespoon sugar

   1 tablespoon Chinese wine vinegar
      or red wine vinegar

   3 garlic cloves, finely chopped

   1 tablespoon minced fresh ginger

   ½ teaspoon crushed red pepper flakes,
      or more to taste

   ½ teaspoon salt

   8 ounces green beans, cut in half
      (2½ cups)

   1 pound spaghetti

   3 scallions, very thinly sliced

1 cucumber, peeled, cut lengthwise,
    seeded, and sliced ¼ inch thick

½ cup roasted cashews, preferably
    unsalted, roughly chopped

3 tablespoons finely chopped cilantro
    (optional)

1. Combine the sauce ingredients in a blender (preferably) or a food processor and process until smooth. Pour into a small bowl. **2.** Bring a large stockpot of water to a boil. Drop in the green beans and cook 5 minutes, or just until tender yet still slightly crunchy. Remove with a strainer, place in a bowl, and cover with cold water to stop any further cooking. Pour off the water and cover again. Let sit a few minutes so they can get completely cold. Drain well, then place on a kitchen towel and pat dry. **3.** Put the spaghetti in the boiling water and cook until al dente, about 12 minutes. Do not overcook it. Drain thoroughly in a colander. Rinse under cold running water until cold. Shake the colander vigorously to remove any excess water. Place the noodles in a very large bowl. **4.** Mix in the green beans, scallions, cucumber, and cashews. Pour on the sauce and use tongs to toss, coating well. Let the noodles marinate at least 30 minutes before serving. Garnish with cilantro, if desired.

TIP: If you prepare this dish more than 30 minutes in advance, pour on only ¾ of the sauce, and then just before serving add the remaining sauce and toss well.

CRUNCHY THAI NOODLE SALAD

Chewy pasta, crunchy vegetables, and an exotic dressing make these Asian-style noodles irresistible. This dish is a good choice on a summer day when you want to keep cooking to a minimum.

SERVES 4 AS A MAIN COURSE

The Dressing:

    3 tablespoons Asian sesame oil

    3 tablespoons canola oil

    ¼ cup tamari soy sauce

    3 tablespoons lime juice

    2 tablespoons tomato paste

    2 tablespoons honey

    1 tablespoon minced fresh ginger

    3 garlic cloves, minced

    ½ teaspoon crushed red pepper flakes

    ½ teaspoon salt

The Salad:

    1 pound spaghetti or linguine

    2 cups mung bean sprouts

    1 cucumber, peeled, seeded, and cut into
        matchsticks

    1 carrot, peeled and grated

    3 scallions, very thinly sliced

    2 tablespoons shredded fresh basil

    2 tablespoons finely chopped fresh mint

2 tablespoons finely chopped cilantro

¼ cup chopped dry roasted peanuts

1. Bring a large stockpot of water to a boil for the noodles. **2.** In a medium-size bowl whisk together all the ingredients for the dressing. **3.** Cook the noodles until al dente. Drain thoroughly in a colander and rinse the noodles under cold running water. Shake the colander vigorously to remove all water. Place the noodles in a very large serving bowl. **4.** Pour on the dressing and toss well. Mix in all the remaining ingredients except the peanuts. Let the noodles marinate at least 30 minutes before serving. Serve with the chopped peanuts sprinkled on top.

TIP: The trio of basil, mint, and cilantro is key to giving this salad its Thai character, so be sure to include all these herbs.

CLASSIC TABBOULI

The discovery among American vegetarians in the 1960s and 1970s of the dynamic way other cultures use grains to create tantalizing meatless creations was liberating; it opened up a new world of possibilities for those of us who thought brown rice was exotic. Middle Eastern tabbouli made with bulgur (precooked cracked wheat) was a revelation—a truly delicious whole grain salad that was also packed with nutrients. This was a prime example of flavor not taking a back seat to nutrition. It is still one of my favorite salads.

SERVES 4 AS A MAIN COURSE

1½ cups bulgur, preferably golden
    and coarse-cut

2 ripe tomatoes, finely diced

1½ cups minced fresh parsley

2 tablespoons minced fresh mint

3 scallions, thinly sliced

The Dressing:

¼ cup lemon juice

½ teaspoon salt

Generous seasoning freshly ground pepper

½ cup olive oil

1. Place the bulgur in a medium-size bowl and pour in enough boiling water to cover by 1 inch. Set a large plate on the bowl and let the bulgur steam for 30 minutes. Spoon the bulgur into a clean cotton kitchen towel in batches and gather into a ball. Squeeze out all the liquid. Place the bulgur in a large bowl. Let cool. **2.** Stir in the tomatoes, parsley, mint, and scallions. **3.** Whisk together the dressing ingredients and pour over the salad. Cover and chill at least 30 minutes or up to 24 hours before serving. Serve cool, not cold.

TIP: Traditional tabbouli is packed with herbs, making it quite green as a result. Take time to mince the parsley and mint to achieve a delicate look and texture.

Vegetarian Classics

BEYOND TABBOULI

Here tabbouli has evolved into a grand salad packed with Mediterranean vegetables and feta cheese, and not a minute of cooking is needed. Great for a hot summer's day.

SERVES 4–6 AS A MAIN COURSE

1½ cups bulgur, preferably golden
    and coarse-cut

6 ripe cherry tomatoes, halved

1 (6-ounce) jar marinated artichoke hearts,
    well drained and halved

1 cucumber, peeled, seeded, and
    finely diced

2 scallions, very thinly sliced

1 yellow or red bell pepper, finely diced

⅔ cup finely diced feta cheese

1 cup minced fresh parsley

2 tablespoons minced fresh mint

The Dressing:

¼ cup lemon juice

⅓ cup olive oil

½ teaspoon salt

Generous seasoning freshly ground pepper

1. Place the bulgur in a medium-size bowl and pour in enough boiling water to cover by 1 inch. Place a large plate on the bowl and let the bulgur steam for 30 minutes. Spoon some bulgur into a clean cotton kitchen towel in batches and gather into a ball. Squeeze out all the liquid. Place in a large bowl and break up any clumps with a large spoon. Let cool completely.

2. Stir in all the remaining salad ingredients.

3. Whisk together the dressing ingredients in a medium-size bowl. Pour over the salad and toss to coat well. Cover and chill at least 30 minutes or up to 24 hours before serving (see Tip). Serve cool, not cold.

TIP: To seed a cucumber, peel it first, then cut it in half lengthwise. Use a teaspoon to scrape out all the seeds. Cut the cucumber into long strips and then dice.

If you make this salad more than 30 minutes in advance, do not add the cucumber until a few minutes before serving because the cucumber tends to get soft as it marinates.

RICE, RED LENTIL, AND WHEAT BERRY SALAD

If you've never tasted red lentils, you're in for a treat. These tiny orange legumes turn a tan color when cooked, and their rich, buttery flavor is incomparable. Because they cook in only 17 minutes, they retain their shape and add a pleasing touch of nubbiness. Indian basmati rice and Thai jasmine rice are both subtly aromatic and will add to the character of this salad. If you have only a domestic long-grain white rice on hand, you can use that and

Main-Course Salads

still create a delicious dish. And, finally, the wheat berries add crunch and a delightful nutty flavor to this salad. You'll be able to find them at any health food store. (See page 17 for more information about them.)

SERVES 4–6 AS A MAIN COURSE

⅓ cup wheat berries

1 teaspoon canola oil

¼ teaspoon salt

¾ cup red lentils, rinsed in a strainer

¾ cup basmati or jasmine rice, rinsed in a strainer

The Dressing:

¼ cup lemon juice

2 large garlic cloves, put through a press or minced

¼ teaspoon salt

Generous seasoning freshly ground pepper

⅓ cup olive oil

1 carrot, minced

1 red bell pepper, very finely diced

½ cup minced fresh parsley

1. Soak the wheat berries overnight in enough water to cover by 2 inches. Alternatively, place them in a medium-size saucepan half-filled with water and boil, uncovered, for 2 minutes. Remove from the heat and let sit 1 hour. Drain and then refill the saucepan halfway with water and cook the wheat berries, partially covered, for 1 hour. When done, the wheat berries will be tender but slightly crunchy. Drain thoroughly and let cool. **2.** Bring 2 cups water, oil, and salt to a boil in a medium-size saucepan. Stir in the lentils and rice, and turn the heat to low. Cover the pan and cook 17 minutes, or until *all* the liquid is absorbed. Do not stir the mixture while it is cooking. Carefully spoon the mixture into a large bowl and let cool to room temperature. **3.** Meanwhile, place the dressing ingredients in a jar with a tight-fitting lid and shake vigorously. Set aside. **4.** When the rice mixture is completely cool, use a large spoon to break up any clumps that have formed. Carefully stir in the wheat berries, carrot, red pepper, and parsley. Pour the dressing on the salad and toss. Let marinate at least 20 minutes before serving.

TIP: The rice greedily soaks up the dressing, so if you want to make this salad from 2 to 24 hours in advance, pour on only half the dressing and then add the remainder about 20 minutes before serving.

CURRIED RICE SALAD WITH ALMONDS AND GRAPES

The nuttiness of brown rice marries well with this piquant dressing and the contrasting sweetness of the grapes and almonds. Begin this classy and refreshing salad with cold rice, and you'll be certain to have fluffy results.

4 cups (approximately) cold, cooked,
long-grain brown rice (1½ quantities
of Perfect Brown Rice, page 26)

1 cup seedless red grapes

½ cup sliced almonds

3 scallions, very thinly sliced

3 tablespoons minced fresh mint or
cilantro

The Dressing:

4 tablespoons lemon juice

1 tablespoon curry powder

½ teaspoon cumin seed

½ teaspoon turmeric

1 tablespoon minced gingerroot

3 garlic cloves, pressed or minced

¾ teaspoon salt

6 tablespoons canola oil

1. Place the cold rice in a large serving bowl. Use a large spoon to break up any clumps that have formed. Stir in the grapes, almonds, scallions, and mint or cilantro. **2.** Place the dressing ingredients in a jar with a tight-fitting lid and shake vigorously. Pour on the rice and toss to coat well. Cover and chill the rice at least 1 hour or up to 24 hours to allow the flavors to meld. Bring to room temperature before serving.

TIP: White rice such as basmati can be substituted, but long-grain brown rice works well here, so this is an opportunity to enjoy this nutritious whole grain.

TUSCAN-STYLE COUSCOUS SALAD

In this aromatic salad couscous, the grainlike pasta from North Africa is combined with white beans, tomatoes, and basil in a garlic-infused dressing to make a splendid summer salad that requires almost no cooking. Crostini spread with goat cheese would be a perfect accompaniment. White wine, anyone?

SERVES 4 AS A MAIN COURSE

1½ cups couscous

½ teaspoon turmeric

2 cups boiling water

¼ cup pine nuts

1 (15-ounce) can small white beans such as
navy or Great Northern, rinsed well
and drained

15 cherry tomatoes, halved, or 1 large ripe
tomato, finely diced

½ cup shredded fresh basil

½ cup slivered red onion

The Dressing:

⅓ cup lemon juice

3 garlic cloves, put through a press
or minced

½ teaspoon salt

Generous seasoning freshly ground pepper

⅓ cup olive oil

1. Place the couscous and turmeric in a large bowl and mix. Pour on the boiling water, stir, and immediately cover the bowl with a large plate. Let sit for 10 minutes. Remove the cover and fluff the couscous with a fork. Let cool. **2.** Place the pine nuts in a small skillet and toast over medium heat, tossing often, until golden, about 5 minutes. Watch them carefully because they can easily burn. Let cool, then mix into the couscous along with the beans, tomatoes, basil, and red onion. **3.** Place the dressing ingredients in a jar with a tight-fitting lid and shake vigorously. Pour over the couscous mixture and toss well. Let marinate at least 30 minutes before serving. Cover and chill if longer than 30 minutes. Serve at room temperature.

T I P : Chickpeas can be substituted for the white beans with good results.

MARINATED PENNE SALAD WITH GREEN BEANS AND TOMATOES

This pasta dish is filled with vegetables that burst with color and flavor. Use perfectly ripe summer tomatoes and tender green beans to create the consummate summer salad that works equally well as a main course or a side dish at a cookout.

SERVES 6 AS A MAIN COURSE

The Dressing:

> 2½ tablespoons red wine vinegar
>
> 3 garlic cloves, put through a press or minced
>
> ½ teaspoon salt
>
> Generous seasoning freshly ground pepper
>
> ½ cup olive oil

The Salad:

> 1 pound green beans, cut in half (4 cups)
>
> 1 pound penne
>
> 3 medium-large ripe tomatoes, cut into ¾-inch dice
>
> 1 yellow bell pepper, cut into thin slivers
>
> ¼ cup minced fresh basil

1. Bring a large stockpot of water to a boil. **2.** Place all the dressing ingredients in a jar with a tight-fitting lid and shake vigorously. Set aside. **3.** When the water boils, drop in the green beans. Cook 5 minutes, or until tender. Taste one to be sure. Use a strainer to scoop out the beans and place them in a large bowl. Fill the bowl with very cold water. Pour out the water, fill again, and let the beans sit in it until they become completely cold. Be sure they stop cooking so they retain their bright green color. Drain the beans and place on a kitchen towel. Pat very dry. **4.** Cook the penne in the same boiling water until al dente. Drain in a colander, then rinse under cold running water to cool. Shake the penne until very dry. Place in a large bowl and mix in the green beans, tomatoes, yellow pepper, and basil. **5.** Pour on the

Vegetarian Classics

dressing and toss well. Let marinate at least 30 minutes before serving.

TIP: You can make the pasta salad a day in advance and refrigerate it. Be sure to bring it to room temperature or at least to a cool temperature before serving it so that the flavors come through.

COLORFUL ORZO SALAD WITH SHIITAKE MUSHROOMS

The rich flavor of mushrooms paired with the creamy, delicate texture of orzo gives this vibrant salad great panache. Serve it at your next barbecue for a real crowd pleaser.

SERVES 6 AS A MAIN COURSE

The Dressing:

> 2 tablespoons lemon juice
>
> 1 teaspoon red wine vinegar
>
> 3 garlic cloves, pressed or minced
>
> 1 teaspoon salt
>
> Liberal seasoning freshly ground pepper
>
> ½ cup olive oil

The Salad:

> 1 tablespoon unsalted butter
>
> 8 ounces shiitake mushrooms, stems discarded and caps wiped clean and thinly sliced

> 8 ounces button (common) mushrooms, thinly sliced
>
> 1 pound orzo (rice-shaped pasta)
>
> ½ cup shredded fresh basil
>
> 2 scallions, very thinly sliced
>
> 1 ripe red tomato, finely diced
>
> 1 ripe yellow tomato, finely diced

1. Place the dressing ingredients in a jar with a tight-fitting lid and shake vigorously. **2.** Bring a large stockpot of water to a boil. **3.** Meanwhile, heat the butter in a large skillet over medium heat. Add the mushrooms and sauté until brown and juicy, about 10 minutes. Set aside to cool. **4.** Drop the orzo into the boiling water and cook, stirring often, until al dente, that is, tender yet still slightly firm. Drain thoroughly in a colander and place in a large bowl. Pour on half the dressing, toss well, and let cool to room temperature. **5.** Mix in the mushrooms, basil, scallions, and tomatoes. Pour on the remaining dressing and toss well. Let marinate at least 30 minutes before serving.

TIP: You can make numerous substitutions with great success. Substitute roasted yellow bell pepper for the yellow tomato, chopped arugula for the basil, and red onion for the scallions. The idea is to fill this salad with dynamic colors as well as flavors.

Pasta: To Rinse or Not to Rinse . . .

The rule of thumb regarding pasta is *never* rinse hot, cooked pasta if you are going to serve it hot. If you are going to serve it cold, as in a pasta salad, rinse it most of the time, depending on the recipe.

Pasta that is going to be served hot should be drained quickly once it has reached the al dente stage, and then immediately tossed with its sauce and served. I don't know where the misconception about rinsing pasta came from. Perhaps it arose from people not cooking their pasta in enough water and getting stuck-together noodles as a result, or perhaps they let their hot pasta sit in the colander while they prepared their sauce and the pasta clumped together. In both cases, rinsing would be the only remedy to unstick the mess. So cook your pasta in plenty of boiling water, stir frequently, and toss with the sauce immediately after the pasta is drained.

When cooking pasta for a cold salad, you want the pasta to stop cooking once it has been drained. To do this you have to rinse it immediately under cold running water. Because the water now adhering to the pasta is cold, it won't evaporate the way hot water will, so you will have to shake it vigorously in the colander to get rid of the excess water.

TORTELLINI SALAD WITH BROCCOLI, RED PEPPER, AND PINE NUTS

This substantial pasta salad is a breeze to prepare. It lends itself to improvisation, but this trio of additions—broccoli, red pepper, and pine nuts—is my favorite.

SERVES 4 AS A MAIN COURSE

The Dressing:

    2 tablespoons red wine vinegar

    2 large garlic cloves, put through a press
        or minced

    ½ teaspoon salt

    ⅓ cup olive oil

The Salad:

    5 cups tiny broccoli florets (from about 1
        bunch broccoli)

    1 red bell pepper, cut into ¼-inch strips
        about 2 inches long

    1 pound frozen cheese tortellini

    ¼ cup toasted pine nuts (see Tip)

1. Place all the dressing ingredients in a jar with a tight-fitting lid and shake vigorously. **2.** Bring a large stockpot of water to a boil. Drop in the broccoli and cook 3–5 minutes, or just until tender yet still crunchy. Taste one to be sure. Drop in the red pepper strips and boil 10 seconds. With a large strainer immediately scoop out the vegetables and place in a large bowl. Fill the bowl with very cold water to stop the vegetables from cooking further. Let sit a few minutes, then pour out the water and fill again with fresh cold water. Let the vegetables sit about 5 minutes, or until completely cold. Remove from the water and place on a cotton kitchen towel. Pat very dry. **3.** Place the tortellini in the boiling water and cook until al dente, about 7 minutes. Drain thoroughly in a colander. Rinse the tortellini under cold running water. Shake the colander vigorously to drain away all the water. Place the tortellini in a large bowl. **4.** Mix in the broccoli and red peppers, pine nuts, and dressing. Toss well. Let marinate at least 20 minutes before serving, or cover and chill up to 24 hours. Bring to room temperature before serving.

TIPS: The red pepper is blanched only a few seconds to tenderize it slightly but keep it crunchy. The broccoli should also be crunchy yet tender. To ensure that the broccoli remains bright green, you must shock it in cold water and get it completely cold. Any remaining warmth will continue to cook the broccoli, and it will turn an olive color.

To toast the pine nuts place them in a small, dry skillet over medium heat. Toss often. Be very watchful because they burn easily.

SUMMER CHICKPEA, TOMATO, AND SPINACH SALAD

Bean salads have evolved over the past thirty years into sophisticated medleys that now include a wide range of beans, vegetables, and herbs. The beans' high-protein content makes them an ideal base for a main-course salad that may serve as a one-dish summer meal.

This is one of my favorite dog-day summer meals because there is no cooking involved and the flavor combination is superb. Tender flat-leaf spinach, usually sold in bunches, works better here than crinkle-leaf spinach sold in bags. If you cannot get spinach, arugula is also a great choice, or you could substitute a few tablespoons of chopped fresh basil. Pass the peppermill with this luscious salad, and accompany it with a chunk of crusty bread to round out the meal.

SERVES 4 AS A MAIN COURSE

The Dressing:

> 2 tablespoons red wine vinegar
>
> 1 large garlic clove, put through a press or minced
>
> ¼ teaspoon salt

Generous seasoning freshly ground
　black pepper

¼ cup olive oil

The Salad:

2 (15-ounce) cans chickpeas, rinsed
　and well drained

2 ripe tomatoes, diced

½ cup slivered red onion

4 cups flat-leaf spinach, stems discarded
　and leaves torn into small pieces

1. Combine all the dressing ingredients in a jar with a tight-fitting lid and shake well, or whisk them together in a bowl. **2.** In a large serving bowl combine the chickpeas, tomatoes, and onion. Pour on the dressing and toss to coat everything thoroughly. Let marinate at least 30 minutes or up to several hours. If serving time is more than 30 minutes away, chill, then bring to room temperature. Add the spinach, toss well, and let the salad sit 10 minutes to slightly wilt the spinach. Serve on large plates or in pasta bowls, accompanied by some chewy European-style bread, if desired.

TIP: Flat-leaf spinach is sometimes referred to as baby spinach, but as many gardeners know, it is actually a different variety from its crinkled-leaf cousin. Its smaller, thinner leaves are ideal for salads.

BLACK BEAN, MANGO, AND JICAMA SALAD WITH CITRUS VINAIGRETTE

Tropical flavors come together here to make a wonderfully flavorful salad that requires no cooking and can be assembled with ease. A great choice for a hot summer day or as a prelude to a Mexican feast. If you are unacquainted with jicama, it's a humble vegetable that resembles a raw potato and gives an intriguing crunch to salads.

SERVES 4 AS A MAIN COURSE

¾ pound (½ of a medium-size) jicama

2 (15-ounce) cans black beans, rinsed well
　in a strainer and drained

1 ripe mango, cut into ½-inch cubes (read
　"Mango Mania," page 156)

½ cup finely diced red onion

2 jalapeño peppers, minced and seeds
　removed (wear rubber gloves) (see
　Tip)

⅓ cup Citrus Vinaigrette (page 71)

2 tablespoons minced cilantro

1. Peel the jicama with a vegetable peeler. Slice into ¼-inch-thick slices, stack, and cut into ¼-inch-thick strips. Cut the jicama into ¼-inch cubes. You should have 1½ cups. **2.** In a large bowl combine the jicama, black beans, mango, red onion, jalapeño peppers, and vinaigrette and toss gently. Let marinate 30 minutes or up to 4 hours to blend the flavors. Stir in the cilantro just before serving.

TIPS: You can substitute ¼ teaspoon crushed red pepper flakes for the jalapeños if you desire.

■ Jicama (pronounced HEE-ca-ma) can be found in most supermarkets.

SICILIAN POTATO AND VEGETABLE SALAD

Red-skin potatoes are chosen for this salad because they are waxy and, consequently, hold together very well when cooked. In the summer this is a main course in our house, and it is especially pleasing when preceded by corn on the cob; however, it would also make an ideal side dish at a barbecue or transport very well to a picnic.

SERVES 4–6 AS A MAIN COURSE

The Dressing:

2 tablespoons red wine vinegar

2 garlic cloves, pressed or minced

½ teaspoon salt

Generous seasoning freshly ground pepper

⅓ cup olive oil

The Salad:

½ pound green beans, tips removed and each bean cut in half

5 medium-large (2 pounds) red-skin potatoes (skins left on), cut into 1½-inch pieces

1 ripe tomato, cut into ½-inch dice

1 (15-ounce) can white beans, such as Great Northern or navy beans, rinsed well and drained, or 1½ cups freshly cooked white beans (page 27)

⅓ cup slivered red onion

16–20 black olives, preferably Niçoise

2 teaspoons drained capers

1. To make the dressing combine all the ingredients in a jar with a tight-fitting lid and shake vigorously. **2.** Fill a stockpot halfway with water and bring to a boil. Drop in the green beans and cook 4–5 minutes, or until tender when tasted. Using a sieve, remove the green beans into a bowl. Keep the water boiling. Cover the green beans with cold running water, drain, and cover again. Let sit until cold throughout, at least 5 minutes. Drain well and place on a cotton kitchen towel to dry. **3.** Drop the potatoes into the boiling water and cook until tender, 10–15 minutes. Do not overcook or they will get mushy. Drain thoroughly in a colander. Place the potatoes in a medium-size bowl and pour on half the dressing. Using a rubber spatula, toss the potatoes gently with the dressing. Let cool to room temperature. **4.** Place the green beans in

Main-Course Salads

a large bowl. Add the tomato, white beans, onion, olives, and capers. Pour on the remaining dressing and toss. When the potatoes are cool, gently fold them into the salad. Serve the salad at room temperature.

COMPOSED SALAD PLATTER

This salad is comprised of a bed of dressed greens topped with an assortment of separate bundles of marinated vegetables such as beets, green beans, and cherry tomatoes, plus roasted tofu, baked goat cheese, and olives. You can let the market dictate what's freshest, but the idea is to create a main-course salad platter that displays individual mounds of beautifully dressed vegetables. Other choices could be marinated mushrooms, potato salad, and marinated peppers. This is an outstanding summer meal that is best when made in stages so it can be easily assembled just before serving.

MAKES 4 MAIN-COURSE PLATTERS

The Dressing:

2½ tablespoons red wine vinegar

1 teaspoon Dijon-style mustard

1 large garlic clove, pressed or minced

¼ teaspoon salt

Generous seasoning freshly ground pepper

⅔ cup olive oil

The Salad:

1 recipe (1 pound) Roasted Tofu
    (page 189)

8 small or 4 medium-size beets, (red,
    striped, or golden variety)

½ pound green beans, tips removed

1 tablespoon minced fresh basil, dill,
    or parsley

12 cherry tomatoes, each cut in half

12 black olives, your favorite kind

1 slice white bread

4-ounce log goat cheese, cut into 4 slices

1 tablespoon olive oil

12 cups mixed greens (such as romaine,
    green leaf, and Boston lettuces,
    and arugula)

½ cup slivered red onion

1. Combine all the ingredients for the dressing in a jar with a tight-fitting lid and shake vigorously. **2.** Make the Roasted Tofu and chill until very cold. **3.** Trim the greens off the beets, leaving a ½-inch stem. Boil the beets until tender. The time will vary depending on the size of the beets. Drain well. Slip their skins off and discard. Cut the beets into bite-size chunks and toss with about 1 tablespoon of the dressing. Chill. **4.** Bring a medium-size saucepan of water to a boil. Drop in the green beans and cook until tender, about 5 minutes.

Place the beans in a large bowl and immediately fill with very cold water. Drain and fill again. When the beans are cold throughout, remove them and dry on a cotton kitchen towel. Place in a bowl and toss with about 1 tablespoon of the dressing and the fresh herb of your choice. Cover and chill. **5.** Toss the cherry tomatoes with a little dressing, and set the olives aside. **6.** Preheat the oven to 425 degrees just before serving the salad. **7.** Place the slice of bread in a blender to make bread crumbs. Pour them onto a small plate. **8.** Lightly brush each slice of goat cheese with the tablespoon of olive oil and press the cheese into the crumbs to coat both sides. Place the cheese on a baking sheet. Bake 10 minutes, or until hot and sizzling but not so that the cheese is runny. **9.** Place the mixed greens and onion in a large salad bowl. Pour on the remaining salad dressing and toss. You can present the salad on four individual dinner plates, or let guests serve themselves from one large platter. Arrange the greens accordingly. On center of the bed of greens place the beets, then surround with mounds of Roasted Tofu (you might not need all of it), green beans, tomatoes, olives, and baked goat cheese. Serve at once.

T I P : The dressing, roasted tofu, and the beets can be prepared up to 3 days in advance.

QUICK BREADS, MUFFINS, SCONES, ETC.

Of all the sensory experiences that elicit feelings of warmth, comfort, and welcome, little can compete with a house filled with the intoxicating aroma of freshly baked bread. It's one of the simple pleasures of the kitchen that even busy cooks can find time to enjoy. The satisfaction one can derive from baking quick breads, muffins, and scones is immense, and the simplest meal can be transformed by the inclusion of a home-baked good.

I often do advance preparation when I am going to bake. For example, when I have overnight guests and want to serve hot, fresh muffins in the morning, I butter the muffin pan and measure out all the dry ingredients in the mixing bowl the night before. It's amazing how this little bit of advance work simplifies the entire task.

Follow the tips below for preparing the items in this chapter, and you'll find that creating sensational muffins, scones, and quick breads is easy to achieve.

A GUIDE TO LIGHT BREADS, FLAKY SCONES, AND TENDER MUFFINS

Baked goods that depend on baking powder as a leavener rather than yeast are meant to be quick and easy, requiring just basic cooking skills. So why do many home cooks who enjoy cooking avoid baking as though it entails some arcane techniques that are beyond their ability? Perhaps a few heavy muffins or a leaden quick bread convinced them that they are hopeless bakers. Are you one of these? Now is the time to overcome any hesitation you have toward baking because what follows are some foolproof baking tips that will ensure success.

MEASURING: There are many specialties in cooking that can succeed and even thrive when one improvises or wishes to toss in ingredients on a whim, such as making soup or preparing a pasta salad. Baking is not one of these. Accuracy and precision are the cornerstones of baking, and measuring properly is the key to obtaining predictable results. To measure flour you need dry measuring cups. Flour can be piled into these individual plastic or metal cups with a spoon and then leveled off with a knife. Glass measuring cups are intended to measure liquid; you can hold the cup at eye level and see that it is filled to the line you desire. Do not use glass measuring cups for flour; you will not get accurate results. Measuring spoons for baking powder and baking soda are used the same way as dry measuring cups: dip the spoon into the container and overfill it. Take a knife and level off the ingredient so that it is perfectly flat across the top of the spoon. If the baking soda is a

bit lumpy, put the measured amount in the palm of your hand and break up the lumps with the back of the measuring spoon before adding it to the mixing bowl.

MIXING: Practically all quick breads, muffins, and so forth, are mixed using the "wet and dry" approach. Carefully measure all the liquid ingredients into one bowl and thoroughly mix them together. Measure all the dry ingredients into another bowl and make sure they are blended perfectly. Combine the wet and dry ingredients and stir just until evenly moistened. Only about 8 strokes of a large spoon are necessary. You want the batter to be mixed thoroughly but handled as little as possible. Use a rubber spatula to scrape the batter into the baking pan.

OVEN HEAT: Your oven temperature needs to be precise so the baked goods will rise properly. If you suspect that your oven is inaccurate, use an oven thermometer and place it in the center of the oven. Always preheat the oven at least 15 minutes before baking, and if you are using a thermometer, read it at this point. Adjust the temperature accordingly. Muffins, quick breads, and corn bread should be placed on an oven rack that is in the center of the oven. Scones and biscuits benefit from being on a rack that is in the upper third of the oven because their bottoms are less likely to darken when they're high above the source of heat.

BAKING PANS: The insides and top of muffin pans should be buttered generously. You don't need any special pan for muffins; the common aluminum pans found in most cookware sections work just fine. Be aware if you have a nonstick pan that the outside of the muffins will be darker and crisper than if an aluminum pan is used. The rule with baking pans is that *dark-colored pans make dark surfaces*. This applies to muffin pans, baking sheets, and loaf pans. Baking scones, biscuits, or cookies on a dark (nonstick) baking sheet makes their bottoms too dark. A baking sheet that is too thin can also cause that problem. To prevent the bottoms of baked goods from burning stack 2 baking sheets together or place the baking sheet on an inverted baking sheet (if it can't be sandwiched because it is a different size); this adds another layer of insulation. Heaviness is a good quality in baking pans (and pots and pans, too) because the result is even heat distribution. If you can

find ceramic loaf pans, by all means use them. They will cook your quick breads beautifully and help create a tender crust.

TESTING FOR DONENESS: When baking, the oven door should remain closed until just a few minutes before the time the baked goods are ready. You don't want to interrupt the rising process by letting heat escape or having a draft enter the oven. Quick breads and muffins should be quickly tested by inserting a thin, pointed knife in their centers and checking to see if any batter adheres. If so, cook a few more minutes and test again. Many people use a thin cake tester to check for doneness, but I have been tricked by these devices because they are so thin. I prefer a thin, narrow knife because it is easy to see whether any batter is adhering to it.

COOLING: Cooling racks are essential for breads because they allow air to circulate. If you keep muffins or breads in their pans, steam will get trapped, causing soggy bottoms. Let the items sit for 5 minutes or so once they are removed from the oven, then remove them from their pan(s) and let cool on a wire cooling rack.

LEMON BREAD WITH LEMON-ALMOND GLAZE

This luscious bread has an electrifying lemon flavor and a smooth, buttery texture. It would serve equally well as part of a brunch or afternoon tea, or as a light dessert.

MAKES 1 LOAF, 10–12 SERVINGS

8 tablespoons (1 stick) unsalted butter, very soft

½ cup sugar

2 large eggs

Zest of 1 lemon

⅓ cup frozen lemonade concentrate, thawed

1 teaspoon vanilla extract

2 cups unbleached flour

2 teaspoons baking powder

½ teaspoon salt

¾ cup half-and-half

Lemon-Almond Glaze:

1 tablespoon melted butter

1 tablespoon fresh lemon juice

1 teaspoon milk

⅛ teaspoon almond extract

¼ teaspoon vanilla extract

¾ cup confectioners' sugar

1. Preheat the oven to 350 degrees. Generously butter and flour a 9 × 5-inch loaf pan. In a large bowl, using an electric mixer, cream the butter and sugar until very smooth. Add the eggs and beat until very fluffy, at least 3 minutes. Add the zest, lemonade concentrate, and vanilla, and beat until mixed. 2. In a medium-size bowl combine the flour, baking powder, and salt. Sprinkle it into the butter mixture and beat a few seconds. Pour in the half-and-half and beat just until the batter is evenly moistened. Scrape the batter into the prepared loaf pan. 3. Bake 50–60 minutes, or until a tester or knife inserted in the center of the bread comes out clean. Cool the bread completely on a wire rack. 4. To make the glaze: combine the butter, lemon juice, milk, and almond and vanilla extracts in a medium-size bowl. Add the confectioners' sugar and beat vigorously with a fork. Let the mixture sit a minute so the sugar can absorb the liquid, then stir again until smooth. Check the consistency. Add 1–2 drops of milk if the glaze is too thick to spread. Spread or drizzle the glaze over the top of the bread. Let harden, about 15 minutes, before slicing the bread.

DRIED CRANBERRY AND ORANGE BREAD

Because this bread freezes so well, I like to double the recipe during the holidays and then give one loaf as a gift and freeze the other for our holiday breakfast. Fresh cranberries are available only from November to January where I live, so I love the fact that this bread relies on tangy dried cranberries that are available year-round.

MAKES 1 LOAF, 10–12 SERVINGS

>   2 cups unbleached flour
>
>   2 teaspoons baking powder
>
>   ½ teaspoon salt
>
>   ½ cup dried cranberries
>
>   6 tablespoons butter, very soft
>
>   ¾ cup sugar
>
>   Zest of 2 oranges
>
>   2 large eggs
>
>   ½ cup orange juice
>
>   ½ cup low-fat milk

1. Preheat the oven to 350 degrees. Butter and flour a 9 × 5-inch loaf pan. **2.** Place the flour, baking powder, and salt in a medium-size bowl and mix well. Put the cranberries in a small bowl and toss with 1 tablespoon of the flour mixture. **3.** In a large bowl, using an electric mixer, beat the butter, sugar, and orange zest together until creamy, at least 2 minutes. Add the eggs and beat until very fluffy, at least 3 minutes more. Alternately add half the flour and half the orange juice and milk. Beat just until mixed, then repeat, mixing only until combined. Fold in the cranberries by hand. Scrape the batter into the loaf pan. **4.** Bake 50–55 minutes, or until a tester inserted in the center of the bread comes out dry. Cool on a wire rack for 5 minutes before unmolding. Let the bread cool completely before slicing, at least 2 hours.

TIP: You can make 3 baby loaves and give them as gifts. Butter and flour 3 disposable 5 × 3 × 2 pans, fill them with the batter, and bake about 40 minutes.

SPICED APPLE RUM BREAD

The rum provides a warm, sweet accent that is subtle but aromatic and delightful. If you prefer, you can substitute apple cider, and you'll still get a moist, flavorful bread that is a real charmer.

MAKES 1 LOAF, 10–12 SERVINGS

>   2 cups unbleached flour
>
>   1 cup sugar
>
>   1 teaspoon baking powder
>
>   1 teaspoon baking soda

1 teaspoon cinnamon

1 teaspoon powdered ginger

¼ teaspoon ground cloves

¼ teaspoon nutmeg

½ cup finely chopped pecans or walnuts

½ teaspoon salt

2 large eggs

½ cup canola oil

1 cup unsweetened applesauce

¼ cup rum or apple cider

1. Preheat the oven to 350 degrees. Butter and flour a 9 × 5-inch (1½-quart) loaf pan. **2.** In a large bowl thoroughly combine the flour, sugar, baking powder, baking soda, cinnamon, ginger, cloves, nutmeg, nuts, and salt. **3.** In a medium-size bowl beat together the eggs, oil, applesauce, and rum. Add to the flour mixture and stir until evenly moistened. Scrape into the prepared pan. **4.** Bake 1 hour, or until a knife inserted in the center of the bread comes out clean. Let stand on a wire rack for 10 minutes before removing from the pan. Cool completely before slicing, about 2 hours.

BANANA BRAN BREAD

I always keep a bag of bran in my freezer to have on hand for baked goods such as this fantastic bread. You can spread a thin layer of cream cheese or peanut butter on slices of banana bread to create tasty sandwiches.

MAKES 1 LOAF

1 cup unbleached flour

½ cup bran

⅔ cup sugar

1 teaspoon baking powder

1 teaspoon baking soda

½ teaspoon salt

½ cup finely chopped walnuts

2 large eggs

1 cup thoroughly mashed ripe bananas (2–3 bananas)

6 tablespoons unsalted butter, melted

1. Preheat the oven to 350 degrees. Butter a 9 × 5-inch (1½-quart) loaf pan. **2.** In a large bowl combine the flour, bran, sugar, baking powder, baking soda, salt, and walnuts. **3.** Whisk the eggs in a medium-size bowl. Thoroughly whisk in the mashed banana and butter. Scrape this into the flour mixture and stir just until evenly moistened. Pour the batter into the prepared pan. **4.** Bake 50 minutes, or until a knife inserted in the center of the loaf comes out clean. Cool on a wire rack for 10 minutes before removing from the pan. Cool completely, at least 2 hours, before slicing.

TIP: The kind of bran you want for this recipe is wheat bran, available in natural foods stores and many supermarkets. You can substitute toasted wheat germ for the bran and get very similar results.

SWEET POTATO BREAD

I love sweet potatoes prepared in every manner, and this bread is no exception. Especially moist and lightly infused with cinnamon and cloves, this quick bread is great for snacks, brunch, and tea time.

MAKES 1 LARGE LOAF, 12–14 SERVINGS

  2 cups unbleached flour

  1¼ cups sugar

  1¼ teaspoons baking powder

  ½ teaspoon baking soda

  ¾ teaspoon salt

  1 teaspoon cinnamon

  ½ teaspoon ground cloves

  ¾ cup finely chopped pecans

  2 large eggs

  ½ teaspoon vanilla extract

  1 cup cooked, well-mashed sweet potato
     (from 1 large potato)

  ½ cup canola oil

  ½ cup low-fat milk

1. Preheat the oven to 350 degrees. Butter and flour a 9 × 5 × 3-inch loaf pan (see Tip). **2.** In a medium-size bowl thoroughly combine the flour, sugar, baking powder, baking soda, salt, cinnamon, cloves, and pecans. **3.** Whisk the eggs in a large bowl until blended. Whisk in the vanilla and sweet potato until very well blended. Whisk in the oil and milk. Add the flour mixture and whisk just until the batter is smooth and blended. Scrape the batter into the prepared pan. **4.** Bake 1 hour and 20 minutes, or until a knife inserted in the center of the bread comes out clean. Remove the loaf from the pan and cool completely on a wire rack before slicing, at least 2 hours.

TIPS: You need a full-size (8-cup) 9 × 5 × 3-inch loaf pan for this bread. If your loaf pan is smaller, spoon a portion of the batter into a tiny foil loaf pan or into muffin cups. Don't fill your loaf pan more than ⅔ full.

To cook the sweet potato, cut it into quarters and boil until tender, about 20 minutes. Cool a few minutes and then slip off the peel. Mash the potato well with a fork.

QUICK OATMEAL RAISIN BREAD

This grain-filled bread is an ideal snack to pack in kids' lunch boxes or to serve as part of a breakfast spread. Make it the night before or early in the day so that it has plenty of time to cool before being sliced.

MAKES 1 LOAF, 10–12 SERVINGS

  1¼ cups quick oats

  ½ cup whole wheat flour

  ¾ cup unbleached flour

  ¼ cup wheat bran

½ teaspoon cinnamon

2 teaspoons baking powder

½ teaspoon salt

⅔ cup raisins

2 large eggs

½ cup firmly packed light brown sugar

¼ cup canola oil

1¼ cups buttermilk

1. Preheat the oven to 350 degrees. Butter a 9 × 5-inch (1½-quart) loaf pan. **2.** In a large bowl thoroughly combine the oats, the two flours, bran, cinnamon, baking powder, and salt. Add the raisins and toss to coat well. **3.** Beat the eggs in a medium-size bowl with a fork or whisk.

Oat Cuisine

Quick oats are regular old-fashioned oats that have been cut to make them thinner. They are just as nutritious as old-fashioned oats because the bran and germ of the oat remain during processing. Oat groats (kernels) are steamed and flattened to make old-fashioned oats. For quick oats the kernels are cut into small pieces before being flattened with rollers. Oats are a powerhouse of nutrients. They contain high-quality protein, B vitamins, iron, calcium, and vitamin E. Oats also are an excellent source of soluble fiber, which is known to lower cholesterol levels in the blood.

Beat in the sugar and oil until well mixed. Beat in the buttermilk until blended. Pour this mixture into the flour mixture and stir just until the batter is evenly moistened. Scrape the batter into the prepared pan. **4.** Bake 50 minutes, or until a knife inserted in the center of the bread comes out clean. Remove the loaf from the pan and cool on a wire rack. Cool to room temperature, at least 2 hours, before slicing.

CLASSIC CORN BREAD

This is classic corn bread in the northern tradition, which is lighter and more cakelike than its southern counterpart. (Southern corn bread has little or no flour in it and is very moist and dense.) Serve this with chili, soups, main-course salads, or as a breakfast offering. It is so easy to prepare and so satisfying that it has become a staple in our house. It can be in the oven at a moment's notice.

SERVES 6

1 cup cornmeal

1 cup unbleached flour

1 tablespoon baking powder

¼ cup sugar

½ teaspoon salt

1 large egg

4 tablespoons unsalted butter, melted

1¼ cups low-fat milk

1. Preheat the oven to 400 degrees. Butter an 8 × 8-inch baking pan. 2. In a large bowl thoroughly whisk together the cornmeal, flour, baking powder, sugar, and salt. 3. Whisk the egg in a medium-size bowl. Whisk in the butter and milk until well blended. Pour into the cornmeal mixture and whisk just until the batter is evenly moistened. Do not overbeat. With a rubber spatula scrape the batter into the prepared pan. 4. Bake 25 minutes, or until very lightly golden on top and a knife inserted in the center of the bread comes out dry. Let cool on a wire rack at least 10 minutes before cutting. Serve warm or at room temperature.

CORN BREAD WITH CHILIES AND CHEESE

Laced with corn, green chilies, and jalapeño pepper cheese, this festive corn bread is almost like a meal unto itself. For an easy portable lunch, pack squares of this corn bread with some slices of cheese such as cheddar or more jalapeño cheese.

SERVES 6

1¼ cups cornmeal

¾ cup unbleached flour

1 tablespoon baking powder

½ teaspoon salt

¼ cup sugar

1 cup frozen corn, thawed

1 (4-ounce) can chopped (mild) green chilies, well drained

1 cup grated Monterey Jack cheese with jalapeño peppers

2 large eggs

1 cup milk

¼ cup canola oil

1. Preheat the oven to 400 degrees. Butter an 8 × 8-inch baking pan. 2. In a large bowl thoroughly combine the cornmeal, flour, baking powder, salt, and sugar. Stir in the corn, chilies, and cheese until well coated. 3. Beat the eggs in a medium-size bowl. Beat in the milk and oil. Pour into the cornmeal mixture and stir just until evenly moistened. Scrape the batter into the prepared pan. 4. Bake 30 minutes. Let cool on a wire rack at least 15 minutes before cutting into squares. Serve barely warm or at room temperature.

CORN BREAD LOAF

Here is an unusual corn bread that my mother often makes—it is filled with corn kernels and baked in a loaf pan. The moist loaf slices beautifully, and sliced leftover corn bread can be toasted until crisp and golden. For corn bread lovers like me, it's a great way to enjoy corn bread that is at once familiar and different.

Vegetarian Classics

Butter for greasing pan

1¼ cups unbleached flour, plus extra for
dusting the pan

1¼ cups cornmeal

½ cup sugar

1 teaspoon baking powder

½ teaspoon salt

2 large eggs

½ cup canola oil

1 cup low-fat milk

1 cup frozen corn kernels, thawed

1. Preheat the oven to 350 degrees. Butter and flour a 9 × 5-inch loaf pan. **2.** In a large bowl thoroughly combine the flour, cornmeal, sugar, baking powder, and salt. **3.** Beat the eggs in a medium-size bowl. Beat in the oil and milk. Pour into the flour mixture and stir just until evenly moistened. Stir in the corn. Scrape the batter into the prepared loaf pan. **4.** Bake 15 minutes. Lower the heat to 325 degrees and bake 1 hour more, or until a knife inserted in the center of the bread comes out clean. Let the loaf cool in the pan for 15 minutes before removing it. Cool on a wire rack until warm or at room temperature before slicing, at least 1 hour.

TIP: This bread keeps fresh-tasting for a few days if well wrapped and refrigerated. Slices can be toasted until golden brown.

IRISH SODA BREAD

When I traveled around Ireland, I tasted countless versions of soda bread, but very few contained raisins and caraway seeds. When I returned to the United States, my friend's Irish-born grandmother had this memorable bread waiting for us. It seems that this is the style favored by Irish Americans. It is filled with raisins and caraway seeds, and has a sweet backdrop.

I like to bake this bread in an 8-inch cake pan because it creates a nicely shaped loaf; however, you will also get good results using a deep 1½-quart baking dish or allowing it to stand freely on a greased baking sheet.

MAKES 1 LOAF, 12–14 SERVINGS

2½ cups unbleached flour, plus extra for
dusting

½ cup whole wheat flour

½ cup sugar

¾ teaspoon salt

2 teaspoons baking soda

4 tablespoons (½ stick) butter, cut into
bits, plus extra for greasing

1 cup raisins

1½ tablespoons caraway seeds

1½ cups buttermilk, or plain yogurt
thinned with milk

Milk for brushing on top

I. Preheat the oven to 350 degrees. Butter and flour a round 8 × 2-inch cake pan. **2.** In a large bowl place the two flours, sugar, salt, and baking soda, and thoroughly mix together. Drop in the butter bits and toss to coat with the flour. Rub the butter into the flour with your fingertips until little pea-size pieces form. Stir in the raisins and caraway seeds. **3.** Pour in the buttermilk and stir to moisten the dough evenly. Sprinkle a little flour on the work surface, then place the dough on it. Knead the dough a few times just to make it pliable. Shape it into a ball, then put it in the baking pan and flatten it. With a sharp knife cut an "x" in it. Use your fingers to coat the surface of the dough with a little milk to give it a slight sheen. **4.** Bake 55–60 minutes, or until a rich golden brown. Remove the bread from the pan and let cool completely on a wire rack, at least 2 hours, before slicing it.

T I P : To make it easier to slice this soda bread, place it in a plastic bag for the last 15 minutes or so of cooling time to soften the crust slightly.

ANGEL BISCUITS

I discovered these biscuits in an old community cookbook, and they are a marvel. The inclusion of both yeast and baking powder and the lack of a warm rising period breaks the rules of classical bread or biscuit making, yet this recipe turns out the best biscuits you could ask for. You can keep the dough for several days in the refrigerator, which just adds to the charm and idiosyncrasy of these biscuits.

MAKES 1 DOZEN BISCUITS

¼ cup warm water

½ packet (about 1⅛ teaspoons)
   dry active yeast

2½ cups unbleached flour

2 tablespoons sugar

½ teaspoon baking powder

½ teaspoon baking soda

¾ teaspoon salt

4 tablespoons unsalted butter, chilled

1 cup buttermilk

1 tablespoon butter, melted

I. Place the water in a small bowl and sprinkle on the yeast. Let sit 2 minutes, then stir it into the water until blended. **2.** Thoroughly combine the flour, sugar, baking powder, baking soda, and salt in a large bowl. Cut the butter into bits and toss it in the flour mixture. Rub the butter into the flour with your fingertips or a pastry cutter until small pellets form. Pour in the yeast mixture and buttermilk, and stir just until evenly moistened. Cover the bowl with plastic wrap and refrigerate at least 1 hour or up to 4 days. **3.** Preheat the oven to 450 degrees. Place the oven rack in the top third of the oven. **4.** Place the dough on a lightly floured surface and knead a few times. Roll it into a ½-inch thickness. Use a 3-inch biscuit cutter to cut out the biscuits and place them on a greased baking sheet. Brush the tops lightly with melted butter. Bake 11–13 minutes, or until deeply golden.

GIANT CORN MUFFINS

These are classic corn muffins baked in a jumbo-size pan. They are moist, slightly sweet, and have just the right texture—not too cakey and not too grainy. If you don't have a large muffin pan, see the Tip about adjusting the cooking time.

MAKES 6 LARGE MUFFINS

>   Butter for greasing
>   1¼ cups unbleached flour
>   ¾ cup cornmeal
>   1 tablespoon baking powder
>   ½ teaspoon salt
>   ⅓ cup sugar
>   1 large egg
>   ¼ cup canola oil
>   1 cup milk

1. Preheat the oven to 400 degrees. Butter a jumbo-size (¾-cup) muffin pan. **2.** In a large bowl thoroughly combine the flour, cornmeal, baking powder, salt, and sugar. **3.** Beat the egg in a medium-size bowl. Beat in the oil and milk. Pour into the dry ingredients and stir just until evenly moistened. Spoon into the prepared muffin cups. **4.** Bake 22 minutes, or until a knife inserted in the center of a muffin comes out clean. Serve warm, not piping hot, for optimum flavor and texture.

TIP: If you use a standard 12-cup muffin pan (the muffin cups usually have a ⅓- to ½-cup capacity), bake about 18 minutes.

ORANGE POPPY SEED MUFFINS

I love the flavor of orange in baked goods, and in these moist, tender muffins it is delightfully pronounced.

MAKES 1 DOZEN MUFFINS

>   1½ cups unbleached flour
>   ¾ cup sugar
>   1½ tablespoons poppy seeds
>   ½ teaspoon salt
>   2 teaspoons baking powder
>   ½ teaspoon baking soda
>   2 tablespoons grated orange zest
>   (about 2 oranges)
>   1 egg
>   1 cup buttermilk
>   6 tablespoons butter, melted
>   2 tablespoons orange juice

Quick Breads, Muffins, Scones, Etc.

1. Preheat the oven to 400 degrees. Generously butter the insides and top of a regular-size (⅓-cup) muffin pan. **2.** In a large bowl thoroughly combine the flour, sugar, poppy seeds, salt, baking powder, baking soda, and zest. **3.** Beat the egg in a medium-size bowl. Beat in the buttermilk, butter, and orange juice. Pour into the flour mixture and stir just until evenly moistened. Do not overmix the batter. Spoon into the muffin pan. Bake 18–20 minutes, or until a tester inserted in a muffin comes out clean. Immediately remove the muffins from the pan and cool on a wire rack. Serve warm or at room temperature.

TIP: It is a good idea and economical to purchase poppy seeds in bulk from a natural foods store and keep them in a plastic bag in the freezer. They are rather perishable, so this will extend their life and make them available to you at a moment's notice.

MIXED BERRY MUFFINS

These muffins are fat and impressive, and have a delicate crumb and irresistible flavor. Use mixed frozen berries that are readily found in most supermarkets in the frozen food section.

MAKES 1 DOZEN MUFFINS

1¼ cups frozen mixed berries

2 cups unbleached flour

½ cup sugar

1 tablespoon baking powder

¾ teaspoon salt

2 large eggs

1 teaspoon vanilla extract

1¼ cups low-fat milk

6 tablespoons butter, melted

1. Preheat the oven to 400 degrees. Generously butter the insides and top of a regular-size (⅓-cup) muffin pan or line the pan with paper muffin cups. With a large, sharp knife cut any large frozen berries, such as strawberries and blackberries, into small pieces, then place the berries in a small bowl. **2.** In a large bowl thoroughly combine the flour, sugar, baking powder, and salt. Sprinkle 1 tablespoon of the flour mixture on the berries and toss to coat. **3.** Beat the eggs in a medium-size bowl. Beat in the vanilla, milk, and melted butter. Pour into the flour mixture and stir a few strokes to evenly moisten the batter, then gently fold in the berries. Do not overmix. **4.** Fill the muffin cups with the batter; it will reach the top of the pan. Bake 20–22 minutes, or until a knife inserted in the center of a muffin comes out dry. These muffins are most flavorful when served at room temperature.

Vegetarian Classics

BANANA GINGER MUFFINS

The flavors of banana and ginger are meant for each other, each enhancing the other's tropical charm. In these muffins bits of candied ginger are strewn throughout the banana batter, creating a tender muffin with lots of spunk.

MAKES 1 DOZEN MUFFINS

> 2 cups unbleached flour
>
> ½ cup sugar
>
> 1 tablespoon baking powder
>
> 1 teaspoon cinnamon
>
> ½ teaspoon salt
>
> ½ cup finely chopped crystallized ginger
>
> 2 large eggs
>
> 1 cup thoroughly mashed ripe bananas (2–3 bananas)
>
> 6 tablespoons butter, melted
>
> ¾ cup low-fat milk

1. Preheat the oven to 400 degrees. Butter the insides and top of a regular-size (⅓-cup) muffin pan. **2.** In a large bowl thoroughly whisk together the flour, sugar, baking powder, cinnamon, salt, and ginger. **3.** Whisk the eggs in a small bowl. Whisk in the mashed banana, butter, and milk until thoroughly combined. Scrape this mixture into the flour mixture and whisk just until evenly moistened. Do not overbeat. Spoon the mixture into the prepared muffin pan. It will reach the top of each cup. **4.** Bake 18 minutes, or until a knife inserted in the center of a muffin comes out dry. Remove the muffins from the pan and let cool on a wire rack. Serve warm or at room temperature.

GLORIOUS MORNING MUFFINS

Jam-packed with grated carrots, apple, and coconut, these flavorful muffins became very popular in the 1980s. Don't worry that the batter completely fills each muffin cup; the muffins rise beautifully and retain a nice shape.

MAKES 1 DOZEN MUFFINS

> 2 cups unbleached flour
>
> ½ cup sugar
>
> 2 teaspoons baking powder
>
> 2 teaspoons cinnamon
>
> ½ teaspoon salt
>
> 1 cup grated carrots (about 2 carrots)
>
> 1 tart apple (such as Granny Smith), peeled, cored, and grated
>
> ½ cup raisins
>
> ⅓ cup sweetened shredded coconut
>
> ½ cup finely chopped pecans
>
> 2 large eggs

½ cup canola oil

1 teaspoon vanilla extract

⅔ cup low-fat milk

1. Preheat the oven to 375 degrees. Butter the insides and top of a regular-size (⅓-cup) muffin pan. **2.** In a large bowl thoroughly combine the flour, sugar, baking powder, cinnamon, and salt. Stir in the grated carrots, apple, raisins, coconut, and pecans, and toss to coat well. **3.** Beat the eggs in a medium-size bowl. Beat in the oil, vanilla, and milk. Add to the flour mixture and stir to blend. Do not overbeat the batter. **4.** Spoon the batter into the muffin cups. Bake 20–22 minutes, or until a knife inserted in the center of a muffin comes out clean. Cool the muffins on a wire rack for 5 minutes, then remove from the pan and let cool some more. These muffins are best served barely warm or at room temperature—not hot.

CRANBERRY OAT MUFFINS

These muffins have a delightful crunch to them and an appealing balance of sweetness and tang. The cranberries are chopped before being added to the batter so they are nicely distributed in small pieces.

MAKES 1 DOZEN MUFFINS

1¼ cups unbleached flour

¼ cup whole wheat flour

1 cup oats

½ cup sugar

1 tablespoon baking powder

½ teaspoon cinnamon

½ teaspoon salt

1 cup fresh or frozen thawed cranberries

1 large egg

1 cup milk

6 tablespoons butter, melted and cooled

1. Preheat the oven to 400 degrees. Generously butter the insides and top of a regular-size (⅓-cup) muffin pan. **2.** In a large bowl thoroughly combine the 2 flours, oats, sugar, baking powder, cinnamon, and salt. **3.** Place the cranberries in a processor and roughly chop them, or place on a cutting board and chop by hand with a large knife. Mix the cranberries into the flour mixture. **4.** Beat the egg in a medium-size bowl. Beat in the milk and butter. Pour into the flour mixture and stir just until the batter is evenly moistened. Do not overmix it. Spoon the batter into the prepared muffin pan. **5.** Bake 18 minutes, or until a knife inserted in the center of a muffin comes out clean. Remove the muffins from the pan and cool on a wire rack. Serve slightly warm or at room temperature.

TIP: Having grown up in eastern Massachusetts near cranberry bog territory, I know that pesticides are used on all cranberries. It's easy and probably common to wash fresh cranberries, but you should do the same for frozen ones as well. Rinse them well in a strainer, then pat them thoroughly dry on a kitchen towel.

APPLE CIDER MUFFINS WITH STREUSEL TOPPING

The essence of apple, both grated and in cider form, defines these spicy muffins. Although my family loves them as is, you can add raisins, dates, or chopped walnuts or pecans with successful results.

Makes 1 dozen muffins

Streusel Topping:

> ¼ cup unbleached flour
>
> ¼ cup sugar
>
> 3 tablespoons chilled unsalted butter, cut into bits

The Muffins:

> 2 cups unbleached flour
>
> ½ cup whole wheat flour
>
> 1 tablespoon baking powder
>
> ½ teaspoon cinnamon
>
> ¼ teaspoon ground cloves or allspice
>
> ½ teaspoon salt
>
> 1 apple, grated (skin left on)
>
> 1 large egg
>
> ½ cup firmly packed light brown sugar

> ⅓ cup canola oil
>
> 1 cup apple cider

1. To make the streusel: combine the flour and sugar in a small bowl. Toss the butter bits with the mixture, then use your fingers to rub the butter into the flour until moist pellets form. Set aside. **2.** Preheat the oven to 400 degrees. Generously butter the insides and top of a regular-size (⅓-cup) muffin pan. **3.** In a large bowl thoroughly combine the 2 flours, baking powder, cinnamon, cloves, and salt. Add the apple and toss with the mixture until it no longer remains in clumps. **4.** Beat the egg in a medium-size bowl. Beat in the brown sugar, oil, and apple cider. Add to the flour mixture and stir just until blended. Spoon the batter into the muffin cups. With your fingers sprinkle some streusel on each muffin, then pat it down lightly. **5.** Bake 17–18 minutes, or until a knife inserted in one of the muffins comes out clean. Cool on a rack for 5 minutes before removing the muffins from the pan. Serve slightly warm or at room temperature.

JAMMIES

These fun muffins nestle a little surprise in their centers—a spoonful of jam that can be spread around the muffins once they are split open. Kids love them, and you can be inventive and vary the types of preserves you place in the center.

2 cups unbleached flour

½ cup sugar

1 tablespoon baking powder

½ teaspoon salt

Pinch nutmeg

1 large egg

6 tablespoons butter, melted and cooled

1¼ cups milk

1 teaspoon vanilla extract

¼ cup jam (approximately)

1. Preheat the oven to 425 degrees. Generously butter the insides and top of a regular-size (⅓-cup) muffin pan. **2.** In a large bowl thoroughly combine the flour, sugar, baking powder, salt, and nutmeg. **3.** Beat the egg in a medium-size bowl. Beat in the butter, milk, and vanilla. Pour into the dry ingredients and stir just until the batter is evenly moistened. Do not overbeat. **4.** Spoon about ⅓ of the batter into all the muffin cups. (They will be less than half filled.) Place a teaspoon of jam in the center of each muffin, then cover with the remaining batter. **5.** Bake 15–20 minutes, or until evenly golden on top. Cool on a wire rack for a few minutes before removing from the pan.

BEST POPOVERS

Because of their uniqueness, it's a challenge to describe popovers to those who have never sampled them. They resemble muffins in shape but have a hollow interior, crisp brown exterior, and somewhat moist cakelike lining. Confusing? Then you'll just have to try these marvels. To bake popovers that puff up into huge golden domes begin cooking them in a cold oven. The intense heat rising from the bottom of the oven will cause the popovers to balloon into giant air-filled shapes.

MAKES 6 POPOVERS

2 large eggs

2 tablespoons butter, melted, plus extra for greasing

1 cup milk

1 cup unbleached flour

2 teaspoons sugar

½ teaspoon salt

1. Butter 6 custard cups (¾ cup capacity) and place on a baking sheet. **2.** Whisk the eggs in a large bowl. Pour in the melted butter and milk, and mix. Add the flour, sugar, and salt, and whisk until the batter is smooth. Do not overmix. **3.** Fill the custard cups with the batter. Place the baking sheet with the custard cups on it in the cold oven, then set the heat at

425 degrees. Bake 40 minutes. Do not peek in the oven before the popovers are done, or they could deflate. Tip the popovers on their sides in the cups and cut a slit in the sides to let steam escape. Serve within 15 minutes.

TIP: Although it is common to serve popovers for breakfast, they are also quite lovely as an accompaniment to soup or dinner.

CLASSIC CURRANT SCONES

I like to serve these scones when I have a special jam that I want to highlight because their delicate flavor allows the distinctiveness of the jam to stand out. Although triangles can be easily cut, the scone dough can also be cut with your favorite biscuit cutter to make plain or scalloped circles. In that case, roll the dough so that it is ½ inch thick.

MAKES 1 DOZEN SCONES

2 cups unbleached flour

⅓ cup sugar

2 teaspoons baking powder

½ teaspoon baking soda

½ teaspoon salt

6 tablespoons unsalted butter, chilled

½ cup currants

1 large egg

¾ cup buttermilk, or yogurt thinned with a little milk

Milk for glazing

1. Place the oven rack in the top third of the oven. Preheat the oven to 400 degrees. Lightly butter a baking sheet. **2.** In a large bowl combine the flour, sugar, baking powder, baking soda, and salt, and mix together thoroughly. Cut the butter into bits and toss them into the flour mixture. Rub the butter into the mixture with your fingertips until small pellets form. Stir in the currants. **3.** Beat the egg in a small bowl. Beat in the buttermilk. Pour into the flour mixture and stir with a fork until the dough is evenly moistened. Sprinkle a little flour on a work surface and drop the dough on it. Gather the dough into a ball and knead once or twice. Pat the dough into a ¾-inch disk. Cut the disk into 12 triangles with a large knife. Brush the top of the scones with a little milk and place on the baking sheet. **4.** Bake 15 minutes, or until lightly golden. Cool on a wire rack before serving.

GINGER CREAM SCONES

Heavy cream is the only moistening agent in these melt-in-your-mouth scones, and it makes them so flaky and delicate that they would be suitable for a royal occasion. Little nuggets of candied ginger add a beguiling charm that makes the accompaniment of jam completely unnecessary. These exquisite scones can stand proudly on their own.

MAKES 1 DOZEN SCONES

  2 cups unbleached flour

  ⅓ cup sugar

  2½ teaspoons baking powder

  ½ teaspoon salt

  ⅓ cup finely diced crystallized ginger

  1⅓ cups heavy cream

  1 teaspoon vanilla extract

  Milk for glazing

1. Place the oven rack in the top third of the oven. Preheat the oven to 400 degrees. Lightly butter a baking sheet. **2.** In a large bowl thoroughly combine the flour, sugar, baking powder, salt, and crystallized ginger. **3.** Mix the cream and vanilla together, then pour into the flour mixture. Stir with a large spoon just until the dough is evenly moistened. Lightly flour a work surface and place the dough on it. Knead 1 or 2 times, then pat into a ¾-inch-thick disk. Cut the disk into 12 triangles. Place the scones on the baking sheet and brush the tops lightly with some milk. **4.** Bake 15 minutes, or until the scones are lightly golden. Cool until slightly warm or at room temperature before serving.

TIP: Although it is not difficult to find candied (crystallized) ginger nowadays—it is sold in most supermarkets—a particularly good source can be a specialty candy or chocolate shop, the ones that sell beautiful chocolate bonbons by the pound.

IRISH WHOLEMEAL SCONES

At Field's market in Skibbereen, County Cork, Ireland, we had the best scones of our trip around the Emerald Isle. These scones resemble Irish brown bread because they are made with the same Irish "wholemeal" flour that is widely used in that country. The closest flour we have here is whole wheat flour, but that lacks the graininess that is so pleasing in their variety. I was thrilled to discover that I could duplicate wholemeal flour by adding some oats and wheat germ or bran to our whole wheat flour. Although filled with whole grain goodness, these memorable scones are light and tender.

MAKES 1 DOZEN SCONES

  1 cup unbleached flour

  ½ cup whole wheat flour (preferably stone-ground)

  ¼ cup oats

  ¼ cup toasted wheat germ or bran

2 tablespoons sugar

2 teaspoons baking powder

½ teaspoon baking soda

½ teaspoon salt

6 tablespoons unsalted butter, chilled

1 large egg

¾ cup buttermilk, or plain yogurt thinned
    with a little milk

Milk for glazing

1. Place the oven rack in the top third of the oven. Preheat the oven to 400 degrees. Lightly butter a baking sheet. **2.** In a large bowl thoroughly combine the two flours, oats, wheat germ, sugar, baking powder, baking soda, and salt. Cut the butter into bits and toss into the mixture to coat the pieces of butter. Rub the butter into the mixture with your fingertips until small pellets form. **3.** Beat the egg in a small bowl. Beat in the buttermilk. Pour into the flour mixture and stir with a fork until the flour is evenly moistened. Let the mixture sit for 1 minute so it can absorb the liquid. **4.** Lightly flour a work surface and place the dough on it. Knead 1 or 2 times, adding flour if it is too sticky. Form into a disk and pat to a ¾ inch thickness. Cut the dough in half, then cut each half into 6 triangles to make 12 scones. Place the scones on the baking sheet. Brush the top of each scone with some milk. **5.** Bake 15 minutes, or until lightly golden. Cool on a wire rack before serving.

DOUBLE ALMOND SCONES

These are luxurious scones, made so by the inclusion of almond paste, which gives them an unbeatable flavor and moistness.

MAKES 1 DOZEN SCONES

7–8 ounces almond paste

1¾ cups unbleached flour

2 tablespoons sugar

Grated zest of 1 orange

2½ teaspoons baking powder

½ teaspoon salt

5 tablespoons chilled unsalted butter,
    cut into bits

½ cup sliced almonds

1 large egg

⅔ cup buttermilk, or plain yogurt thinned
    with a little milk

Milk for brushing

1. Place the oven rack in the top third of the oven. Preheat the oven to 400 degrees. Lightly butter a baking sheet. **2.** Place the almond paste in a food processor and process until it is the texture of coarse sand. Scrape it into a large bowl and thoroughly mix in the flour, sugar, orange zest, baking powder, and salt. Add the butter bits and toss to coat with the flour mixture. Rub the butter into the flour with your fingertips until coarse crumbs form. Stir in the

Quick Breads, Muffins, Scones, Etc.

sliced almonds. **3.** Beat the egg in a small bowl. Beat in the buttermilk. Pour into the flour mixture and stir just until evenly moistened. **4.** Lightly flour a work surface and drop the dough on it. Knead 2 or 3 times, then pat into a ¾-inch-thick disk. Cut the disk in half with a large, sharp knife and cut each half into 6 triangles to make 12 scones. Place the scones on the baking sheet. Brush the top of each scone with some milk. **5.** Bake about 17 minutes, or until golden. Cool completely on a wire rack before serving.

TIP: Although almond paste and marzipan are similar, almond paste is less sweet and intended for baking, whereas marzipan is not meant to be cooked.

CHEESE SCONES

Serve these richly flavored scones alongside a steamy bowl of soup, such as Vegetable Chowder (page 46) or Kale Soup (page 47), as a welcome alternative to French bread or rolls.

MAKES 24 SMALL SCONES

> 2½ cups unbleached flour
>
> 1 tablespoon baking powder
>
> ½ teaspoon dry mustard
>
> ¾ teaspoon salt
>
> ⅛ teaspoon cayenne pepper

> 6 tablespoons chilled unsalted butter, cut into bits
>
> 1½ cups grated extra-sharp cheddar cheese
>
> 2 large eggs
>
> ¾ cup plus 2 tablespoons low-fat milk

1. Place the oven rack in the top third of the oven. Preheat the oven to 400 degrees. Lightly butter a large baking sheet. **2.** In a large bowl thoroughly combine the flour, baking powder, mustard, salt, and cayenne. **3.** Drop in the butter bits and toss to coat them with the butter. With your fingertips rub the butter into the flour mixture until it is the texture of very coarse crumbs. Add 1 cup of the cheese and use your fingertips to coat the cheese pieces with the mixture. **4.** In a medium-size bowl, beat the eggs. Beat in the milk. Pour this into the flour mixture and stir until the dough is evenly moistened. **5.** Lightly flour your work surface and drop the dough onto it. Knead two or three times, then form into a ball and divide it into two pieces. Pat each piece into a disk ½–¾ inch thick (no thicker). With a large, sharp knife cut each disk in half, and cut each half into 6 triangles to make 24 scones. Place the scones on the baking sheet (if your baking sheet is small, bake the scones in two batches) and place some of the remaining grated cheese on top of each scone. **6.** Bake on the top rack for 10–12 minutes, or until golden. Remove the scones from the baking sheet and cool slightly on a wire rack. Serve warm.

BREAKFAST, BRUNCH, AND EGG DISHES

It is heartwarming to begin the day coddled with a breakfast that's more than a cup of coffee and a bowl of cereal. And whether it's a batch of muffins or a sophisticated brunch, its a treat to share well-made food that is homespun and satisfying.

If you want to offer your family or guests a hearty breakfast or brunch but are concerned that it will be too much work in the early morning hours, do some advance preparation the night before to simplify matters tremendously. Butter muffin pans (if you are including muffins from the Quick Breads chapter), measure dry ingredients for muffins or pancakes in a bowl and cover with plastic wrap, chop any vegetables (except potatoes because they discolor), and cut and chill any fruit you plan to serve. Another option is to select an overnight casserole from this chapter; all you'll have to do is pop it in the oven when you awake. So choose a strategy that allows you to enjoy breakfast preparation as well as its benefits.

YOGURT FRUIT PARFAIT

This is an ideal fruit salad to serve at the beginning of a special brunch or breakfast. Perfectly ripe chunks of fruit are layered with a sweet yogurt "cream." Use decorative goblets or large wineglasses to display the colorful layers and make an elegant presentation. The fruits that work best are the tender, delicate ones, such as berries, melons, and banana. Avoid apples and citrus fruit because their textures and flavors will clash with the suggested fruits.

SERVES 4

1 cup plain yogurt

1½–2 tablespoons honey

Dash cinnamon

4 cups (approximately) assorted fruit (such
as melon, berries, kiwi, banana,
mango, and pear), cut into bite-size
pieces

Mint sprigs or sliced almonds for garnish

1. Combine the yogurt, 1½ tablespoons honey, and cinnamon in a bowl and mix well. Taste for sweetness and add more honey if necessary. 2. Fill 4 decorative goblets or large wineglasses about halfway with the fruit. Spoon on a layer of yogurt. Top with more fruit and again cover with yogurt. Garnish with a mint sprig or a few sliced almonds. Serve within 1 hour.

TIPS: You can sweeten the yogurt with sugar instead of honey, but you will have to wait a few minutes for it to dissolve in the yogurt before pouring it on the fruit. You can also use a flavored yogurt.

The amount of fruit is approximate because it will depend on the size of your serving glasses.

If you don't use bananas (which darken) in your mixture, you can wait even longer before serving the parfait. Refrigerate the parfaits if you make them more than 1 hour in advance.

PERFECT PANCAKES

Slightly crisp on the edges, thin but not too thin, and melt-in-your-mouth tender—these are my requirements for perfect pancakes. Be certain to oil your griddle or frying pan adequately and regulate the heat carefully so these pancakes will be golden underneath when the bubbles burst on top. This will ensure "perfect pancakes."

SERVES 4 HUNGRY ADULTS

2¼ cups unbleached flour

¼ cup sugar

2¼ teaspoons baking powder

¾ teaspoon salt

3 large eggs

2¼ cups milk

4 tablespoons (½ stick) butter, melted

Oil for greasing the pan

Maple syrup (optional; see Tip)

1. In a large bowl whisk together the flour, sugar, baking powder, and salt. 2. Whisk the eggs in a medium-size bowl. Whisk in the milk and melted butter. Pour into the flour mixture and whisk just until combined. The batter should be a little lumpy, not perfectly smooth. 3. Cover the griddle or frying pan with a thin film of oil. Heat the pan over medium heat until a drop of water dances when flicked on the pan.

While making a homemade breakfast for family or friends is usually much appreciated, it can be tense for the cook if she has to tend the food at the stove the whole time. If you want to serve pancakes, waffles, or French toast to your family or guests all at once, preheat the oven to 300 degrees before you begin cooking. Place a baking sheet in the oven so it can heat up as well. As each batch is cooked, place it in 1 layer on the warm baking sheet and then serve all at once.

Spoon a few tablespoons of batter on the pan for each pancake. When the bubbles on the surface of the pancakes have formed and most of them have burst, and the pancakes are golden underneath, flip over and cook until golden. Heat regulation is one of the keys to properly cooking pancakes. The pan should be hot enough so the batter sizzles when poured on it, yet not so hot that the pancakes get brown underneath before the bubbles burst on top. Keep adjusting the heat throughout cooking. Serve immediately or place on a baking sheet and keep warm in a preheated 300-degree oven. Continue to lightly oil the pan in between batches of pancakes. Serve with warm maple syrup, if desired.

Perfect Blueberry Pancakes: Mix into the batter 1 cup fresh blueberries or well-drained and defrosted frozen blueberries.

Perfect Banana Pancakes: Substitute ¼ cup maple syrup for the sugar. Pour the batter into the hot pan and place thin slices of barely ripe banana on top. Spoon tiny amounts of batter on each banana slice, and use the back of a spoon to spread it out to cover the slices. Flip the pancakes over when the bubbles burst.

TIP: To warm maple syrup, put the jar or tin in a saucepan or heat-proof measuring cup filled with very hot tap water. Do this when you start frying the pancakes. Replace the water occasionally with hotter water.

PUMPKIN PANCAKES

These pancakes resemble traditional pancakes in texture but flaunt the irresistible flavor of pumpkin pie. Be certain to cook them through by waiting until some bubbles burst before flipping them.

SERVES 4 GENEROUSLY

2 large eggs

½ cup canned pumpkin (puree)

¼ cup canola oil

2¼ cups low-fat milk

2¼ cups unbleached flour

¼ cup sugar

2½ teaspoons baking powder

¾ teaspoon salt

1 teaspoon cinnamon

¾ teaspoon allspice

¼ teaspoon nutmeg

Canola oil for frying

Maple syrup for topping

1. Whisk the egg in a medium-size bowl. Add the pumpkin, oil, and milk, whisking until smooth. **2.** In a large bowl thoroughly whisk together the flour, sugar, baking powder, salt, cinnamon, allspice, and nutmeg. Pour the egg mixture into these dry ingredients and whisk until just blended and with a few lumps remaining. Do not overbeat. **3.** Pour a thin film of oil in a large skillet and heat over medium heat until a drop of water dances when dropped on the surface. Lower the heat to a little less than medium, and it should be just right. Spoon on some batter to make a few pancakes; they shouldn't be too thick. When some bubbles have appeared and burst and the bottom of the pancake is a rich golden color, flip them over and cook until golden brown. Repeat with the remaining batter. Serve with maple syrup.

TIP: You can freeze the remaining pumpkin in a plastic container. If you like, you can measure out ½-cup portions and freeze them individually for future batches of Pumpkin Pancakes.

BUTTERMILK CORN PANCAKES

Like classic pancakes these corn-filled flapjacks go well with maple syrup and are equally satisfying for breakfast or supper.

SERVES 3

1¼ cups unbleached flour

¼ cup cornmeal

2 tablespoons sugar

1¼ teaspoons baking powder

¼ teaspoon baking soda

1 teaspoon salt

2 large eggs

1¾ cups buttermilk

3 tablespoons butter, melted

1 cup frozen corn, thawed

Oil for greasing

Maple syrup

1. In a medium-size bowl whisk together the flour, cornmeal, sugar, baking powder, baking soda, and salt. **2.** Whisk the eggs in a large bowl and then whisk in the buttermilk and melted butter. Gently whisk in the flour mixture and the corn just until the batter is evenly moistened. Do not overbeat. **3.** Pour a thin film of oil on a griddle or large skillet and heat over medium heat. Test to see if the pan is hot enough by flicking a drop of water on it; it should sizzle. When the pan is ready, put a few tablespoons of batter on the pan to make 3-inch pancakes. Flip the pancakes over when they are golden brown underneath; this should take a few minutes on each side. Unlike classic pancakes, this batter doesn't bubble up as it cooks. Repeat with the remaining batter, lightly oiling the pan in between batches. Serve the pancakes with maple syrup.

WHOLE-GRAIN WAFFLES

Waffles can be an efficient homemade breakfast at a moment's notice if you get into the habit of freezing a few each time you make them. Just pop them into the toaster or heat in the oven when the time comes; you don't have to thaw them first.

MAKES 1 DOZEN 6-INCH WAFFLES

½ cup oats

½ cup whole wheat flour

1 cup unbleached flour

1 tablespoon sugar

½ teaspoon salt

1½ teaspoons baking powder

1 teaspoon baking soda

4 large eggs

2 cups buttermilk

8 tablespoons (1 stick) butter, melted

Maple syrup (see Tip)

1. Preheat the waffle iron. **2.** Place the oats in a blender or food processor and grind into a powder. Pour into a large bowl and thoroughly mix in the 2 flours, sugar, salt, baking powder, baking soda, and salt. **3.** Beat the eggs in a medium-size bowl. Beat in the buttermilk and melted butter. Pour this mixture into the dry ingredients and stir just until blended but still a little lumpy. Do not overbeat. **4.** Cook the waffles according to the manufacturer's directions. Serve immediately

TIP: Although these waffles can be served for breakfast with maple syrup drizzled on them, they are also delicious as a dessert topped with ice cream and fruit or syrup.

GRAND MARNIER FRENCH TOAST

French toast with spirits—a great brunch dish when you want something comforting yet special. You won't need much maple syrup as a topping because there is so much flavor and lingering sweetness from the Grand Marnier.

SERVES 4

4 large eggs

⅔ cup low-fat milk

¼ cup Grand Marnier or Triple Sec (or
other orange liqueur)

¼ cup sugar

Oil for frying (preferably canola)

8 slices good-quality white bread

Maple syrup

1. In a medium-size bowl thoroughly beat the eggs until perfectly blended. Beat in the milk, Grand Marnier, and sugar. Pour into a shallow dish such as a glass pie plate. 2. Pour a thin film of oil in a frying pan and heat over medium heat until a drop of water dances when dropped on it. 3. Place the slices of bread one by one in the egg mixture and let sit a few seconds. Carefully turn each one over and moisten the other side. Place a slice of soaked bread in the frying pan and repeat with another slice. Cook on both sides until golden brown and cooked through. Regulate the heat so the bread doesn't brown too fast. Serve with a bit of maple syrup.

TIP: Using 2 large skillets makes the process move quickly.

Experiment with different breads such as challah or French bread. If using supermarket bread, select a good-quality white bread such as Pepperidge Farm Hearty White.

BAKED APPLE FRENCH TOAST

This sumptuous French toast casserole has a layer of caramelized apples on the bottom that gets flipped over at serving time so it becomes the topping. You don't need to serve maple syrup with this version because the topping is so moist and flavorful. It is quick and easy to prepare and is the ideal dish when you have overnight guests or are serving a buffet brunch. Maybe best of all, it can all be prepared the night before.

SERVES 4 GOOD EATERS

4 tablespoons (½ stick) unsalted butter

3 medium-large apples (such as Cortland,
Macoun, or Empire), peeled and
thinly sliced (4–4½ cups) (see Tips)

¾ cup firmly packed light or dark brown
sugar

2 tablespoons water

1 teaspoon cinnamon

6–8 slices Italian or wide French bread
(4–5 inches in diameter), cut 1 inch
thick (see Tips)

4 large eggs

1¼ cups milk

2 teaspoons vanilla extract

1. Melt the butter in a large skillet and add the apple slices. Sauté 5 minutes, tossing often. Mix in the brown sugar, water, and cinnamon. Cook, stirring, 8–10 minutes, or until the apples are very tender. Scrape the mixture into a 13 × 9 × 2-inch Pyrex baking dish or other shallow 3-quart casserole. **2.** Cover the apples with the bread slices, trimming the bread if necessary, to entirely cover the surface. **3.** Beat the eggs thoroughly, then beat in the milk and vanilla. Pour all over the bread. Cover the dish with plastic wrap and refrigerate overnight. **4.** Remove the dish from the refrigerator in the morning and let sit at room temperature while you preheat the oven to 375 degrees. Bake the casserole, uncovered, for 30–35 minutes, or until the bread is golden and firm. Let sit 10 minutes before unmolding. **5.** Run a knife around the edges of the dish. If you have a platter or tray large enough to fit over the casserole, place it on top and carefully flip over the baking dish to unmold it. Otherwise, cut the French toast into individual portions and, using a spatula, lift one portion from the dish. Invert a serving plate and place on the French toast portion, then flip over so the apple layer is on top.

TIPS: Experiment with the bread. Try challah, a firm sourdough bread, or other home-made-type bread. Do not slice it more than 1 inch thick.

I avoid Granny Smith and Golden Delicious apples for this dish because they are so firm, and Red Delicious apples tend to be mealy.

PANETTONE FRENCH TOAST

Panettone, the rich, Italian Christmas bread that is studded with raisins and citrons, can now easily be found in stores in the United States during the holiday season. It is imported from Italy and contains only fresh ingredients with no additives. My family enjoys it on Christmas morning, and we have discovered that it makes delicious French toast. Because the bread is rich and large, 1 or 1½ slices per person will satisfy most appetites.

SERVES 4

> 6 large eggs
> ½ cup low-fat milk
> Canola oil for frying
> 4–6 slices (cut ¾ inch thick) panettone
> Maple syrup

1. Beat the eggs thoroughly in a medium-size bowl. Beat in the milk until blended. Pour the mixture into a shallow dish large enough to hold a slice of panettone. **2.** Pour a thin layer of oil in 1 or 2 large frying pans and heat over medium heat until a drop of water flicked on the pan sizzles. **3.** Dip 1 slice of panettone into the egg mixture, then quickly turn it over to soak the other side. Because the panettone is so soft and porous, you'll need to moisten it quickly so it

Breakfast, Brunch, and Egg Dishes

doesn't get too saturated and break. Place the slice immediately in the hot oil. Repeat with another slice if you are using 2 pans. Cook until a rich golden brown, flip over, and cook again until browned. Serve with maple syrup.

TIP: Because panettone is so sweet, it browns very quickly when fried. Regulate the heat so that the French toast has enough time to cook inside before becoming too brown on the outside.

ZUCCHINI, TOMATO, AND BASIL FRITTATA

This frittata has a wonderful blend of Mediterranean flavors and also a special tender texture from the bits of juicy tomato scattered throughout. It's delicious at room temperature as well as cold, so don't hesitate to pack it for a picnic or make into a portable lunch.

SERVES 4

3 tablespoons olive oil

1 large onion, finely diced

1 (14-ounce) can ready-cut diced tomatoes, drained well and juice reserved

2 small zucchini, halved lengthwise and thinly sliced

8 large eggs

⅓ cup grated Parmesan cheese

2 tablespoons minced fresh basil, or ½ teaspoon dried

½ teaspoon salt

Liberal seasoning freshly ground pepper

1. Heat 2 tablespoons oil in a 10-inch skillet, preferably nonstick, over medium heat. Add the onion and sauté until softened, about 10 minutes. Add the drained tomatoes and cook slowly with the onions until the onions are very tender, about 10 minutes. Stir in the zucchini and cover the pan. Cook, stirring often, until the zucchini is tender, about 10 minutes. Add a little of the reserved cooking liquid if the vegetables begin to stick. Scrape the mixture into a bowl and let cool.
2. Clean the skillet in which the vegetables were cooked. Pour in the remaining tablespoon of oil and swirl it around the pan to coat the sides as well as the bottom. If your pan isn't nonstick, you will probably need a bit more oil. Heat the pan over medium heat. 3. Meanwhile, beat the eggs thoroughly. Beat in the cheese, basil, salt, and pepper. Stir in the zucchini mixture. Pour into the prepared pan. After about 5 minutes, when the edges begin to set, loosen the edges of the frittata with a rubber spatula and tilt the pan to allow the uncooked egg to reach the bottom. It should take about 15 minutes for the frittata to become almost completely set. 4. Meanwhile, preheat the broiler. When the frittata is about 80 percent cooked, slide it under the broiler for a minute or so, until the top is set. (If the handle of your pan isn't ovenproof, wrap a few layers of foil around it before placing it under the broiler.) Let the frittata cool 10 minutes before cutting it into wedges.

SWISS CHARD AND POTATO FRITTATA

Almost any leafy green will do in this savory frittata. Spinach, kale, escarole, and broccoli rabe are alternatives, although I love the ease with which Swiss chard can be used and the way it blends harmoniously with the browned onions and potatoes.

SERVES 3

6 large Swiss chard leaves

1 tablespoon olive oil

1 medium onion, diced

1 garlic clove, minced

1 medium boiling (waxy) potato, peeled and diced into ½-inch cubes (no bigger)

6 large eggs

¼ cup grated Parmesan cheese

¼ teaspoon salt

Generous seasoning freshly ground pepper

1 tablespoon unsalted butter

1. Wash the Swiss chard and pat very dry. Cut off and discard the stems, then gather the leaves into a tight bundle and finely chop them. **2.** Heat the oil in a 9- or 10-inch nonstick skillet over medium heat. Add the onion and garlic, and sauté until the onion turns golden, about 10 minutes. Mix in the potato and cover the pan. Cook, shaking the pan occasionally, until the potato is tender and the onions are brown, about 10–15 minutes. Remove the cover and pile on the Swiss chard. Cover again and cook, tossing occasionally, until the leaves are wilted, about 5 minutes. Scrape this mixture onto a plate and let cool. Wipe the pan clean. **3.** Beat the eggs thoroughly in a large bowl. Beat in the cheese, salt, and pepper. Stir in the cooled vegetable mixture. **4.** Melt the butter in the skillet over low heat and swirl it around to coat the sides of the pan. Pour in the egg mixture. After about 5 minutes, when the edges begin to set, help the liquid egg pour over the sides of the frittata by occasionally loosening the edges with a rubber spatula and tilting the pan. It should take about 15 minutes for the frittata to become almost completely set. **5.** Preheat the broiler. When the frittata is about 80 percent cooked, slide it under the broiler for a minute or so, until the top is set. (If the handle of your pan isn't ovenproof, wrap a few layers of foil around it before placing it under the broiler.) Let the frittata cool 10 minutes before cutting it into wedges.

T I P : Any variety of Swiss chard will do in this frittata—white ribbed, Ruby chard, or the new rainbow chard.

"BACON" AND ONION FRITTATA

Many fake meat products miss the mark and are better left untouched, but not tempeh "bacon." This soy-based product (sometimes called "smoked tempeh strips") is delicious in sandwiches and as a flavor enhancer in casseroles and egg dishes. Spicy Oven Fries (page 152) or Mixed Potato Home Fries (page 153) are ideal accompaniments.

SERVES 4

2 tablespoons olive or canola oil, divided

3 strips tempeh "bacon"

1 medium-large onion, finely diced

8 large eggs

⅓ cup grated Asiago or Parmesan cheese

¼ teaspoon salt

Freshly ground pepper to taste

1 tablespoon unsalted butter

1. Heat 1 tablespoon oil in a 10-inch (preferably nonstick) skillet over medium-high heat. Lay the tempeh strips in the hot oil and fry on both sides until brown and crisp. Remove the strips with tongs, place on a large plate, and chop into ½-inch pieces. **2.** Pour the remaining oil into the skillet. Add the onion and lower the heat to medium. Sauté until the onion is very soft and golden brown, about 10 minutes. Scrape the onion onto the plate containing the bacon. **3.** Beat the eggs in a large bowl until well blended. Beat in the cheese, salt, and pepper. Stir in the bacon and onion. **4.** Melt the butter in the skillet over low heat, swirling the pan around so the butter also coats the sides. Pour in the egg mixture. After about 5 minutes, when the edges begin to set, help the liquid egg pour over the sides of the frittata by occasionally loosening the edges with a rubber spatula and tilting the pan. It should take about 15 minutes for the frittata to become almost completely set. **5.** Meanwhile, preheat the broiler. When the frittata is about 80 percent cooked, slide it under the broiler for a minute or so,

Vegetarian Classics

until the top is set. (If the handle of your pan isn't ovenproof, wrap a few layers of foil around it before placing it under the broiler.) Let the frittata cool 10 minutes before cutting it into wedges.

TIP: Asiago is a buttery nutty-flavored cheese that is reminiscent of Parmesan but a little more mellow.

SPANISH TORTILLA

Although this classic Spanish egg creation bears the same name as the common Mexican flatbread, the resemblance is in name only. A Spanish tortilla is like a frittata—that is, a firm, round omelet cooked in a skillet—and in this case is filled with fried potatoes and onions. I like to make this for breakfast, brunch, or supper; however, you can treat it the way the Spanish do and serve it at room temperature as a nibble (*tapas*) to accompany drinks.

SERVES 3

4 tablespoons olive oil, divided

2 medium boiling potatoes, peeled and cut into ¼-inch dice (2 cups diced)

Salt to taste

Freshly ground pepper to taste

2 medium onions, diced

6 large eggs

1. Heat 3 tablespoons oil in a 9- or 10-inch nonstick skillet over medium-high heat. When the oil is hot but not smoking, add the potatoes and cook until golden brown all over and tender, at least 10 minutes. If the potatoes become brown before they are tender, turn the heat to medium-low and cook a few minutes more. Season generously with salt and pepper. Remove the potatoes with a slotted spoon and place on a plate, leaving any oil behind. **2.** Add the onions to the skillet and cook until very tender and golden brown, at least 10 minutes. Spoon onto the plate containing the potatoes. Wipe the skillet clean, pour in the remaining tablespoon of oil, and place the pan over medium heat. **3.** Beat the eggs in a large bowl. Mix in the potatoes and onions. When the skillet is hot but not smoking, pour in the egg mixture. Let set a few minutes, then loosen the edges with a spatula. Cook the tortilla until it is about 90 percent set. Shake the pan occasionally to make sure the tortilla doesn't stick to the bottom. Lower the heat a little if it is getting too brown. Place a plate over the skillet and invert the skillet so the tortilla is bottom side up on the plate. Quickly slide the tortilla back onto the skillet. Cook 1 or 2 minutes. Slide the tortilla back onto the plate and cut into wedges.

Breakfast, Brunch, and Egg Dishes

MUSHROOM, ONION, AND SMOKED CHEESE OMELET

The trio of ingredients in this omelet has flavors that are made for each other. The earthiness of the mushrooms and the rich, smoky flavor of the cheese juxtapose nicely with the sweet onions. I use common button mushrooms for this savory omelet, but any type of mushroom or a mixture also works well.

SERVES 2

> 1 tablespoon olive oil
>
> 1 medium onion, halved and very thinly sliced
>
> 2 cups (6 ounces) thinly sliced mushrooms
>
> 4 large eggs
>
> ¼ teaspoon salt
>
> 2 tablespoons water
>
> 2 teaspoons unsalted butter
>
> ½ cup grated smoked Gouda cheese

1. To make the filling: heat the oil in a medium-size skillet over medium heat. Add the onion and cover the pan. Sauté, stirring occasionally, until the onion is very tender and golden, about 10 minutes. Mix in the mushrooms and sauté, uncovered, until brown and juicy, about 10 minutes. Keep warm over low heat. **2.** Beat the eggs thoroughly with the salt and water in a medium-size bowl. **3.** Make 1 omelet at a time. Heat 1 teaspoon butter in an 8-inch skillet, preferably nonstick, over medium-high heat. When the pan is very hot but not yet smoking, pour in half of the egg mixture. It will immediately begin to set at the edges. Use an inverted spatula to push the edges toward the center of the omelet while tipping the pan to allow the liquid egg to run onto the hot pan. When very little of the uncooked egg remains, spoon half of the hot mushroom filling onto one side of the omelet. Cover with half of the grated cheese. Immediately fold the omelet in half, then slide onto a plate. Repeat to make one more omelet.

TIP: Make certain the filling is very hot when you add it to the omelet to help melt the cheese quickly.

EGG AND PEPPER BREAKFAST BURRITOS

Such a simple concept, yet so delicious, these burritos are good for breakfast, lunch, or supper. The recipe can easily be doubled or tripled for a crowd. Spicy Oven Fries (page 152) alongside them would add just the right touch.

SERVES 2

1 tablespoon olive oil

1 small onion, finely diced

1 small to medium green bell pepper, finely diced

2 (8-inch) flour tortillas

4 eggs, well beaten

Salt to taste

⅔ cup grated Monterey Jack cheese with jalapeño peppers

1. Heat the oil in a small skillet over medium heat. Add the onion and green pepper, and cook 2 minutes. Cover the pan and cook until the green pepper is very soft and an olive color, at least 10 minutes. **2.** Meanwhile, heat the tortillas using a method outlined on page 258. **3.** When the peppers are cooked, pour in the eggs and stir with a spoon until scrambled. Season with salt and remove the pan from the heat. **4.** Place each warm tortilla on a large plate and sprinkle half the cheese down the center of each one. Cover with the eggs, then tightly roll up, burrito-style. Serve at once.

SPINACH, ARTICHOKE, AND RED PEPPER STRATA

(Overnight Breakfast Casserole)

If you're expecting a large crowd for breakfast or brunch, nothing beats the convenience of a strata. Cubed bread, cheese, and vegetables are baked in a quichelike custard until firm and golden brown. A generous serving of either Spicy Oven Fries (page 152) or Mixed Potato Home Fries (page 153) is a great match.

SERVES 8

1 tablespoon olive oil

1 large red bell pepper, cut into thin strips 2 inches long

1 (10-ounce) package frozen chopped spinach, thawed

9 large eggs

3½ cups low-fat milk

½ cup grated Parmesan cheese

¼ teaspoon nutmeg

1 teaspoon salt

Generous seasoning freshly ground pepper

2½ tablespoons butter, softened

9 slices (approximately) firm white bread (see Tips)

2 (6-ounce) jars marinated artichoke hearts, well drained

2 scallions, very thinly sliced

3 cups grated extra-sharp cheddar cheese

1. Heat the oil in a medium-size skillet over medium heat and sauté the red pepper until tender, about 7 minutes. Set aside. **2.** Place the thawed spinach in a strainer and press out all of its liquid with the back of a large spoon. Set aside. **3.** Thoroughly beat the eggs in a

Breakfast, Brunch, and Egg Dishes

large bowl. Beat in the spinach, milk, Parmesan cheese, nutmeg, salt, and pepper. **4.** Using ½ tablespoon butter, grease a 13 × 9 × 2-inch baking dish. With the remaining 2 tablespoons butter, coat 1 side of each slice of bread. Cut the bread into 1-inch cubes. You will need 9 cups of cubed bread. **5.** Place half of the bread cubes in the baking dish. Sprinkle on half of the red pepper strips, 1 jar of artichokes, and half of the scallions. Ladle on half of the spinach mixture, then sprinkle on half of the cheddar cheese. Repeat this layering and end with the cheddar cheese. Cover the dish with plastic wrap or foil and refrigerate overnight. **6.** Remove the dish from the refrigerator at least 30 minutes before baking. Preheat the oven to 350 degrees. Bake the strata, uncovered, for 1 hour, or until golden brown on top and firm in the center. Let the strata sit 15 minutes before cutting it into squares.

T I P S : Choose a firm homemade-style bread such as sourdough, a Tuscan-style chewy bread, or a day-old loaf of Italian or French bread. Avoid very soft packaged bread.

Make sure the strata is cooked enough when you remove it from the oven. Test it like a cake. A knife inserted in the center should come out clean.

MIXED PEPPER STRATA

(Overnight Breakfast Casserole)

Eggs and peppers enhance each other, and combined with jalapeño pepper cheese they create a breakfast dish with a Mexican accent and dynamic flavor. As with Spinach, Artichoke, and Red Pepper Strata, serve this with home fries, such as Spicy Oven Fries (page 152) or Mixed Potato Home Fries (page 153).

SERVES 6

> 2 teaspoons olive oil
>
> 1 red bell pepper, cut into ½-inch dice
>
> 1 green bell pepper, cut into ½-inch dice
>
> 1 onion, finely diced
>
> 2 tablespoons butter, softened
>
> 6 slices (approximately) firm white bread, such as sourdough
>
> 2 cups grated Monterey Jack cheese with jalapeño peppers
>
> 5 large eggs
>
> 1 cup light cream
>
> 1 cup milk
>
> ¾ teaspoon salt
>
> ½ teaspoon dried oregano

1. Heat the oil in a large skillet over medium heat. Add the peppers and onion, and sauté until very tender, about 10 minutes. Set aside to cool.

2. Using 1½ tablespoons butter, coat 1 side of each slice of bread. Cut the bread into 1-inch cubes. You need 6 cups of cubed bread. **3.** Using ½ tablespoon butter, grease a 12 × 7 × 2-inch shallow 2½-quart baking dish (such as a Pyrex glass dish). Scatter the bread cubes in the dish, spread on the peppers, and then sprinkle on the cheese. **4.** Beat the eggs in a bowl. Beat in the cream, milk, salt, and oregano. Pour the mixture all over the bread mixture. Cover the casserole with foil or plastic wrap and refrigerate overnight. **5.** Remove the dish from the refrigerator at least 30 minutes before baking. Preheat the oven to 350 degrees. Bake the strata, uncovered, for 35 minutes, or until golden brown on top and firm in the center. Let the strata sit 15 minutes before cutting it into squares.

TIPS: Select bread that is firm.

Although the cheese has jalapeños in it, this is not a fiery hot dish, just a bit spunky.

EASY STICKY BUNS

Sticky buns have long been my son Daniel's favorite breakfast treat, but I am leery of serving him bakery-made sticky buns because they are usually so rich and sweet. This quick version, made with frozen bread dough, contains just the right amount of caramel to make them worthy of their name without being cloying. These sticky buns are sensational.

MAKES 1 DOZEN ROLLS

1 cup firmly packed light brown sugar, divided

¼ cup water

4 tablespoons (½ stick) unsalted butter, at room temperature, divided

1 pound frozen bread dough, thawed

Flour for dusting

2 teaspoons cinnamon

½ cup chopped pecans

1. Set out a shallow 10-inch baking dish. **2.** In a small saucepan combine ⅔ cup brown sugar, the water, and 2 tablespoons butter. Heat, stirring often, just until the sugar has melted and the mixture blends. Pour all but 3 tablespoons of the caramel into the baking dish and spread it around. **3.** On a lightly floured surface shape the dough into a rectangle. With a rolling pin roll it into a 16 × 10-inch rectangle. (If the dough resists being stretched, let it rest a few minutes and roll again.) Spread the remaining 2 tablespoons butter all over the dough. Sprinkle on the remaining ⅓ cup brown sugar, the cinnamon, and pecans. Drizzle with the remaining 3 tablespoons of caramel. Starting at the long end, roll the dough into a log. Tightly pinch the seam together. With a serrated knife and using a sawing motion, cut the log crosswise into 12 pieces. Place the buns, cut side up, on the caramel in the baking dish. Let rise 30 minutes. **4.** Preheat the oven to 350 degrees. Bake the buns 30 minutes, or until golden. Cool on a wire

Breakfast, Brunch, and Egg Dishes

rack for 5 minutes, then cover the baking dish with a platter and invert the buns so the caramel is on top. Serve warm, not piping hot.

TIPS: To thaw the dough, place it in the refrigerator for 12 hours or keep at room temperature for about 2 hours. If you thaw it in the refrigerator, bring to room temperature before beginning the recipe.

Frozen bread dough can easily be found in supermarkets. It should contain only flour, water, yeast, and salt and no preservatives.

CLASSIC GRANOLA

This is a richly flavored granola that is not too sweet and has a wonderful tender texture. I love it as is, with raisins and walnuts, but you can vary the nuts and dried fruit to your liking and get good results. It's very easy to make, and you'll find it far superior to commercial granolas. Consider giving a batch as a holiday gift; it looks very appetizing packed in a large glass jar.

MAKES 12 CUPS

½ cup canola oil

½ cup honey

6 cups old-fashioned oats

⅓ cup bran

⅓ cup toasted wheat germ

½ teaspoon salt

1 tablespoon cinnamon

1½ cups unsweetened coconut (purchased at a natural foods store)

¼ cup sunflower seeds

¼ cup sesame seeds

2 cups chopped walnuts

1⅓ cups raisins

1. Preheat the oven to 350 degrees. **2.** Combine the oil and honey in a large stockpot and heat, stirring often, just until blended. You don't want the mixture to boil. Stir in all the remaining ingredients except the raisins. Mix well to coat everything evenly. **3.** Bake the granola in 3 batches. Spread ⅓ of the mixture evenly on a large baking sheet (with sides). Bake 15–20 minutes. For the last 5–10 minutes toss the granola occasionally with a spatula to allow it to cook evenly. The granola tends to burn along the sides of the pan, so be watchful. When done, the granola will be lightly browned but still soft. **4.** Place this batch in a bowl and stir in ⅓ of the raisins. Let cool completely before storing in jars. Repeat with the remaining 2 batches of granola.

TIPS: You can't bake the raisins or they'll get rock hard. They have to be mixed into the granola once it is out of the oven.

Make sure the granola is completely cooled before placing it in jars or else it will get soft from the trapped warmth.

Store granola in airtight jars or containers for up to 1 week at room temperature or refrigerate up to 1 month. Serve at room temperature.

SNACKS AND DRINKS

This chapter offers a hodgepodge of fun snacks and drinks, from after-school treats for youngsters to healthful fruit smoothies for diet-conscious adults and sophisticated biscotti that can rightfully sit alongside a demitasse of espresso. Many of these goodies can be purchased in stores, but no commercial version can compete with the quality of homemade treats. Several recipes are ideal activities for parent and child to share, such as Soft Pretzels (see below) and Best-Ever Doughnuts (page 129), because they naturally arouse kids' curiosity. Turn to this chapter when you want to serve an out-of-the-ordinary snack or drink, and I'm sure you'll add many of these items to your list of favorites.

SOFT PRETZELS

These excellent pretzels are crisp on the outside and soft and chewy inside. Their superb texture comes from the immersion of the pretzel dough in water for a few seconds before they are baked (similar to making bagels). They are not difficult to make; in fact, you'll be surprised at how easy it is to create such an impressive snack. Kids love them, and they can have fun helping you shape them into traditional pretzel shapes or other designs of their choice. They go well with a glass of beer or make a great treat on their own.

MAKES 18 FAT PRETZELS

> ½ cup warm water
>
> 1 packet active dry yeast
>
> 2 cups milk (preferably whole milk)
>
> ¼ cup sugar
>
> Salt
>
> ¼ cup canola oil

6 cups unbleached flour

Butter for greasing

1 egg white

Kosher (coarse) salt

1. Place the warm water in a small bowl and sprinkle on the yeast. Let sit a few minutes to soften, then stir it into the water. Let sit 5 minutes more. **2.** Warm the milk to a lukewarm temperature. Pour into a large bowl (or the bowl of a mixer if you have a dough hook) and stir in the sugar, 1½ teaspoons salt, oil, and the yeast liquid. Sprinkle in the flour and stir to form an evenly moistened dough, or use the dough hook on your mixer and mix until moistened. Knead the dough for 8–10 minutes, or until pliable, or use the mixer to knead it for 8 minutes. **3.** Lightly grease a large bowl. Press the dough into the bowl, then flip it over so it is greased-side up. Cover the bowl with plastic wrap and let rise until double in size, about 1 hour. **4.** Punch down the dough. On a lightly floured surface roll it into a 12 × 18-inch rectangle. Cut the dough into 18 strips. With your hands roll the strips into round ropes. Shape into pretzel shapes. (I make an inverted "U," crisscross the ends, and then pick them up and firmly press them into the top of the "U.") Place the pretzels on baking sheets and let rise 30 minutes. **5.** Fill a large pot halfway with water plus 2 tablespoons salt and bring to a boil. Position the oven racks so one is in the center and one is above it. Preheat the oven to 400 degrees. **6.** At this point a little organization will go a long way. Place a large cooling rack on a large tray or a smaller rack on a plate. (This is for the pretzels when they are removed from the water.) Place a baking sheet containing the pretzels nearby. With a large spatula lift up a pretzel and lower it into the boiling water. Let sit 5 seconds, then lift it out of the water with the spatula and drain on the cooling rack. Repeat until the cooling rack is filled. Place the boiled pretzels on plates or a work surface so you can make room on the cooling rack for the next batch. Repeat with all the pretzels. **7.** Butter 2 baking sheets. Place the pretzels on the sheets, leaving a 1-inch space between them. Lightly brush with the egg white, then sprinkle generously with kosher salt. Place 1 sheet on the center rack and 1 on the rack above it, and bake 17 minutes, or until lightly golden. Switch the position of the baking sheets halfway during the cooking time. Cool the pretzels on a cooling rack. Serve warm.

TIP: Leftover pretzels can be brought to room temperature and frozen in plastic bags. Thaw before serving and heat in a moderate oven until warm.

Vegetarian Classics

BEST-EVER DOUGHNUTS

These outstanding doughnuts are easy and fun to make, and may be the ideal rainy day project to tackle with children. Although they are fried in oil, their batter is not overly rich or sweet, so they are a wonderful alternative to their calorie-laden commercial cousins.

MAKES 1 DOZEN

> 3 cups unbleached flour
>
> 1 tablespoon baking powder
>
> ½ teaspoon cinnamon
>
> ⅛ teaspoon nutmeg
>
> ½ teaspoon salt
>
> 2 large eggs
>
> ¾ cup sugar
>
> 3 tablespoons butter, melted
>
> ½ cup milk
>
> 1 teaspoon vanilla extract
>
> Oil for frying

For Dipping:

> ½ cup sugar
>
> 1¼ teaspoons cinnamon

1. In a medium-size bowl thoroughly combine the flour, baking powder, cinnamon, nutmeg, and salt. **2.** Whisk the eggs and sugar together in a large bowl until light and smooth. Whisk in the butter, milk, and vanilla. Add the dry ingredients, whisking just until blended. Do not overmix. **3.** Turn the dough onto a lightly floured surface (it will be soft) and knead 2 or 3 times. Use a rolling pin to roll the dough a hair less than ¾ inch thick (no thinner). Cut out the doughnuts with a floured 2½-inch doughnut cutter. Roll the little center pieces into balls to form doughnut "holes." You should get about 12 doughnuts and holes. **4.** Fill a 3-quart saucepan or deep frying pan with about 3 inches oil. Heat over medium heat until a tiny pellet of dough dropped in the oil sizzles and immediately rises to the surface, about 370 degrees. Meanwhile, combine the sugar and cinnamon in a bowl and set aside. **5.** When the oil is ready, fry a few doughnuts at a time until golden brown, turning once. It will take about 1 minute on each side. Remove with tongs and drain on paper towels or brown paper bags. While still hot, dip in the cinnamon-sugar mixture until well coated. Fry the doughnut holes in the same manner. Serve warm, preferably, or at room temperature.

Snacks and Drinks

TIPS: Use a ruler to accurately measure the thickness of the rolled dough.

The temperature of the oil is crucial to frying the doughnuts properly. If the oil isn't hot enough, the dough will absorb the oil and make the doughnuts greasy. If the oil is too hot, the doughnuts will brown before they are cooked inside. Regulate the heat so the doughnuts take a full minute on each side to brown—a medium setting on an electric stove and a bit lower on a gas stove. If the oil gets too hot when cooking the doughnuts, remove the pot from the heat for a few seconds to cool it down quickly.

MAPLE OATCAKES

Scottish oatcakes, with their unique grainy texture, are superb when topped with jam and served with a steamy cup of tea. These also make a popular snack for children and are a good choice when you want to serve them something fun yet nutritious.

MAKES 16 OATCAKES

> 3 cups old-fashioned oats
>
> ½ teaspoon salt
>
> 1 stick (8 tablespoons) unsalted butter, at room temperature, plus extra for greasing
>
> ⅓ cup heavy cream
>
> ⅓ cup pure maple syrup

1. Place the oats and salt in the container of a food processor and process until as fine as flour. Pour the mixture into a large bowl. **2.** Put the butter, cream, and maple syrup in the processor and process until blended. Pour the oats back into the processor and process until combined with the butter mixture, about 30 seconds. **3.** Preheat the oven to 325 degrees. **4.** Lightly butter the bottom and a little bit up the sides of two 9-inch round cake pans. Divide the oat mixture into 2 portions. Using your fingers, press a portion into each pan, making them as evenly thick as possible. Use a rubber spatula to smooth over the tops. With a sharp knife cut almost all the way through to make 8 triangles in each pan. **5.** Bake 30 minutes. Remove from the oven and cut all the way through to separate the triangles. Remove the triangles with a spatula and place on a baking sheet. (The easiest way to remove the triangles is by sliding the spatula under their sides.) Lower the oven heat to 275 degrees. **6.** Return the oatcakes to the oven and bake 30 minutes more, or until dark beige all over. Cool thoroughly and store in a covered tin.

TIPS: Oatcakes are fragile, so handle with care. To store, place them in layers between sheets of wax paper. You can refrigerate them up to 1 month, but be sure to serve at room temperature.

If you don't have a food processor, you can grind the oats in a blender and then cream the butter and make the "dough" with an electric mixer.

ORANGE-ALMOND BISCOTTI

Although you can now purchase biscotti in most supermarkets, none compare to home-made versions that allow you to combine intriguing flavors and ingredients. Biscotti get their characteristic crispness by being baked twice—first in the form of a log and then in slices. Packed in pretty cellophane bags, they make a welcome food gift.

MAKES ABOUT 40

> ¾ **cup almonds**
>
> 2 **cups unbleached flour**
>
> 1 **teaspoon baking powder**
>
> ¼ **teaspoon salt**
>
> 2 **large eggs**
>
> 1 **cup sugar**
>
> ½ **teaspoon vanilla extract**
>
> ¼ **teaspoon almond extract**
>
> **Grated zest of 1 orange**

1. Preheat the oven to 350 degrees. **2.** Place the almonds in a shallow baking dish and toast until fragrant and golden, about 8 minutes. Let cool completely, then use a large knife to chop them coarsely. Meanwhile, line a baking sheet with parchment paper or butter and flour it.

3. In a small bowl combine the flour, baking powder, and salt. **4.** In a large bowl combine the eggs, sugar, vanilla and almond extracts, and orange zest. Beat with an electric mixer until pale and creamy **5.** Add the almonds and dry ingredients, and beat just until combined. Gather the dough into 2 balls. Place the balls on the baking sheet and shape each one into a smooth 12 × 2-inch log. **6.** Bake 35 minutes, or until lightly golden. Remove the pan from the oven and lower the heat to 325 degrees. Let the loaves cool a full 10 minutes; they will crumble if they are sliced when too hot. **7.** Place the loaves on a cutting board and use a serrated knife to cut the loaves on a sharp diagonal into ½-inch-thick slices. Place the slices, cut side down, on the baking sheet. **8.** Return the biscotti to the oven and bake 15–20 minutes more, turning each slice over after 10 minutes. The biscotti will be lightly golden when done, yet still somewhat soft. They will harden upon cooling. Transfer the biscotti to a cooling rack and cool thoroughly before storing in a covered tin for up to 2 weeks.

TIP: If you prefer biscotti with a more cookie-like texture, beat 4 tablespoons of very soft butter with the sugar before adding the extracts and zest. These biscotti won't have the storing qualities of butter-free biscotti, so refrigerate them if you keep them longer than a few days.

SUGAR AND SPICE NUTS

These tasty nuts are not overly sweet or candylike and so are suitable as nibbles with wine before dinner as well as an afternoon snack. Packed in a decorative jar, they also make an appealing holiday gift.

MAKES 4 CUPS

> ½ cup sugar
>
> 1 tablespoon cinnamon
>
> 1 teaspoon ground cloves
>
> 1 teaspoon ground ginger
>
> Dash salt
>
> 6 tablespoons unsalted butter
>
> 1 teaspoon vanilla extract
>
> 1 pound (4 cups) pecans

1. Preheat the oven to 300 degrees. **2.** Combine the sugar, cinnamon, cloves, ginger, and salt in a small bowl. **3.** Melt the butter and vanilla in a large skillet over medium heat. Stir in ⅓ of the sugar mixture until blended. Add the pecans and toss well to coat them thoroughly. With a rubber spatula scrape the nuts onto a baking sheet and spread them out so they don't touch each other. Bake 15 minutes, or until thoroughly toasted but not dark. **4.** Drop the nuts into a large bowl. Sprinkle on the remaining sugar mixture and toss. Let cool completely before storing in a tightly covered container.

TIP: These will keep up to 2 weeks if refrigerated in an airtight container.

PARMESAN GARLIC BREAD

This is a favorite snack in our house. My thirteen-year-old son, Daniel, is a garlic bread aficionado, and this rendition gets high marks from him. Partially cooking the garlic first before broiling the bread intensifies the garlic flavor, as does a somewhat generous sprinkling of salt. You can slather on the garlic butter up to a few hours in advance, but don't broil the bread until just before serving.

MAKES 1 LOAF, SERVES 4–6

> 1 loaf French bread (about 16 inches long)
>
> 2 tablespoons olive oil
>
> 4 garlic cloves, put through a press
>
> 2 tablespoons butter, softened
>
> 2 tablespoons grated Parmesan cheese
>
> Salt to taste

1. Cut the bread in half horizontally. **2.** Pour the oil into a small saucepan or skillet and heat over medium heat. Add the garlic and cook only about 30 seconds, or until hot throughout and not at all colored. Immediately pour the garlic oil into a small bowl. Let cool to room temperature. **3.** Stir the soft butter and cheese into the oil. Spread the flavored butter all over the cut sides of the bread. Sprinkle with salt. **4.** Preheat the broiler. Broil the bread until golden brown on top. Serve immediately.

MIXED BERRY SMOOTHIE

Using frozen mixed berries makes this drink especially easy to prepare, and you can serve it any time of the year because the berries are always available in the frozen food section of your supermarket. This is another one of my son's favorites.

MAKES 2 GLASSES

> ½ (12-ounce) package frozen mixed
>   berries (about 1⅔ cups) (see Tip)
>
> 1½ cups lemonade or orange juice
>
> 2 tablespoons sugar
>
> 4 ice cubes

1. Combine the berries, lemonade or orange juice, and sugar in the container of a blender and let sit 5 minutes to partially soften the berries. **2.** Add the ice cubes and blend until perfectly smooth. You will probably have to turn off the blender every so often to stir the contents that have adhered to the sides. Taste the drink to see if it needs additional sugar. If so, blend again. Serve in glasses with straws.

TIP: Frozen mixed berries contain strawberries, blueberries, raspberries, and blackberries. You can make variations of this drink by using just one or two of the frozen fruits, which are also sold individually.

CANTALOUPE MILK SHAKE

When we were in Mexico, this drink became my son's favorite breakfast treat. It's a great way to get your child to eat a sizable portion of fruit.

MAKES 1 TALL MILK SHAKE

> ½ very ripe medium-large cantaloupe
>
> ¼ cup milk
>
> 2 teaspoons sugar (only if fruit is not
>   sweet)

1. Use a spoon to scoop the flesh out of the cantaloupe; you should get about 2 cups. Place in a bowl and chill until very cold. **2.** Combine the cantaloupe and milk in a blender and blend until smooth. Taste the drink. You might need to add the sugar and blend again for a few seconds. Let the milk shake rest a few minutes before pouring it in a tall glass so the foam can deflate. Serve with a straw.

TIP: Although it is best to begin with cold cantaloupe, you can serve the milk shake over ice if you don't have time to chill the fruit.

MANGO LASSI

A lassi is a tangy chilled yogurt drink from India. It can be flavored in many different ways, including with rosewater, but mango lassi is my favorite. To my son Daniel, this is the much-awaited treat during an Indian meal.

MAKES 2 GLASSES LASSI

> 1 cup whole-milk yogurt
>
> 1 cup mango nectar or juice (such as the Goya brand)
>
> 2 tablespoons sugar
>
> Ice cubes

Combine the yogurt, mango nectar, and sugar in the container of a blender and blend 1 minute, or until the sugar is dissolved. Fill 2 glasses with ice cubes and pour in the lassi. Serve immediately.

TIP: You can make the lassi a few hours in advance and chill it. Just don't add the ice until serving time, because you don't want to dilute the lassi.

MASALA CHAI

Masala chai is the wonderfully aromatic spiced tea served in India. Although it is a treat any time of day, it is especially welcome following an Indian meal. To me, this recipe has just the right balance of spiciness and sweetness. Taste the chai before serving and adjust it according to your preference.

MAKES 4 CUPS TEA

> 2⅔ cups water
>
> 1½ cups milk, preferably low-fat
>
> 2–3 teaspoons loose black tea (depending on strength of tea), or 3 tea bags
>
> 1 teaspoon garam masala, *or* 1 cinnamon stick, 4 cloves, and 4 cardamom pods, *or* ¼ teaspoon *each* ground cinnamon, cloves, and cardamom (see Tip)
>
> 2 tablespoons sugar

Combine the water and milk in a medium-size saucepan and bring to a boil over medium heat. As soon as the mixture begins to froth up, add the tea, spices, and sugar. Cover the pot, and remove the pan from the heat. Let steep 3 minutes. Strain the tea through a fine strainer and serve immediately.

TIP: Garam masala is an Indian spice blend that can be found in specialty food shops and health food stores.

ICED GINGER TEA

I am a great fan of both hot and cold drinks made from fresh ginger. Iced ginger tea has a delightfully spicy undertone that is especially appealing on a hot summer day.

MAKES 2 TALL GLASSES TEA

2½ cups water

3 tablespoons finely chopped fresh ginger, skin left on

3 tablespoons sugar

1 cup cold water

Combine the water and ginger in a small saucepan and bring to a boil. Reduce the heat and simmer 10 minutes. Strain into a glass jar or pitcher and stir in the sugar until dissolved. Mix in the cup of cold water. Chill until ice cold. Serve in tall glasses over ice.

TIP: Mint Iced Ginger Tea is a refreshing variation. Add 1 peppermint tea bag, 1 teaspoon loose peppermint tea, or 2 tablespoons chopped fresh peppermint to the Iced Ginger Tea when you add the sugar. Remove the tea bag or strain the tea after the mint has steeped for 3 minutes.

THE SANDWICH BOARD

Here is a collection of hot and cold sandwiches, ones that travel well for picnics and for work, some that are best eaten as soon as they are prepared, a few that depend on perfectly ripe summer tomatoes, and some that are great all year long. What unites all these sandwiches is their reliance on very fresh and flavorful ingredients, including high-quality bread. Whether you are using pita bread, French bread, or slices from a whole-grain loaf, a sandwich must have delicious bread in order for it to rise out of the ordinary and be truly satisfying.

Many of these sandwiches make excellent suppers as well. A quick accompaniment that I often rely on is canned chickpeas, white beans, or kidney beans, drained and tossed with vinaigrette, scallions or red onion, and parsley or other fresh herb. Other delicious companions are Provençal Green Bean Salad (page 68) or a mixed green salad.

Whether you serve these sandwiches for lunch or supper, you'll find that they are immensely satisfying and will expand your visions of what a sandwich can be.

See also:

- Classic Tofu "Eggless" Salad (page 198)

- Roasted Tofu Sandwiches (page 198)

- Classic Tempeh Sandwich Spread (page 200)

- Golden Tempeh Sandwich (page 200)

- Barbecued Tempeh Cutlets for Sandwiches (page 201)

CLASSIC VEGETABLE MELT

It's hard to beat the vegetable melt of the 70s for a hearty, nutritious sandwich. It is also an improvisor's dream because it's fun to use what vegetables you have on hand and match them with a special cheese to make a tasty combination. Here I've selected a favorite trio—spinach, red pepper, and mushrooms—and topped it with Monterey Jack cheese with jalapeños to construct a dynamic open-faced sandwich.

MAKES 4 SANDWICHES

1 tablespoon olive oil

3 cups (8 ounces) thinly sliced mushrooms

1 onion, thinly sliced

1 red bell pepper, cut into thin strips

1 (10-ounce) bag triple-washed spinach, stems discarded

2 teaspoons tamari soy sauce

Salt to taste

4 slices homemade-style bread, such as sourdough or multigrain

3 tablespoons mayonnaise

1 cup grated Monterey Jack cheese with jalapeño peppers

1. Heat the oil in a large skillet over medium heat. Add the mushrooms, onion, and red pepper, and sauté until tender, about 10 minutes. 2. Pile on the spinach and cover the pan. Cook just until the spinach wilts, about 3 minutes. Sprinkle on the tamari and salt, and remove from the heat. 3. Preheat the broiler. 4. Toast the bread in a toaster. Spread the mayonnaise on one side of each piece, then lay them on a baking sheet and top with the vegetable mixture. Sprinkle on the cheese. 5. Broil the sandwiches just until the cheese is melted. Serve immediately. This is a sandwich to eat with a knife and fork.

TIP: You can cook the vegetables in advance and set them aside. Reheat just before you assemble the sandwiches.

The Origin of the Sandwich

Sandwiches have been popular in the United States since the late 1800s. The idea of placing meats, cheese, lettuce, vegetables, or condiments between 2 slices of bread began in the mid-1700s with a notorious English gambler, John Montagu, the Fourth Earl of Sandwich. During his betting marathons he would order "meals" of sliced bread and meat that he could eat without interrupting his gambling. The combination was soon named after him, but it only became popular in America much later. When white loaf bread became a staple of the American diet in the 1920s, it took on an alternate name, "sandwich bread."

PORTOBELLO MUSHROOM SANDWICHES WITH LEMON GARLIC MAYONNAISE

Although it's tempting to place a whole Portobello mushroom on a sandwich, the texture of these impressive fungi is markedly improved when the caps are thinly sliced before being sautéed. Stacked on a sandwich they are utterly satisfying.

MAKES 2 SANDWICHES

½ tablespoon unsalted butter

2 large (5-inch diameter) Portobello mushrooms, stems discarded, caps wiped clean, and thinly sliced

Salt to taste

3½ tablespoons mayonnaise

1 very small garlic clove, put through a press or minced

1 tablespoon lemon juice

Generous seasoning freshly ground pepper

4 slices Tuscan-style bread or 2 sandwich rolls

1 small- to medium-size ripe tomato, thinly sliced

10 leaves arugula, each torn in half

1. Melt the butter in a medium-size skillet over medium heat. Add the mushrooms and sauté until brown all over and juicy, about 10 minutes. Season with salt and let cool. 2. Combine the mayonnaise, garlic, lemon juice, and pepper in a small bowl. 3. To make the sandwiches, spread some of the mayonnaise mixture on each bread slice. Place the mushrooms, tomato slices, and arugula on 2 of the slices and top with the remaining bread. Serve at once.

CALIFORNIA AVOCADO SANDWICHES

During the 1960s, avocado became a popular addition to meatless salad sandwiches because they added texture and flavor. Although in New England sandwiches made with avocado are often associated with California, we encountered this delicious sandwich in Mexico and liked it so much we went back to the restaurant many days in a row and had it for both breakfast and lunch. Use a pebbly-skinned Haas avocado for its buttery texture and perfectly ripe tomatoes, and you'll have a hit.

2 SANDWICHES

¼ cup mayonnaise

2 (6-inch) chunks French bread, each sliced horizontally

1 ripe Haas (dark, pebbly-skinned) avocado, peeled and thinly sliced

1 ripe tomato, thinly sliced

8 thin slices cucumber

2 paper-thin slices red onion

Salt to taste

Liberal seasoning freshly ground pepper

Spread the mayonnaise on the cut sides of the
French bread. Layer the avocado, tomato,
cucumber, and red onion on the bottom halves
of the bread, and season with salt and pepper.
Close to make a sandwich, then cut in half.
Serve at once.

TIP: This sandwich is also fabulous served
open-faced. End the layering with the avocado
on top and then season with salt and pepper.

EGGPLANT AND TOMATO SANDWICHES WITH PESTO MAYONNAISE

For many years eggplant in sandwiches was
restricted to its use in hot eggplant Parmesan
grinders (also called submarines and heroes).
Having discovered that breaded eggplant slices
are delicious cold, with little effort we can now
create glorious sandwiches that have a compatible Provençal theme. This one's a winner.

1 small- to medium-size eggplant, peeled
and sliced ½ inch thick

⅓ cup olive oil

⅓ cup dry bread crumbs

Salt to taste

Freshly ground pepper to taste

⅓ cup mayonnaise

⅓ cup Classic Pesto (page 19)

4 (6-inch) pieces French bread, each halved
horizontally

1 ripe tomato, thinly sliced

1. Preheat the broiler. **2.** Place the eggplant
slices in front of you, the oil in a small bowl,
and the bread crumbs on a small plate. Using a
pastry brush, coat both sides of the eggplant
slices with some oil, then press the slices into
the bread crumbs to coat on both sides. Place
the slices on a baking sheet. **3.** Broil the eggplant on both sides until golden brown and
very tender. Season with salt and pepper, and
let cool to room temperature. **4.** Combine
the mayonnaise and pesto in a small bowl and
stir until well blended. Spread some of this mixture on each slice of French bread. Stack eggplant and tomato slices on the bottom pieces of
the French bread and cover with the top sections. Cut each sandwich in half and serve
within 2 hours.

MEDITERRANEAN STUFFED SANDWICH

(Pan Bagna)

"Pan bagna" means bathed bread, and that describes the way olive oil and garlic saturate a hollowed-out loaf of Italian or French bread which then encases vegetables, cheese, olives, and herbs to make one of the most luscious sandwiches known. If you need a sandwich to transport, you can't beat pan bagna because it is meant to be made in advance so the flavors can meld.

MAKES 4 SANDWICHES

  1 wide loaf Italian or French bread (about 24 inches long)

  8 tablespoons olive oil (approximately)

  2 large garlic cloves, put through a press or minced

  2 tablespoons minced fresh basil

  1 teaspoon dried oregano

  Freshly ground pepper to taste

  8 ounces very thinly sliced cheese, preferably provolone or a smoked cheese

  2 large ripe tomatoes, sliced

  1 (7-ounce) jar roasted red peppers, drained very well and patted dry

  1 green bell pepper, thinly sliced into rings

  4 thin slices red onion

  20 black olives (your favorite type), pitted (see page 12)

1. Slice the bread lengthwise and remove some of the inner bread to make 2 somewhat hollow shells. Drizzle the oil over the cavity of both pieces of bread and spread it around with a knife. Sprinkle on the garlic, basil, oregano, and pepper. **2.** Layer all the remaining ingredients on one half of the bread. Top with the other piece of bread. Cut it into 4 sandwiches. Tightly wrap each sandwich in plastic wrap and let marinate at least 1 hour or up to 4 hours. If the sandwiches are going to sit more than 1 hour, refrigerate them and bring to room temperature before serving.

TIP: The bread for these sandwiches should be only somewhat crusty so that the sandwich doesn't fall apart when you bit into it. A commercial French or Italian loaf is best for this.

GRILLED JALAPEÑO CHEESE, TOMATO, AND ROASTED PEPPER SANDWICH

To my mind new versions of grilled cheese sandwiches that are generous with vegetables and light on the cheese are a welcome improvement to the traditional all-cheese version. The secret to creating a grilled cheese sandwich that has a crisp exterior and molten center is to cook it slowly on medium-low heat until it is a rich golden brown and the cheese begins to ooze. Here is a simple combination of ingredients that will produce a sandwich with a dynamic flavor.

MAKES 2 SANDWICHES

> **4 slices good-quality white bread, such as Tuscan-style, sourdough, or Vienna**
>
> **12 thin slices (about 5 ounces) Monterey Jack cheese with jalapeño peppers**
>
> **½ (7-ounce) jar roasted red peppers, patted very dry and thinly sliced**
>
> **4 thin slices ripe tomato**
>
> **1½ tablespoons very soft unsalted butter**

1. Heat a large skillet over medium-low heat. **2.** Place 2 slices of bread in front of you. Lay 3 cheese slices on each slice of bread. Top with the red pepper strips, tomato slices, and remaining 6 slices of cheese. Cover with the other 2 slices of bread to make 2 sandwiches. Using half the butter, spread a thin layer on the top 2 pieces of bread. **3.** Place each sandwich buttered side down in the hot skillet. Butter the tops of the sandwich with the remaining butter. Cook until golden brown, at least 5 minutes, then flip and cook the other side. Make certain the sandwich cooks slowly so the cheese melts properly. Cut in half and serve.

ROASTED SWEET POTATO AND BLACK BEAN QUESADILLAS

A quesadilla is best described as a Mexican grilled cheese sandwich made with tortillas. It can be the perfect vehicle for improvising by including cooked vegetables and fresh herbs you have on hand. Sweet potatoes lend a heftiness to these southwestern-style quesadillas, making them a satisfying choice for a light supper as well as lunch. Cilantro, sweet potatoes, and black beans are a trio of superbly compatible flavors. My stepdaughter, Susanne, counts this among her all-time favorite sandwiches.

SERVES 4

> **2 medium (1 pound total) sweet potatoes (preferably dark orange), peeled, quartered lengthwise, and thinly sliced**
>
> **1 tablespoon olive oil**
>
> **Salt to taste**
>
> **8 (6-inch) flour tortillas**
>
> **1 cup canned black beans, rinsed in a strainer**
>
> **2 large scallions, very thinly sliced**
>
> **4 tablespoons finely chopped cilantro**
>
> **2 cups grated Monterey Jack cheese with jalapeño peppers**
>
> **Butter for greasing the pan**

The Sandwich Board

1. Preheat the oven to 425 degrees. 2. Combine the sweet potatoes and oil in a large bowl and toss to coat evenly. Spread the sweet potatoes out on a baking sheet in 1 layer. Bake about 15 minutes, or until tender. Season lightly with salt, then let cool. Turn off the oven. 3. Place 4 of the tortillas on a work surface in front of you. Sprinkle ¼ of the sweet potatoes, beans, scallions, cilantro, and cheese on each tortilla. Cover with the remaining tortillas and press down gently to help them adhere. 4. If your tortillas are flaky and tender, you will probably not need to add butter to the skillet. Otherwise, melt a little butter in a large skillet over medium heat. Place 1 quesadilla in the skillet and cook until golden underneath, pressing down with a spatula on occasion to help the quesadilla stick together. Spread some butter very lightly on top of the quesadilla, then carefully flip and cook the other side until golden. Remove and cut into wedges. Repeat with the remaining quesadillas. Wait a few minutes before serving because the quesadillas trap a lot of heat and could burn your mouth.

MUSHROOM AND SWISS CHEESE QUESADILLAS

Mushrooms, browned onions, and Swiss cheese are a classic combination because their flavors are so complementary. I like to serve a dark beer alongside these Mexican-style grilled cheese sandwiches.

SERVES 2

> 1 tablespoon olive oil
>
> 1 large onion, halved and thinly sliced
>
> 8 ounces (3 cups) thinly sliced mushrooms
>
> Salt to taste
>
> Freshly ground black pepper to taste
>
> 4 (8-inch) flour tortillas
>
> 1¼ cups grated Swiss cheese
>
> Butter for greasing the pan

1. Heat the oil in a large skillet over medium heat. Add the onion and sauté until golden, about 10 minutes. Mix in the mushrooms and sauté until they are brown and juicy and the onion has browned. Season with salt and pepper. Remove from the heat and let cool. 2. Place 2 tortillas on a work surface. Divide the mushroom mixture between them and spread it around evenly. Sprinkle each with half the Swiss cheese. Top with the remaining tortillas. 3. Melt some butter in a medium-large skillet over medium heat. Place 1 quesadilla in the pan and cook until golden underneath. Press the quesadilla down with a spatula to help the melted cheese adhere. Lightly butter the top of the quesadilla, then carefully flip it over to cook on this side. When golden brown, slide onto a plate and cut into wedges. Repeat with the remaining quesadilla.

Vegetarian Classics

CUCUMBER AND WATERCRESS SANDWICHES WITH WASABI MAYONNAISE

The classic British tea sandwich gets a snazzy twist with the inclusion of wasabi to perk up the mayonnaise. Arugula could be substituted for the watercress with good results.

MAKES 4 SANDWICHES

2 teaspoons wasabi powder (see page 16)

2 teaspoons water

½ cup mayonnaise

8 slices chewy Tuscan-style sourdough or other good-quality bread

1 small cucumber, peeled and thinly sliced

1 bunch watercress, stems discarded

1. Combine the wasabi and water in a small bowl and stir to make a paste. Let sit 10 minutes for the flavor to develop. Stir in the mayonnaise. **2.** Spread the wasabi mayonnaise on all the bread slices. Lay the cucumber slices on half of the bread slices. (You might have some cucumber left over.) Place some watercress on top of the cucumber, then cover with the remaining bread to make sandwiches. Slice the sandwiches and serve within 1 hour.

VEGETABLE SUBS

Depending on what part of the country you live in, this popular vegetarian sandwich could be called a sub, hero, or grinder. Whatever its name, it is made with a long sandwich roll and, in this case, stuffed with salad vegetables and sliced cheese. This delicious sandwich has become a staple in my house because I can easily keep the rolls in the freezer to have on hand, and my vegetable bin always contains some lettuce and other salad ingredients. Don't hesitate to improvise here. You can include sliced olives, roasted red peppers, scallions, hot peppers, sprouts, mushrooms, and your favorite cheese.

MAKES 2 SANDWICHES

2 submarine (grinder) rolls, sliced horizontally almost all the way through

2 tablespoons mayonnaise (see Tips)

Freshly ground black pepper to taste

4 lettuce leaves

4 thin slices tomato

2 thin slices red onion

4 thin rings green or red bell pepper

8 thin slices cucumber

6 thin slices smoked Gouda (see Tips)

1. Spread the bread halves with the mayonnaise, then season generously with pepper. **2.** Divide the ingredients in half. Layer them in each sandwich and close tightly, pressing down on the bread gently to help it adhere. Slice each sandwich in half.

TIPS: Smoked cheese gives this sandwich a rich, dynamic flavor that is hauntingly good. Other cheeses will also work well, such as Muenster, Provolone, Monterey Jack with jalapeño peppers, and Swiss, to name just a few.

If you are going to pack these sandwiches for lunch or a picnic, wrap the tomato slices separately and then place them in the sandwiches just before eating.

Vinaigrette dressing is a wonderful substitute for the mayonnaise.

HOT EGG AND PEPPER GRINDERS

This omelet sandwich has been served in Greek-owned pizza parlors in the United States since the 1970s, and I have been making it for my family ever since. It is equally good for breakfast, lunch, or a light supper.

MAKES 2 SANDWICHES

4 teaspoons olive oil

1 green bell pepper, cut into thin strips

2 grinder, hero, or submarine rolls, sliced open

1 tablespoon mayonnaise

2 large eggs, beaten

Salt to taste

¼ cup grated smoked Gouda cheese

1. Preheat the oven to 350 degrees. **2.** Heat 2 teaspoons oil in a large nonstick skillet over medium heat. Add the green pepper and cover the pan. Cook until very soft and tender, about 10 minutes. Place on a plate and let cool a little. **3.** Heat the rolls in the oven for a few minutes until hot. Remove and let cool a bit. **4.** Spread a thin layer of mayonnaise on each half. **5.** Heat the remaining 2 teaspoons oil in the skillet over medium-high heat. Mix the pepper into the egg. Pour the mixture into the skillet. Let cook undisturbed for a few minutes, then flip the omelet over. Cook just until set. Season with salt. Cut the omelet in half and place each piece in a grinder roll. Sprinkle on the cheese and close the sandwich. Cut in half and serve.

FALAFEL

Falafel are little patties or balls of ground chickpeas, grains, and spices. They are fried until crisp and served with a sauce either as an entree or in pocket bread as a sandwich. Although they can be made from scratch, I have found that the falafel mix one can buy at a natural foods store or Middle Eastern grocery shop is an easy and authentic way to prepare this delicacy. These sandwiches are so filling that they can easily serve as a quick supper with no side dishes or accompaniments needed.

MAKES 4 SANDWICHES

1 (10-ounce) box falafel mix

The Sauce:

½ cup tahini (sesame butter)

½–¾ cup water

¼ cup lemon juice

1 large garlic clove, put through a press or minced

Salt to taste

Oil for frying

4 pita breads, each cut in half to make pockets

2 ripe tomatoes, finely diced

8 lettuce leaves, shredded

1. Prepare the falafel according to the package directions and let sit 15 minutes to absorb the liquid. Shape the mixture into 24 balls, then flatten into patties. **2.** To make the sauce: place the tahini in a medium-size bowl. With a fork slowly beat in the ½ cup water, lemon juice, garlic, and salt. Check the consistency; it should be pourable like honey. Beat in more water if needed. **3.** Pour about ¼ inch of oil in a large skillet and heat over medium heat until hot but not smoking. Fry the patties on both sides until golden brown. Drain on paper towels. **4.** To make the sandwiches heat the pita halves in the oven or a toaster for just a few minutes, or until warm and soft. **5.** Fill each pita half with 3 patties, some tomato, and lettuce. Drizzle the sauce over the filling. Serve immediately.

TIP: The tahini will look thick and somewhat curdled when you begin to beat the water into it. Just keep beating and adding more liquid, and it will transform into a satiny smooth sauce.

An alternative to the tahini sauce is a sauce of plain yogurt, a dash of lemon juice, and a minced garlic clove. Thin with a little water and pour over the falafel filling. It is quick, delicious, and also traditional.

VEGETABLE WRAPS

In the world of sandwiches the "melt" of the 1970s has been replaced by the "wrap" of the 1990s. Although both vegetable-based sandwiches are hearty and flavorful, the wrap has the added advantage of being portable, a real bonus to those who pack lunches.

To make a single round of pita bread, use scissors to cut the bread along the outer edge to separate it into 2 disks.

MAKES 3 SANDWICHES

1 (8-ounce) package Neufchâtel (light cream cheese), at room temperature

2 scallions, very thinly sliced

1 small garlic clove, pressed or minced

½ teaspoon minced fresh dill, or 1 teaspoon dried

3 single rounds large (10-inch) pita bread

½ cucumber, quartered and very thinly sliced

½ red bell pepper, cut into paper-thin strips

1 small tomato, thinly sliced

½ cup very thinly sliced red onion

3 romaine lettuce leaves, torn into small pieces

Salt to taste

Freshly ground pepper to taste

1. In a medium-size bowl combine the cream cheese, scallions, garlic, and dill, and beat together with a fork until nice and creamy. **2.** Divide the mixture into 3 portions and spread a portion on the inner (rough) side of each pita disk, leaving a 1-inch border all around. Sprinkle ⅓ of the cucumbers, peppers, tomatoes, onion, and lettuce all over each pita. Season with salt and pepper. Starting at the end in front of you, tightly roll each pita into a log. Cut in half on the diagonal before serving.

TIP: As an alternative to pita bread you can use mountain bread or a flour tortilla. In both cases you should heat the bread slightly by wrapping it in foil and placing in a 350-degree oven for 5 minutes. Let cool slightly before making the sandwich.

VEGETABLE BURGER ROLL-UPS

One day my husband cooked a vegetable burger but then discovered we had no sliced bread or rolls in the house. He heated a tortilla, crumbled up the cooked burger, sprinkled it on the tortilla, topped it with fresh tomato slices and onions, and then rolled it up. To our surprise, it was great! It has since become our favorite way to eat veggie burgers. The chewy tortilla adds to the texture and charm of the sandwich.

MAKES 2 ROLL-UPS

2 (8-inch) flour tortillas

1 tablespoon canola oil

2 vegetable-style burgers (your favorite kind; mine is frozen Gardenburgers)

3 tablespoons mayonnaise

1 tomato, thinly sliced

2 thin slices red onion, separated into rings

1. Preheat the oven to 350 degrees. **2.** Wrap the tortillas in foil. Heat in the oven until hot throughout, about 5 minutes. **3.** Warm the oil in a medium skillet. Cook the burger according to package directions. **4.** Place the tortillas on large plates. Spread each with half the mayonnaise. Crumble up the burger and sprinkle it on the bottom half of the tortilla. Top with the tomato and onion. Roll up the sandwich tightly, then cut it in half on the diagonal. Serve immediately.

TIPS: As an option the tortillas can be folded gently in half and heated in a toaster for 30 seconds or so.

Other filling additions or substitutions are shredded lettuce, sautéed mushrooms, and diced avocado. Russian dressing is a delicious alternative to plain mayonnaise. To make it, mix mayonnaise, ketchup, and relish together until blended.

ROASTED RED PEPPER AND CREAM CHEESE SPREAD

(For Bagels)

When I have company for the weekend and I'm in need of a quick and easy lunch that everyone will love, I ask my husband to get fresh bagels and I whip this spread together in minutes. It is always a big hit. Fill little bowls with cucumber spears, olives, and mini carrots to offer as accompaniments.

ENOUGH FOR 4 SLICED BAGELS (8 HALVES)

¼ cup roasted red peppers (half of a 7-ounce jar)

1 (8-ounce) package Neufchâtel (light cream cheese), at room temperature

2 tablespoons minced red onion

½ teaspoon sweet paprika

1 teaspoon minced fresh dill, or ½ teaspoon dried

Dash cayenne pepper

Dash salt

1. Place the peppers in a cotton kitchen towel and gather the towel into a ball. Squeeze out all the moisture. Drop the peppers onto a cutting board and mince; the pepper pieces must be very tiny. **2.** Place the peppers in a bowl with all the remaining ingredients and beat with a fork until whipped and very smooth. Cover the bowl with plastic wrap and chill at least 1 hour so the flavors can meld. Serve with bagels.

TIPS: This recipe can be easily doubled or tripled.

The peppers must be dry so their liquid doesn't dilute the spread.

The peppers and onion should be minced, not diced, to achieve the best texture.

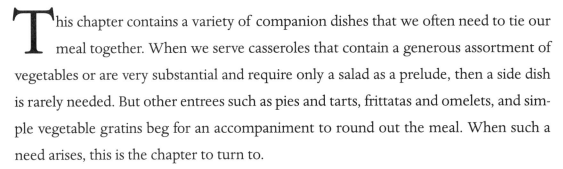

SIDE DISHES

This chapter contains a variety of companion dishes that we often need to tie our meal together. When we serve casseroles that contain a generous assortment of vegetables or are very substantial and require only a salad as a prelude, then a side dish is rarely needed. But other entrees such as pies and tarts, frittatas and omelets, and simple vegetable gratins beg for an accompaniment to round out the meal. When such a need arises, this is the chapter to turn to.

When you select a side dish, be sure that its texture, color, and richness complement and do not clash with the entree it will accompany. For example, Shiitake Mushroom and Goat Cheese Quiche (page 159) would be enhanced by Egg Noodles with Garlic and Herbs (opposite) but overshadowed by the cheesiness of Orzo Pilaf. It's all a question of balance. So dip into this chapter when you need to find that perfect little dish to complete your menu, or you can put together some of your favorite side dishes to create an informal, delectable meal.

ORZO PILAF

Similar to risotto with its creamy texture, this pilaf is a welcome departure from more familiar side dishes. Orzo is, after all, a pasta, yet it has the characteristic stubbiness of rice, making it an ideal accompaniment to all types of entrees. Remember this pilaf for your next special occasion.

SERVES 4 AS A SIDE DISH

> 3 cups vegetable stock, store-bought or homemade (page 18)
>
> 8 ounces (1 cup) orzo (rice-shaped pasta)

½ tablespoon unsalted butter

3 tablespoons grated Parmesan cheese

2 tablespoons minced fresh parsley or 1 tablespoon minced fresh basil or dill

¼ teaspoon salt

Freshly ground black pepper to taste

1. Bring the stock to a boil in a medium-size, heavy-bottomed saucepan. Stir in the orzo and lower the heat. Cook the orzo at a lively simmer for 20 minutes, stirring often. During the last 5 minutes of cooking you'll have to lower the heat again and stir more frequently to prevent the orzo from sticking. When done, the orzo will have absorbed almost all the stock and should be al dente, that is, slightly firm in the center, not mushy. **2.** Stir in the remaining ingredients. If the orzo has become dry instead of creamy, mix in a few tablespoons of stock. Serve immediately.

EGG NOODLES WITH GARLIC AND HERBS

Egg noodles, which are sold in packages in every supermarket, make a sumptuous side dish, and you can count on requests for seconds. Here they have a light dressing of sautéed garlic and some snipped fresh herbs of your choice.

SERVES 4

8 ounces wide egg noodles

1½ tablespoons unsalted butter

1 tablespoon olive oil

1 large garlic clove, put through a press or minced

Salt to taste

¼ cup minced fresh parsley or 2 tablespoons minced chives or fresh basil

1. Bring a stockpot of water to a boil. Drop in the noodles and cook, stirring frequently, until al dente, about 5–7 minutes. **2.** Melt the butter with the oil in a small skillet or saucepan. Add the garlic and cook about 1 minute, or until hot throughout but not at all colored. Immediately remove the pan from the heat. **3.** Drain the noodles in a colander and return to the pot. Pour on the garlic butter and toss well. Add the salt and parsley, and toss again. Serve immediately.

TIP: You can make the noodles in advance and gently reheat them with a few tablespoons of water to create steam.

COUSCOUS PILAF WITH TOASTED PINE NUTS

The deep, rich flavor of onions permeates this couscous side dish, which also has a textural contrast—the soft couscous and the crunchy pine nuts.

1 tablespoon unsalted butter

1 medium onion, minced

¼ cup pine nuts

1½ cups vegetable stock, either store-
bought or homemade (page 18)

¼ teaspoon salt

1 cup couscous

1. Melt the butter in a medium-size saucepan over medium heat. Add the onion and sauté until soft, about 5 minutes. Add the pine nuts and, stirring often, toast them until golden, about 5 minutes. **2.** Pour in the vegetable stock and salt, and bring to a boil. Stir in the couscous, cover the pot, and remove from the heat. Let the couscous sit at least 5 minutes and up to 15 minutes. Fluff with a fork before serving.

ISRAELI COUSCOUS WITH BUTTER AND CHEESE

Israeli couscous, also called Middle Eastern couscous, has a completely different texture from the more common North African version. It resembles tiny white pearls in appearance and tastes like pasta (which, in fact, it is) or, more precisely, orzo. It makes a delicious side dish and cooks up in just a few minutes.

1 teaspoon olive or canola oil

1 cup Israeli couscous (sometimes called
"pearl pasta")

2 tablespoons unsalted butter

¼ teaspoon salt

Freshly ground pepper to taste

⅓ cup grated Parmesan cheese

1. Fill a medium-size saucepan ⅔ full with water and bring to a boil. Add the oil and couscous, and return to a boil. Lower the heat slightly and cook the couscous until al dente, about 8 minutes. Drain thoroughly in a strainer or colander. **2.** Immediately return the couscous to the pot. Stir in the butter, salt, pepper, and cheese. Serve at once.

TIP: Minced fresh parsley, basil, dill, and chives are delicious additions to this couscous.

ISRAELI COUSCOUS WITH TOMATO AND SCALLIONS

Here's another way to serve Israeli couscous, and a good choice when you want to add a splash of color to your plate.

SERVES 4

1 teaspoon olive or canola oil

1 cup Israeli couscous (sometimes called "pearl pasta")

2 tablespoons unsalted butter

1 plum tomato, very finely diced

2 scallions, very thinly sliced

¼ teaspoon salt

Freshly ground black pepper to taste

¼ cup grated Parmesan cheese

1. Fill a medium-size saucepan ⅔ full with water and bring to a boil. Add the oil and couscous, and return to a boil. Lower the heat slightly and cook the couscous until al dente, about 8 minutes. Drain in a strainer or colander. **2.** Immediately melt the butter in the saucepan. Stir in the tomato and scallion, and cook 2 minutes. Mix in the couscous, salt, pepper, and cheese. Toss well and serve.

PESTO MASHED POTATOES

This recipe alone is good enough reason for me to freeze pesto in the summer so I can have it on hand throughout the year to lace these mashed potatoes luxuriously.

SERVES 4–6

5 large (3 pounds) boiling potatoes (preferably Yukon Gold), peeled and cut into even-size pieces

½ cup milk

1 tablespoon unsalted butter

½ cup Classic Pesto (page 19)

1. Bring a stockpot of water to a boil and add the potatoes. Cook, partially covered, until tender. The time depends on the size of the potato pieces. Drain the potatoes in a colander. **2.** Immediately pour the milk in the stockpot and heat it. Return the potatoes to the pot. Use an electric mixer (my favorite method) or a potato masher to mash the potatoes until smooth. Heat gently over low heat until piping hot. **3.** Stir in the butter until it melts. Spoon on the pesto and stir it in gently just until streaks are formed; you don't want it perfectly blended. Serve immediately.

TIP: I prefer to use boiling rather than baking potatoes to make mashed potatoes, and I don't recommend red-skinned potatoes because they are too waxy.

WASABI MASHED POTATOES

I had these fabulous mashed potatoes at a local restaurant one night, and I thought about them for days. The wasabi adds a gutsy zing without being too dominant. These potatoes will surely draw raves.

SERVES 4 VERY GENEROUSLY
(AS YOU'LL WANT THEM SERVED)

The Scoop on Potatoes

There are essentially three types of potatoes, and selecting the right one for your recipe can make a world of difference. *Boiling* potatoes (also called waxy) have a low starch content and a firm flesh that enables them to keep their shape when boiled. These are ideal for soups and potato salads where you want the individual cubes of potato to remain intact. Red-skinned potatoes and round white potatoes are the most common "boilers." *Baking* potatoes have a high starch content and fluffy, mealy flesh when cooked. These long, oval-shaped tubers are perfect for baking and frying. Russet and Idaho are the baking potatoes we are most familiar with.

The third category is the *all-purpose* potato. As you can imagine, when these potatoes are cooked, their texture falls somewhat between waxy and mealy. Yukon Gold has recently become a very popular all-purpose potato and is my first choice for mashed potatoes.

Many cooks choose baking potatoes for mashing because their fluffiness is considered desirable, but I find that it makes them too light in texture. I think that all-purpose potatoes have the best consistency for mashing—neither too light nor too heavy.

---

5 large (3 pounds) boiling potatoes
(preferably Yukon Gold), peeled
and quartered

1 tablespoon wasabi powder
(see page 16)

1 tablespoon water

⅔ cup milk (approximately)

3 tablespoons unsalted butter

½ teaspoon salt

1. Bring a stockpot of water to a boil and add the potatoes. Cook, partially covered, until tender, about 20 minutes. The time will depend on the size of the potato pieces. **2.** Combine the wasabi and water in a small bowl and let sit at least 15 minutes to develop its flavor. **3.** Drain the potatoes in a colander. **4.** Heat the milk in

the pot in which the potatoes cooked. Add the potatoes and turn the heat to low. Use an electric hand mixer to whip the potatoes until smooth. Add a little more milk if the potatoes are too thick. Stir in the butter and salt. Keep warm until ready to serve. Just before serving, stir in the wasabi.

SPICY OVEN FRIES

Just a little oil is needed to bake these home fries into crispy morsels. Serve them alongside a sandwich or at breakfast or brunch with an egg dish.

SERVES 4

4 baking (Idaho or russet) potatoes

3 tablespoons olive oil

2 teaspoons chili powder

Salt to taste

1. Preheat the oven to 425 degrees. **2.** Peel the potatoes and slice them in half lengthwise. Cut each section into ¼-inch-thick slices. Place on a baking sheet and drizzle with oil. Use your hands to toss the potatoes so they become well coated. **3.** Bake 20–25 minutes, tossing after 15 minutes. When done, the potatoes will be golden and very tender. Sprinkle the chili powder all over the fries and toss well with a spatula to coat them evenly. Season generously with salt and serve.

TIPS: Be certain to cook these in 1 layer so they can brown evenly. If your baking pan is small, use 2 to prevent overcrowding.

You will get the optimum flavor from the chili powder by adding it after the potatoes are roasted.

Although I usually cook these potatoes at a high oven setting, they are successful in an oven as low as 350 degrees; you'll just have to cook them about 10 minutes longer. This is sometimes necessary when baking something simultaneously that requires a lower oven setting.

MIXED POTATO HOME FRIES

Sweet potatoes combined with white potatoes makes a colorful and tasty accompaniment to many breakfast dishes. If you are making an entree at the same time and it is to be cooked at a lower temperature, you can place these home fries on the bottom rack of the oven at that temperature; you'll just have to cook them about 10–15 minutes longer.

SERVES 4–6

2 large sweet potatoes (preferably dark orange), peeled, quartered lengthwise, and sliced ¼ inch thick

2 large baking (Idaho or russet) potatoes, peeled, quartered lengthwise, and sliced ¼ inch thick

1 large onion, cut into 1-inch dice

3 tablespoons olive oil

Salt to taste

1. Preheat the oven to 425 degrees. **2.** Combine the potatoes, onion, and oil in a large bowl and toss to coat evenly with the oil. Spread on a large baking sheet or in a roasting pan in 1 layer. **3.** Bake 25–30 minutes, tossing with a spatula after 15 minutes. When done, the potatoes will be tender and brown. Season with salt before serving.

TIPS: As soon as you cut the potatoes, toss them in oil to prevent darkening.

Be certain to cook these in 1 layer so they can brown evenly. If your baking pan is small, use 2 to prevent overcrowding.

Kale

One of the hardiest of vegetables, kale actually benefits from being harvested after a frost, which improves its flavor. You can keep growing kale in the Northeast until after Christmas and enjoy walking through your snow-covered garden during the holidays to harvest it. Surprisingly, kale also grows well in the heat of the American South. The adaptability of this member of the cabbage family probably explains its popularity in two contrasting climates in Europe—the cool countries of Scandinavia, Germany, Holland, and Scotland, and warm Portugal.

SAUTÉED KALE

Kale is a vegetable that deserves to move into the spotlight. It has a nutty flavor, is easy to clean and cook, and is a good source of calcium and vitamin A. In addition, its leafy texture enhances soups and casseroles. Cooked here with garlic and a splash of balsamic vinegar, it becomes an accompaniment to be savored.

SERVES 4

1½ pounds kale (including 4-inch stems)

3 tablespoons olive oil

3 garlic cloves, minced

⅓ cup water

1½ tablespoons balsamic vinegar

Salt to taste

1. Wash the kale by running individual leaves under cold water. Tear the leaves off the stems and discard the stems. Chop the kale into bite-size pieces. You should get about 16 cups of leaves. **2.** Heat the oil in a large skillet over medium heat. Add the garlic and sauté about 1 minute, or just until it begins to sizzle. Use tongs to mix in the kale, coating it with the garlic and oil as much as possible. Add the water and cover the pan. **3.** Steam the kale until it wilts and gets tender, about 5–7 minutes. Remove the cover and toss it around occasionally. When it is tender and almost all the water has evaporated, drizzle with the vinegar and season with salt. Cook a few seconds and then serve.

ZUCCHINI AND RED PEPPER GRATIN

The vegetables in this gratin bake slowly and caramelize, creating a soft, tender mélange.

SERVES 6

> 3 medium zucchini, halved lengthwise and sliced ¼ inch thick on the diagonal
>
> 2 red bell peppers, cored, halved, and very thinly sliced
>
> 2 medium onions, halved vertically, very thinly sliced, and sections separated
>
> ¼ cup olive oil
>
> 3 tablespoons tomato sauce, store-bought or Easy Marinara Sauce (page 25)
>
> Salt to taste
>
> Freshly ground black pepper to taste

The Topping:

> 2 slices bread, whole wheat or white
>
> 1 tablespoon olive oil

1. Preheat the oven to 400 degrees. **2.** In a large bowl combine the zucchini, red peppers, onions, oil, and tomato sauce. Sprinkle with salt and pepper. Place the mixture in a shallow 2½-quart casserole (such as a 12 × 7 × 2 Pyrex dish) and flatten the top. **3.** Bake 45 minutes, tossing the mixture after the first 30 minutes. Flatten again. **4.** Meanwhile, place the bread in a food processor and process to make crumbs. Drizzle on the oil and rub it into the crumbs with your fingers. Sprinkle the crumbs all over the vegetables and bake 15 minutes more, or until golden brown on top. Let the gratin sit 15 minutes before serving so the juices can settle and thicken.

TIPS: The red peppers and onions take longer to cook than the zucchini, so be certain to slice them very thinly.

The tomato sauce is used sparingly to create a glaze rather than being a dominant flavoring agent.

BANANA MINT RAITA

A raita is a yogurt "salad" that accompanies an Indian meal and serves as a contrasting and soothing component to the spicy entree. No Indian meal is complete without one. Use a very ripe banana—that is, one with many brown spots—in this raita so it will be sweet enough to balance the tangy yogurt.

SERVES 6

> 1 cup plain yogurt, preferably low-fat (not fat-free)
>
> 1 small- to medium-size ripe banana, finely diced
>
> 1 tablespoon finely chopped fresh mint, or 1 teaspoon dried
>
> ¼ teaspoon sugar
>
> Dash salt
>
> Mint sprig for garnish

Combine all the ingredients except the mint sprig in a bowl. Cover and chill at least 30 minutes but not more than 2 hours before serving. Garnish with a mint sprig, if available.

CUCUMBER AND TOMATO RAITA

A generous amount of grated cucumber provides a refreshing tone to this raita, making it an ideal partner to a spicy curry.

SERVES 4–6

½ cucumber, peeled

½ cup very finely diced tomato

1 cup plain yogurt

¼ teaspoon salt

Pinch ground cumin

Cut the cucumber piece in half lengthwise. With a small spoon scoop out all the seeds and discard them. Grate the cucumber using a hand grater and place in a serving bowl. Stir in the remaining ingredients. Cover and chill at least 30 minutes or up to 2 hours before serving.

Mango Mania

Until recently this tropical fruit, which is extremely popular in more than half the world, was rarely seen in U.S. markets. Thanks to a new appreciation of Asian and Carribean cuisines, mangoes have made considerable inroads in American kitchens, and we have come to appreciate this highly nutritious fruit with its sweet perfume, silky yellow-orange flesh, and rich tropical flavor. When ripe, a mango has a yellow-rose blush to its skin and the flesh gives when gently pressed with the thumb. If the skin is wrinkly, the mango is too ripe and will have mushy flesh. To cut a mango visualize a large, somewhat flat stone in the center. Stand the fruit upright and cut from top to bottom just off center along the side of the stone. Repeat on the other side of the stone. You'll now have 2 halves free from the stone. With a sharp, pointed knife cut horizontal and vertical slits into the flesh almost all the way through to the skin. It will look like a checkerboard pattern. Bend the flesh backward as though you were going to turn the mango inside out. The cubes of flesh will protrude. You can now cut off the cubes with a sharp knife.

If you prefer to cut a mango into large strips, stand it upright and slice the skin off the fruit with a very sharp knife, cutting from the top down. Once the entire skin is removed, slice the flesh away from the stone, again from the top downward, leaving the stone behind.

FRESH MANGO CHUTNEY

A fresh chutney, as opposed to a cooked, preserved version, is made no more than a few hours before serving and is composed of raw ingredients. This delightful "relish" has the clean, bright taste of mango with a good dose of spiciness. Serve a small spoonful alongside Classic Vegetable Curry (page 243) for a glorious combination.

SERVES 4

1 ripe mango

1 tablespoon minced cilantro

A few dashes cayenne pepper

A few dashes salt

1. To cut the mango, read Mango Mania, opposite. **2.** Place all the ingredients in the container of a food processor and pulse a few times just until the mixture is coarsely chopped. Place in a bowl, cover, and chill at least 30 minutes but no more than a few hours before serving.

SAVORY PIES, TARTS, AND QUICHES

There is something intrinsically rustic and comforting about pies, whether they are savory or sweet, and because of this you can count on them to draw enthusiasm from family and guests alike. My favorite way to serve a main-course pie or tart is with all the "fixins," such as mashed potatoes, side vegetables, and biscuits. This creates a hearty, well-rounded meal that is utterly satisfying both to vegetarians and non-vegetarians alike.

The pies and tarts in this chapter range from ultra-quick versions with bread crumb "crusts" to equally quick puff-pastry renditions and more classic pies made with rolled pie crusts. They all are delicious, so let your whim, the seasons, or your schedule dictate which one you choose.

A TART BY ANY OTHER NAME...

What is the difference between a pie and a tart? Why are some vegetable pies called tarts and others quiches? Generally speaking, the choice of the baking medium defines the result. A pie is baked in a pie plate or pie tin and can have a single or double crust. A tart has a slightly different shape, usually with straight rather than sloping sides, and the sides are rippled. Tart pans often have removable bottoms, though not always.

A quiche can be a tart or a pie, and it is defined by the generous amount of custard and cheese it contains. If there are more vegetables than custard, it is usually called a vegetable tart rather than a quiche.

SHIITAKE MUSHROOM AND GOAT CHEESE QUICHE

For American vegetarians the discovery of quiche in the early 1970s was a godsend because it could be changed so easily into a sensational meatless dish—for example, substituting a tasty vegetable for the bacon in the classic Quiche Lorraine. I have never fully understood why quiche has become the object of jokes by some people. Perhaps it's because it became cliché in the 80s or because so many poorly made versions surfaced during the height of its popularity. To me a well-made quiche is something to savor. When this pie is at its best, a crisp, flaky crust holds a luxurious silken custard, as in this updated version. Here two sensational foods—shiitake mushrooms and goat cheese—create an unbeatable combination.

SERVES 6

Flaky Pie Crust (page 23), savory version

½ tablespoon unsalted butter

6 ounces shiitake mushrooms, stems discarded and caps thinly sliced (3 cups sliced)

4 large eggs

1 cup light cream, or ½ cup heavy cream and ½ cup milk

½ teaspoon salt

Generous seasoning freshly ground black pepper

⅛ teaspoon grated nutmeg

½ cup crumbled goat cheese (such as Montrachet)

½ cup grated Swiss cheese

1. Prepare the pie crust according to directions. Line a 9-inch tart pan with a removable rim or a glass pie plate with the pastry and prick it all over with a fork. Chill at least 30 minutes. **2.** Preheat the oven to 375 degrees. **3.** Line the pastry with aluminum foil and fill it with pie weights, dried beans, or raw rice to hold it in place. Bake 15 minutes. Remove the foil and weights and return the crust to the oven. Bake 5 minutes more. Let cool. Keep the oven on. **4.** Melt the butter in a medium-size skillet over medium heat. Add the mushrooms and sauté until brown and juicy. Let cool. **5.** To make the filling beat the eggs in a large bowl. Beat in the cream, salt, pepper, nutmeg, and mushrooms. Carefully stir in the goat cheese so the pieces stay intact rather than blend with the custard. **6.** Place the tart pan on a baking sheet to transport it to the oven easily. Sprinkle the Swiss cheese on the bottom of the crust. Carefully ladle in the filling. Bake 30 minutes, or until golden on top. Cool on a wire rack. Serve warm, not hot.

TIP: The secret to a great flaky quiche is to precook the crust sufficiently before adding the filling. A limp crust will result if you rush through step 3.

SPINACH, RED PEPPER, AND FETA CHEESE QUICHE

The combination of spinach, red pepper, and feta cheese is as pleasing to look at as it is to eat. Quiche is wonderful served at room temperature, so remember this quiche for a portable lunch, picnic, or afternoon snack.

SERVES 6

Flaky Pie Crust (page 23), savory version

2 teaspoons olive oil

1 red bell pepper, cut into very thin 2-inch-long strips

1 (10-ounce) package triple-washed spinach, stems discarded and leaves torn, or one 10-ounce box frozen chopped spinach, defrosted and squeezed dry

3 large eggs

¼ cup grated Parmesan cheese

½ cup heavy cream

½ cup milk

¼ teaspoon salt

Generous seasoning freshly ground black pepper

⅔ cup (3 ounces) crumbled feta cheese

1. Prepare the pie crust according to directions. Line a 9-inch tart pan with a removable rim or a glass pie plate with the pastry and prick it all over with a fork. Chill at least 30 minutes. **2.** Preheat the oven to 375 degrees. **3.** Line the pastry with aluminum foil and fill it with pie weights, dried beans, or raw rice to hold it in place. Bake 15 minutes. Remove the foil and weights and return the crust to the oven. Bake 5 minutes more. Let cool. Keep the oven on. **4.** To make the filling: heat the oil in a large skillet over medium heat. Add the red pepper and sauté until tender, about 7 minutes. If you are using fresh spinach, pile it on and tightly cover the pan. Cook just until the spinach wilts, about 3 minutes. (If there is any liquid in the pan at this point, boil it away on high heat.) If you are using cooked spinach, add it and cook, uncovered, until all liquid has evaporated, about 2 minutes. Remove the pan from the heat. **5.** Beat the eggs in a large bowl. Beat in the Parmesan cheese, cream, milk, salt, and pepper. Stir in the cooled spinach mixture and the feta cheese. Place the tart pan on a baking sheet to carry it to the oven. Pour the filling into the crust. **6.** Bake 30–35 minutes, or until a knife inserted in the center of the filling comes out clean. Remove the outer rim of the tart pan. Cool the quiche on a wire rack for 15 minutes before serving.

CARAMELIZED ONION TART

With the availability of commercially made frozen puff pastry, homemade pies and tarts can now be prepared in a flash and with great results.

This onion tart is one of the best I've ever eaten. For a homey meal I love to serve it alongside mashed potatoes and a brightly colored vegetable such as sautéed carrots or green beans. Caramelized Onion Tart is also an ideal picnic food (served at room temperature) and makes a fabulous finger-food appetizer when cut into small wedges.

SERVES 6

1 sheet (half of a 17-ounce package) frozen puff pastry

1 tablespoon olive oil

2 pounds onions, thinly sliced (9 cups sliced)

2 large eggs

½ cup heavy cream

Dash cayenne pepper

½ teaspoon salt

½ cup grated Swiss cheese

1. Remove the puff pastry from the package and let thaw at room temperature for about 30 minutes, or until no longer frozen but still cool. **2.** To make the filling: heat the oil in a large stockpot over medium heat. Add the onions and partially cover the pot. Cook, stirring often, for 40 minutes, or until the onions are a deep caramel color and very soft. Turn down the heat a little once the onions begin to soften so they can cook slowly, and scrape the bottom of the pot as necessary. When done, the onions will be evenly brown and almost jamlike. Let cool. (The onions can be prepared and refrigerated up to 48 hours in advance. Bring to room temperature before placing in the filling.) **3.** Lightly butter a dark-colored 9-inch tart pan with a removable rim or a glass pie plate. On a lightly floured surface roll the puff pastry into an 11-inch square. Fit it into the tart pan or pie plate. Use scissors to trim off the overhanging pieces of pastry. Refrigerate the crust 15 minutes or cover and refrigerate up to 8 hours. **4.** Preheat the oven to 425 degrees. **5.** Beat the eggs in a large bowl. Beat in the cream, cayenne, and salt. Stir in the cheese and onions. **6.** Spoon the mixture into the tart pan or pie plate. Bake 30–35 minutes, or until the custard is set and the crust is deeply golden. If your pie plate is glass, you can peek at the bottom of the crust to make sure it is cooked in the center. When the tart is done, remove the outer ring if you used a tart pan with a removable rim. Cool the tart on a wire rack for 15–20 minutes before serving because it should be served warm, not hot.

TIPS: If the top edge of the crust gets too dark in any area, you can shave off the dark spot with a serrated knife.

Puff Pastry Tarts

Puff pastry makes a delicious and quick crust for tarts, and it can be the ideal solution when you aren't in the mood or don't have enough time to make a crust from scratch. The key to any successful tart or pie, however, is a perfectly cooked flaky crust, and to achieve this with puff pastry you must use the right pan. Bright metal tart pans, such as aluminum ones, are too shiny and are poor conductors of heat for puff pastry, and they will prevent the crust from browning properly. If you use a black or dark tart pan with a removable rim or a glass pie plate, the puff pastry crust will be noticeably darker and flakier underneath, where it really matters.

This challenge with puff pastry occurs only with tart making because the pastry lines the pan rather deeply. You won't have any problems browning your puff pastry crust when you make flat, freestanding tarts on a baking sheet, such as Spinach and Pesto Tart (below), Individual Vegetable Tarts (page 166), and Shiitake Mushroom Tarts in Puff Pastry (page 167), because their openness and shallow depth exposes them more evenly to the oven heat.

This tart is also spectacular when baked in Flaky Pie Crust (page 23). Prebake a crust that has been lined with foil and filled with dried beans or pie weights at 375 degrees for 15 minutes. Remove the foil and beans, and bake 10 minutes more. Fill the crust with the onion custard and bake at 375 degrees for 40 minutes.

SPINACH AND PESTO TART

Here is a luscious tart in puff pastry made for me one day by Maureen Fox, my Scottish friend who lives in London. She noted that it lends itself to much variation. This version contains layers of pesto, sliced potatoes, and a savory spinach topping. Sautéed mushrooms, red peppers, zucchini, or broccoli could be added or substituted with great results. A large rectangle of puff pastry serves to encase the filling while providing an ultra-flaky layer. Couscous Pilaf with Toasted Pine Nuts (page 149) would be a fitting side dish.

SERVES 4–6

- 1 sheet frozen puff pastry (half of a 17-ounce package)
- 2 (10-ounce) bags triple-washed fresh spinach, stems discarded
- 2 medium-size boiling potatoes, peeled and sliced ¼ inch thick
- 2 large eggs
- 2 scallions, very thinly sliced
- 1 cup grated Gruyère or other Swiss cheese

¼ teaspoon salt

Generous seasoning freshly ground black pepper

Butter for greasing

½ cup Classic Pesto (page 19)

1. Let the puff pastry thaw at room temperature for about 30 minutes, or until defrosted but still slightly cold. **2.** Place the spinach in a large stockpot with a few tablespoons of water and cook over medium heat just until wilted, about 4 minutes. Drain the spinach in a colander. Let cool until room temperature. Squeeze all the moisture from the spinach with your hands. **3.** Fill a medium-size saucepan with water and bring to a boil. Drop in the potatoes and cook until tender, about 8 minutes. Drain thoroughly. **4.** Beat the eggs in a medium-size bowl. Remove about 2 tablespoons of egg and place in a small bowl to use later as an egg wash. Mix the spinach, scallions, cheese, salt, and pepper into the beaten eggs. **5.** Preheat the oven to 375 degrees. Butter a large baking sheet. **6.** Lightly flour a work surface. Use a rolling pin to roll the sheet of puff pastry until it is about 12 × 14 inches. Place on the baking sheet; a little will overhang. Spread the pesto on the puff pastry, leaving a 1½-inch border. Cover the pesto with the sliced potatoes. Spoon the spinach mixture all over the potatoes, again leaving a border. Fold the border over the filling. Using a pastry brush coat the border with the reserved egg. (You can chill the tart up to 4 hours before baking.) **7.** Bake 25 minutes, or until the pastry is

a rich golden brown. Let sit 10 minutes before cutting into squares and serving.

EASY ZUCCHINI, TOMATO, AND CHEESE TART

Using store-bought puff pastry for the crust makes this tart quick to prepare and provides a flaky, crisp base for this special pie. I love the flavor that the smoked cheese imparts; however, you can successfully substitute other cheeses, such as cheddar, Swiss, or Monterey Jack with jalapeño peppers to give this tart a whole new character.

SERVES 4–6 AS A MAIN COURSE

1 sheet (half of a 17-ounce package) frozen puff pastry

2 tablespoons olive oil

1 onion, finely diced

2 garlic cloves, minced

2 medium zucchini, quartered lengthwise and thinly sliced

1 (14-ounce) can ready-cut diced tomatoes, well drained

3 large eggs

1 cup grated smoked Gouda cheese

½ teaspoon salt

Generous seasoning freshly ground black pepper

Savory Pies, Tarts, and Quiches

1. Remove the puff pastry from the package and let thaw at room temperature for about 30 minutes, or until no longer frozen but still cool. **2.** Meanwhile, heat the oil in a large skillet over medium heat. Add the onion and garlic, and cook 5 minutes, or until the onion is slightly tender. Stir in the zucchini and sauté just until it begins to soften, about 5 minutes. Mix in the drained tomatoes and raise the heat to medium-high. Cook, stirring often, until the zucchini is tender but not mushy and the juices have evaporated. Let cool. **3.** Lightly butter a dark-colored 9-inch tart pan with a removable rim or a glass pie plate. **4.** On a lightly floured surface roll the puff pastry into an 11-inch square. Fit it into the tart pan or pie plate. Trim off the overhanging pieces of pastry with scissors. Refrigerate the crust, uncovered, for 15 minutes, or up to 8 hours, covered. **5.** Preheat the oven to 425 degrees. **6.** Beat the eggs in a large bowl. Stir in the cheese, salt, pepper, and cooled vegetables. **7.** Spoon the mixture into the tart pan. Bake 25–30 minutes, or until the pastry is brown and a knife inserted in the center of the tart comes out clean. Remove the outer rim of the tart pan. Let the tart cool on a wire rack for 20 minutes before slicing. It's best to serve this tart very warm rather than piping hot.

T I P : For a good match serve with Orzo Pilaf (page 148), Couscous Pilaf with Toasted Pine Nuts (page 149), or buttered egg noodles.

LEEK TART

I wish leeks were as familiar in the United States as they are in most European countries because their natural sweetness makes them one of the most delectable of vegetables. This simple yet sophisticated tart with a puff pastry base is outstanding both as a main course, especially when accompanied by a potato side dish (try Wasabi Mashed Potatoes, page 151), or as a first course to an elegant meal.

SERVES 4–6 AS A MAIN COURSE

> 1 sheet (half of a 17-ounce package) frozen puff pastry
>
> 3 large leeks (about 2 pounds)
>
> 1½ tablespoons unsalted butter, plus extra for greasing
>
> ½ cup heavy cream
>
> ½ teaspoon salt
>
> Freshly ground black pepper to taste
>
> 3 large eggs
>
> 1 large egg yolk
>
> ½ cup whole milk

1. Remove the puff pastry from the package and let thaw at room temperature for about 30 minutes, or until no longer frozen but still cool. **2.** Meanwhile, cut the roots off the leeks and all but 2 inches of their green tops. Slice the leeks in half vertically and rinse very well under cold run-

A Look at Leeks

Leeks, considered the "poor man's asparagus" all over Europe, are as common there as onions are here. Leeks have an unbeatable sweetness and subtlety, and although they are a member of the onion family and share some of the onion's pungency, they really can't be replaced by onions in recipes without forfeiting the lively sweet edge they contribute to the finished dish.

Leeks resemble giant scallions, but unlike scallions they harbor a lot of dirt in their leaves. This is a result of dirt being mounded around the leek while it is growing so it can "blanch" the bottom of the vegetable, keeping it white and tender. The bottom white part and the first 2 inches of the green are the edible portions. To clean leeks thoroughly you must slice them in half lengthwise and hold their leaves under cold running water, being careful to expose any dirt lodged there.

"Beware of spring leeks" is a saying that I memorized so that I can avoid purchasing leeks during the spring months when they are often inedible. Leeks are at their prime during the fall and winter months. In the spring, they sometimes send up a hard stalk through their centers as a preparation for "setting seed." You must discard this fibrous shoot, so you are left with only a small portion of edible leaves. If you need leeks for a recipe in the spring, flip through the top part of each leek to see if a woody stalk is hiding there. If so, don't purchase them.

ning water to get rid of the sand. Use your fingers to flip through the leaves to reveal any hidden dirt. Drain well. Slice the leeks thinly crosswise, using all the white part and a little of the light green inner leaves. You need 5 cups sliced leeks. **3.** Melt the butter in a large skillet over medium heat. Add the leeks and sauté 5 minutes, or until they begin to soften. Pour in the cream and cook 5 minutes more. Stir in the salt and pepper, and remove the pan from the heat. Let cool. **4.** Lightly butter a dark-colored 9-inch tart pan with a removable rim or a glass pie plate. On a lightly floured surface roll the puff pastry into an 11-inch square. Fit it into the tart pan or

pie plate. Trim off the overhanging pieces of pastry with scissors. Refrigerate the crust, uncovered, for 15 minutes, or up to 8 hours, covered. **5.** Preheat the oven to 425 degrees. **6.** Beat the eggs and yolk together in a large bowl. Stir in the milk and the leek mixture. Pour this into the cold pie shell. Bake 25–30 minutes, or until richly golden. Remove the outer rim of the tart pan. Let the tart cool on a wire rack for 15 minutes before slicing. Serve warm, not hot.

TIP: For maximum value when purchasing leeks, choose those that are predominantly white with just a little green on top rather than the other way around.

Savory Pies, Tarts, and Quiches

BROCCOLI AND MUSHROOM TART

The jalapeño cheese gives this tart a subtle zip without making it spicy, so by all means include it.

SERVES 4–6

> 1 sheet (half of a 17-ounce package) frozen puff pastry
>
> 1 tablespoon olive oil
>
> 3 cups thinly sliced mushrooms (8 ounces)
>
> 3½–4 cups tiny broccoli florets (no stalks)
>
> ¼ cup water
>
> 3 large eggs
>
> ¼ cup milk
>
> ½ teaspoon salt
>
> 1 cup grated Monterey Jack cheese with jalapeño peppers

1. Remove the puff pastry from the package and let it thaw at room temperature for about 30 minutes, or until no longer frozen but still cool. **2.** Meanwhile, heat the oil in a large skillet over medium heat. Add the mushrooms and sauté until brown. Mix in the broccoli and water, and cover the pan. Cook the broccoli until tender yet still bright green, about 5 minutes. Remove the cover and cook until all the liquid evaporates. Remove the pan from the heat and let the vegetables cool to room temperature. **3.** Lightly butter a dark-colored 9-inch tart pan with a removable bottom or a glass pie plate. On a lightly floured surface roll the puff pastry into an 11-inch square. Fit it into the tart pan. Trim off the overhanging pieces of pastry with scissors. Refrigerate the crust 15 minutes, or cover and chill up to 8 hours. **4.** Preheat the oven to 425 degrees. **5.** Beat the eggs in a large bowl. Stir in the milk, vegetables, salt, and cheese. **6.** Spoon the mixture into the tart pan. Bake 25–30 minutes, or until the pastry is brown and a knife inserted in the center of the tart comes out clean. Remove the outer rim of the tart pan if you are using such a pan. Let the tart cool on a wire rack for 15 minutes before slicing. Serve the tart hot but not piping hot.

TIP: To create a tart with a delicate texture, be certain to cut the florets as tiny as possible— about the size of a peanut in its shell.

INDIVIDUAL VEGETABLE TARTS

These elegant tarts are flaky and delicate. A layer of garlic-infused tomato pesto is topped with thinly sliced potato and zucchini, and baked until golden brown. They are not difficult to prepare and can be easily assembled in stages. Orzo Pilaf (page 148) would be the perfect side dish to accompany these wonderful tarts.

SERVES 4

1 sheet (half of a 17-ounce package)
   frozen puff pastry

Sun-Dried Tomato Pesto (page 21)

1 medium-large boiling potato (preferably
   Yukon Gold), peeled, halved, and
   sliced ¼ inch thick

2 tablespoons olive oil

1 medium zucchini, sliced ¼ inch thick

1. Defrost the puff pastry for 45 minutes, or until thawed but still cold. **2.** Meanwhile, make the Sun-Dried Tomato Pesto and set aside. **3.** Fill a saucepan halfway with water and bring to a boil. Drop in the potato slices and cook until tender but not mushy, about 5 minutes. Drain and spread out on a plate to let cool. **4.** Heat the oil in a large skillet until hot but not smoking. Fry the zucchini slices until golden on each side. Remove to a plate and let cool. **5.** On a lightly floured surface roll the puff pastry into an 11 × 11-inch square. Using a 5-inch cutter or inverted bowl, cut 4 disks from the pastry. Place the disks on a baking sheet and pierce all over with a fork. Keep refrigerated until you are ready to assemble the tarts. **6.** Preheat the oven to 400 degrees. **7.** Spread 2 tablespoons pesto on each pastry disk, leaving a ½-inch border. You will have some pesto left over; refrigerate for another use (see Tip). Cover the pesto with some potato slices, then cover the potatoes with zucchini slices arranged in a circle. You may have some potato and zucchini

left over. **8.** Bake 15–20 minutes, or until the pastry is golden brown. Serve at once.

T I P : Leftover pesto is delicious spread on slices of toasted French bread and also tossed on pasta.

SHIITAKE MUSHROOM TARTS IN PUFF PASTRY

These tarts are a variation of a *New York Times* recipe featuring porcini mushroom tarts by the esteemed chef Jean Georges Vongerichten. His layering of an onion-walnut puree beneath sautéed mushrooms and glazing the tops with garlic oil creates one of the most memorable tarts I've ever had. These little pies will be a knockout at any party. Serve them with Wasabi Mashed Potatoes (page 151) or Pesto Mashed Potatoes (page 151) and a colorful sautéed vegetable for a great match.

SERVES 4

2 garlic cloves, minced

5 tablespoons olive oil

1 sheet (half of a 17-ounce package)
   frozen puff pastry

2 medium onions, thinly sliced

½ cup chopped walnuts

Salt to taste

Freshly ground black pepper to taste

6 ounces shiitake mushrooms, stems discarded and caps thinly sliced (3 cups sliced)

4 ounces common white mushrooms, thinly sliced (1½ cups sliced)

1. Defrost the puff pastry for 45 minutes, or until thawed but still cold. **2.** Combine 3 tablespoons oil with the garlic in a small bowl and let sit at least 45 minutes. **3.** Heat 1 tablespoon oil in a skillet. Add the onions and sauté until golden brown and very soft, about 15 minutes. Stir in the walnuts and cook 2 minutes. Season with salt and pepper. Puree the mixture in a food processor and let cool. **4.** Heat the remaining tablespoon of oil in the skillet and sauté the mushrooms until brown, about 10 minutes. Let cool. **5.** On a lightly floured surface roll the puff pastry into an 11 × 11-inch square. Using a 5-inch cutter or inverted bowl, cut 4 disks from the pastry. Place them on a baking sheet and chill until you are ready to assemble the tarts. **6.** Strain the garlic oil through a strainer. Discard the garlic and set aside the oil. **7.** Preheat the oven to 400 degrees. **8.** Spread ¼ of the onion mixture on each pastry disk, leaving a ½-inch border. Cover each tart with ¼ of the mushrooms. Brush a little garlic oil on each tart. Bake 15–20 minutes, or until the pastry is golden brown. Brush the tarts again with some oil before serving. Serve immediately.

GREENS, POTATO, AND FETA CHEESE PIE

This quick pie, made with a crust of bread crumbs, contains a savory filling resembling that of the popular Italian *torta verde*. It is equally delicious made with Swiss chard, spinach, or a combination of both.

SERVES 4

½ tablespoon unsalted butter, at room temperature

¼ cup dry bread crumbs

2 medium boiling potatoes (such as red-skinned), peeled and cut into ¼-inch dice (about 1½ cups)

6–7 large leaves Swiss chard, removed from stems, or one 10-ounce package fresh spinach, stems discarded, or a combination of both

1½ tablespoons salt

1 cup crumbled feta cheese

2 scallions, thinly sliced

2 tablespoons chopped fresh parsley

Generous seasoning freshly ground black pepper

2 large eggs, well beaten

¼ cup milk

2 tablespoons olive oil

1. Coat the bottom and sides of a 9-inch pie plate with the ½ tablespoon butter. Sprinkle the crumbs on the plate, then rotate the plate until they cover the entire bottom and sides. This will form the crust. 2. Place the potatoes in a medium-size saucepan and cover with water. Bring to a boil, then lower the heat to a simmer. Cook the potatoes until tender, about 10 minutes. Drain well and place in a large bowl. 3. Wash the Swiss chard or spinach and place in a colander. Sprinkle the salt all over the leaves and let sit for 30 minutes; this will cause the juices to "sweat." With your hands gather the leaves into a ball and squeeze out all the juices. Chop the leaves roughly and add them to the potatoes. Mix in all the remaining ingredients. 4. Preheat the oven to 375 degrees. 5. Place the greens mixture in the prepared pie plate. Bake 40 minutes, or until a knife inserted in the center of the pie comes out clean. Let sit 10 minutes before serving.

CRUSTLESS YELLOW SQUASH, RED PEPPER, AND SPINACH PIE

Here's another easy pie with a bread crumb crust. The three vegetables mentioned in the title of this pie are noteworthy for their compatible flavors and stunning color contrasts. A wedge of this savory tart is superb alongside a mount of Pesto Mashed Potatoes (page 151).

SERVES 4

½ tablespoon butter, at room temperature

¼ cup dry bread crumbs

1 tablespoon olive oil

1 red bell pepper, cut into ½-inch dice

4 large garlic cloves, minced

3 medium yellow squash, quartered vertically and thinly sliced

1 (10-ounce) package triple-washed spinach, stems discarded and leaves torn, or one 10-ounce box frozen chopped spinach, defrosted and squeezed dry

3 large eggs

¼ cup milk

¼ teaspoon salt

Generous seasoning freshly ground black pepper

1½ cups grated Swiss cheese

1. Slather the butter all over the inside of a 9-inch pie plate. Sprinkle the bread crumbs on the plate, then rotate the plate so the crumbs adhere to the sides and bottom. A thicker layer of crumbs on the bottom is okay. 2. Heat the oil in a large skillet over medium heat. Add the red pepper and cover the pan. Cook 5 minutes, tossing occasionally. Add the garlic and cook, uncovered, for 2 minutes. 3. Mix in the squash and sauté, tossing often, until the squash is tender, about 10 minutes. 4. If you are using fresh spinach, pile it on and cover the pan. Cook 2 minutes, or until the spinach wilts.

If any juices are on the bottom of the pan, raise the heat and let them evaporate. If you are using frozen spinach, add it and cook until all its liquid evaporates, about 3 minutes. Let the mixture cool. **5.** Preheat the oven to 375 degrees. **6.** Beat the eggs in a large bowl. Stir in the milk, salt, pepper, and cooled vegetables. Spoon half the mixture into the prepared pie plate. Sprinkle on 1 cup cheese. Spoon on the remaining mixture and top with the remaining cheese. **7.** Bake 30 minutes, or until a knife inserted in the center comes out clean. Cool 15 minutes before cutting the pie into wedges.

SHEPHERD'S PIE

This British pie with a mashed potato topping has been a favorite vegetarian dish for decades. Here a thick, luscious stew made with zucchini, corn, tomatoes, and beans replaces the traditional lamb filling, and it rests under a canopy of creamy mashed potatoes that is baked until golden and crusty. This dish is easy to prepare and would be a good choice to serve a crowd.

SERVES 4–6

> 3 tablespoons olive oil
>
> 3 garlic cloves, minced
>
> 1 cup canned crushed tomatoes or tomato puree

> ½ cup water
>
> 1 cup fresh or frozen green beans, cut into 1-inch lengths
>
> 1 cup cooked chickpeas or white beans, rinsed well if canned
>
> 2 tablespoons minced fresh basil, or 1 teaspoon dried
>
> ½ teaspoon salt
>
> Generous seasoning freshly ground black pepper
>
> 2 medium zucchini, quartered lengthwise and thinly sliced
>
> 1 cup fresh or frozen corn

The Topping:

> 4 large (2½ pounds) boiling potatoes, peeled and quartered
>
> ¼ cup milk (approximately)
>
> 2 tablespoons unsalted butter
>
> ¼ teaspoon salt
>
> 3 tablespoons grated Parmesan cheese

1. Heat the oil in a 3-quart saucepan over medium heat. Add the garlic and cook 1–2 minutes, or until softened but not at all colored. Stir in the crushed tomatoes, water, green beans, chickpeas, basil, salt, and pepper, and cook, stirring often, for 10 minutes. Add the zucchini and corn, and simmer 10 minutes more, or until the vegetables are tender but not mushy. **2.** Meanwhile, cook the potatoes in boiling water until tender. Drain very well in a colander and return to the pot. Add the milk (see Tip), butter, and salt, and mash with an electric mixer or potato masher until smooth, adding a little more milk if necessary. **3.** Preheat the oven to 375 degrees. **4.** Pour the stew into a shallow 2½-quart baking dish, such as a 12 × 7 × 2 Pyrex dish. Spread the mashed potatoes all over the top of the stew, being careful to go to the edge of the casserole. Sprinkle the top with the Parmesan cheese. **5.** Bake 30 minutes, or until bubbly and brown on top. Let sit 10 minutes before serving.

TIPS: Be careful with the amount of milk you add to the potatoes when you mash them. You want them to be creamy but somewhat thick because the steam from the casserole will moisten them further and thin them a little.

You can easily prepare this pie in stages. The stew can be cooked up to 24 hours in advance. The potatoes can be placed on top up to 8 hours in advance. If refrigerated, bring to room temperature before baking.

CLASSIC VEGETABLE POT PIE

When vegetarians who were brought up eating meat crave a homey dish from their childhood, vegetable pot pie is a favorite choice. Although I like to accompany this pie with mashed potatoes, you can instead add 1½ cups of diced potatoes to the carrots when you cook them and have your potatoes right in the pie.

SERVES 4

2 cups water

2 carrots, thinly sliced

1 celery rib, thinly sliced

1 cup diced green beans, fresh or frozen

2 tablespoons olive oil

1 medium onion, finely diced

3 cups (8 ounces) sliced mushrooms

1 red bell pepper, cut into ½-inch dice

⅓ cup unbleached flour

1 cup milk

1 tablespoon tamari soy sauce

¼ teaspoon dried basil

Pinch dried oregano

½ teaspoon salt

Generous seasoning freshly ground pepper

1 sheet (half of 17-ounce box) puff pastry

Flour for dusting

1 egg beaten with 1 tablespoon water

1. Place the water in a medium-size saucepan and bring to a boil. Add the carrots and celery, and cook 2 minutes. Add the green beans and simmer until the vegetables are tender, about 5 minutes. Set aside. (Do not drain the vegetables.) **2.** Heat the oil in a large skillet over medium heat. Add the onion, mushrooms, and red pepper, and sauté until the mushrooms are juicy and the peppers are tender, at least 10 minutes. **3.** Sprinkle the flour over the vegetables. Toss and cook, stirring constantly, for 2 minutes. The vegetables will be dry and the flour will brown slightly. **4.** Pour in the carrot and liquid mixture, milk, and soy sauce, and stir continuously until the gravy comes to a boil. Scrape the bottom of the skillet to remove and incorporate any crusty tidbits. Boil 1 minute, or just until the mixture thickens. Stir in the basil, oregano, salt, and pepper. Scrape the mixture into a shallow 2½-quart baking dish (such as a 12 × 7 × 2-inch Pyrex dish). Let cool to room temperature. **5.** Meanwhile, thaw the puff pastry at room temperature for 30 minutes, or until completely defrosted but still cool. **6.**

Preheat the oven to 400 degrees. **7.** Lightly flour a work surface and the top of the pastry sheet. Roll the pastry until it is a little larger than the top of the baking dish. Place the pastry on the cooled filling and let it extend 1 inch or so up the sides of the dish. Trim it with scissors to fit evenly. With a sharp knife cut a few slits in the pastry to create steam vents. Brush the pastry with the beaten egg mixture. (You can prepare the pie to this point and refrigerate up to 2 hours. Bring to room temperature before cooking.) **8.** Bake the pie 30 minutes, or until the pastry is a rich golden brown. Serve at once.

Vegetarian Classics

PIZZAS AND CALZONES

THE ALLURE OF PIZZA

Although pizza parlors are strewn all across the United States and many of them now offer sophisticated, wood-fired, brick oven pizzas with artisan-style crusts, nothing can quite compare to the satisfaction of creating a perfect pizza at home. *Perfect*? It's true that everyone has his and her own idea of what constitutes perfection when it comes to this beloved pie, but the idea is to be able to obtain the results that you want and to do so not by chance but through knowledge and skill.

Pizza is the ultimate vehicle for improvisation, and so with a lively imagination you can create custom-made pies that are culinary works of art. After much experimentation I have come up with an assortment of pizzas and calzones that I think are sensational, from Classic Pizza to Caramelized Onion Pizza with a Beer Crust. The pizza toppings in this chapter can be easily divided to cover just one pizza, so you can mix and match to create different pizzas from one batch of dough. The tips below will help you create pizzas and calzones that you'll be proud of because of their superlative texture and flavor.

Making and Rolling the Dough

Making a batch of pizza dough is a simple, easy task. Once the ingredients are combined, all that remains to be done is kneading the dough to develop the gluten. This accounts for the elasticity or chewiness in the crust. You can knead the dough in a sturdy food processor, with a dough hook in an electric mixer, or by using your hands. To knead the dough by hand, you should lightly flour a work surface if the dough is sticky. Use the heels of your hands to push the dough away from you, then fold the dough in half facing you. After you knead it and fold it this way a few times, the dough will become elongated horizontally. Give the dough a half turn so it is now vertical. Fold it over in half, then repeat with the pattern of pushing with the heels of your hands and then folding it. Do this for 10 minutes. Now the dough is ready to rise in a warm place until it doubles in bulk.

After you punch down the risen dough, it is ready to be stretched and rolled. Divide the dough into 2 or 3 equal-size portions, depending on your recipe. Roll one portion into a ball and then flatten into a perfectly round disk. With a rolling pin roll the disk into an 11- or 12-inch circle, turning the dough as necessary to keep the circle even. Here is a tip: If the dough resists being rolled and stretched and keeps shrinking back, let it rest a few minutes to relax the gluten. It will then be much easier to roll. If after rolling the dough some more it resists again, let it rest again for a few minutes, then roll again.

Cooking the Pizza

The ideal way to cook a pizza at home is to re-create the hot oven floor of pizza parlors. Pizza stones are available for the home cook for this purpose. A pizza stone, a large stone slab, is placed in the oven so the pizza can sit directly on it instead of in a pan. Pizza stones can be found in cookware shops and work well, but I am a fan of an alternative cooking base: *quarry tiles*. These clay tiles can be easily stacked in a cabinet and take up less storage space. They are inexpensive (six 6-inch tiles cost about $7.00) and easy to use. You can purchase quarry tiles from a tile store.

Once you have your pizza stone (or tiles), you must preheat them in a hot (450-degree) oven for 45 minutes before you slide your pizza on it. A hot stone will set the crust of thinly-rolled pizza dough and make it crisp.

To slide the pizza onto the pizza stone you need to use a pizza peel (paddle). Sprinkle cornmeal all over the surface of the peel; this is essential to make the pizza slide off easily without sticking. Place the rolled dough on the peel and cover with toppings of your choice. Shake the peel occasionally to make certain the crust still moves freely and isn't sticking at any spot. To get the pizza onto the hot pizza stone takes a little skill but can be mastered after just a few tries. Place the edge of the pizza peel right on the fur-thest edge of the pizza stone and with a quick jerk of your hand pull the peel back; the pizza will slide off onto the center of the stone.

Vegetarian Classics

Cook the pizza until the underneath crust is golden brown. Remove the pizza by sliding the peel under the entire crust.

Baking Sheets

If you don't have a pizza stone or tiles, dark baking sheets are the next best choice. Dark metal absorbs heat and causes baked goods to darken quickly. This is undesirable when you are baking cookies, but for pizza it is an asset. Bright silvery baking sheets are the least desirable for pizza because so much heat is reflected that browning takes place very slowly.

A Relaxed Pizza Party

Although I have been making pizza from scratch for more than twenty years, only recently have I discovered the secret to throwing a pizza party with ease. What do I do differently now? My new laid-back pace hinges on one key step: rolling out the dough and freezing the disks at least 1 day in advance. By having this task completed before the party, and also preparing the toppings early in the day, all that needs to be done when the guests arrive is assembling the pizzas on the frozen crusts and popping them in the oven. What a difference.

Pizza Party Strategy

■ Make the dough a few days in advance and roll it into 11- or 12-inch disks, or several small individual (7-inch) rounds. Freeze on baking sheets. When frozen, remove and place in individual plastic bags. Remove from the bags when it is time to thaw them out.

■ The day before the party grate the cheese, chop the vegetables for the toppings, and prepare the sauce(s).

■ The day of the party sauté vegetables for toppings, make a salad, and make dessert.

■ When guests arrive, assemble the pizzas. If you are cooking the pizzas on a pizza stone, wait until the last minute to place the crust on the pizza peel because if it sits there too long, moisture can build up and the pizza won't glide freely on the cornmeal. If you are using greased baking sheets to cook the pizzas, you can place the crusts on them at any time and add the toppings of your choice.

■ To serve the pizzas easily, slide the cooked pizza onto a large cutting board and cut it with a pizza wheel or large knife. Slide the whole pizza onto a large round platter and bring it to the table. The cutting board is now free for the next pizza.

To freeze the crusts place each one on a baking sheet and put the sheet in the freezer until the crust is frozen solid, about 1 hour. Remove the crust from the sheet, seal it in a plastic bag, and return it to the freezer. Repeat with the remaining crusts. Thirty minutes before you're ready to cook the pizzas you can remove the crusts from their bags, allow them to thaw on your work space, and then place on a baking sheet or pizza peel. (If you assemble and bake the pizzas on frozen crusts, you'll find that the toppings cook before the crust has enough time to brown.)

CLASSIC PIZZA DOUGH

This all-purpose pizza dough works equally well creating thin or thick crusts, and also provides a base for calzones. It's easy to prepare and has a wonderful chewy and crisp finish.

FOR 2 (12-INCH) PIZZAS

- 1 cup warm water, divided
- 1 teaspoon sugar
- 1 packet (2¼ teaspoons) active dry yeast
- 3 tablespoons olive oil, plus extra for greasing
- 2½ cups unbleached flour, plus extra for dusting
- ½ teaspoon salt

1. Place ¼ cup warm water in a small bowl. Add the sugar and stir until dissolved. Sprinkle the yeast onto the surface of the water. Let the yeast sit undisturbed for 1 minute, then stir it into the water until blended. Let the yeast "proof" for 10 minutes; it should become somewhat bubbly because of the presence of the sugar. If it doesn't bubble at all, it is outdated and inactive. **2.** Pour the yeast into a large bowl and stir in the remaining water, oil, flour, and salt. Mix the dough with a wooden spoon until it forms a ball. Lightly flour a work surface and place the dough on it. Knead the dough for 10 minutes, or until it is smooth and elastic. Flour the work surface as necessary to prevent the dough from sticking. **3.** Coat the inside of a large glass or ceramic bowl with oil. Press the ball of dough into the bottom of the bowl, then flip the dough over so the oiled side is on top. Cover the bowl with plastic wrap and let the dough rise in a warm place until it doubles in bulk, about 1½ hours. **4.** Punch down the dough and knead it a few times. Divide it in 2, then proceed with your recipe.

TIP: If you are not ready to make your pizzas at this point, you can place the dough in a plastic bag or in a bowl covered with plastic wrap and refrigerate it a few hours. The cold will delay further rising. Bring the dough to room temperature before rolling it out.

SEMOLINA PIZZA DOUGH

Semolina gives this crust a nutty flavor and golden color, while rendering the texture both crisp and chewy. Look for semolina that is similar to very fine cornmeal in its coarseness.

FOR 3 (11-INCH) PIZZAS

> 1¼ cups warm water, divided
>
> 1 teaspoon sugar
>
> 1 packet (2¼ teaspoons) active dry yeast
>
> 2 tablespoons olive oil, plus extra for greasing
>
> ½ teaspoon salt
>
> 2 cups unbleached flour, plus extra for dusting
>
> 1 cup semolina (see page 13)

1. Place ¼ cup warm water in a small bowl. Stir in the sugar until dissolved. Sprinkle the yeast onto the surface of the water. Let the yeast sit undisturbed for 1 minute, then stir it into the water until blended. Let the yeast "proof" for 10 minutes; it should become somewhat bubbly because of the presence of the sugar. If it doesn't bubble at all, it is outdated and inactive. 2. Pour the yeast into a large bowl. Mix in the remaining water, oil, and salt. Add the flour and semolina, and stir with a wooden spoon until a ball of dough forms. 3. Turn the dough onto a lightly floured surface and knead about 10 minutes. Flour the work surface as necessary to prevent the dough from sticking. When ready, the dough should be smooth and elastic. 4. Lightly oil a large ceramic or glass bowl. Place the dough inside, then flip it over so the oiled side is on top. Cover with plastic wrap and place in a warm place to rise until it doubles in bulk, about 1½ hours. Proceed with your pizza recipe.

QUICK BAKING POWDER PIZZA DOUGH

This pizza dough has no yeast in it and relies on baking powder as a leavener, creating a surprisingly crisp yet tender base for a delicious last-minute pizza. The dough is so easy to handle that you could easily make small, individual pizzas—a perfect solution, perhaps, to a kids' pizza party.

FOR 4 (8-INCH) PIZZAS

> 2½ cups unbleached flour, plus extra for dusting
>
> 1½ teaspoons baking powder
>
> ½ teaspoon salt
>
> 4 tablespoons unsalted butter, chilled and cut into pieces
>
> 1 cup low-fat milk
>
> Olive oil for greasing or cornmeal for sprinkling

Pizzas and Calzones

1. Place the flour, baking powder, and salt in a large bowl. Add the butter and toss to coat. Rub the butter into the flour with your fingertips until the mixture resembles coarse meal. You can do this in a food processor, if desired. Add the milk slowly and mix just until the dough is evenly moistened. 2. Turn the dough onto a lightly floured surface and knead 2 or 3 times, or just until it is pliable. Divide the dough into 4 balls. 3. Lightly oil a large baking sheet, or if you will be using a pizza stone, sprinkle some cornmeal on a pizza peel. Using a lightly floured rolling pin, roll out each ball into an 8-inch circle. Place 2 on the baking sheet or 1 on the pizza peel. Proceed with your recipe.

TIP: If you want to make the dough in advance, just roll it out and place it on a baking sheet, then pop it in the freezer until you are ready for dinner. Let it thaw at room temperature for 30 minutes or so before covering it with your toppings.

BEER PIZZA DOUGH

This quick pizza dough was in my last book, *Simple Vegetarian Pleasures,* and I have become so fond of it that I am offering it again with a fabulous new topping combination (see Caramelized Onion, Walnut, and Goat Cheese Pizza with a Beer Crust, page 184). The beer adds a lightness to the crust while imparting a slight yeast flavor. Although you can use a dark beer with good results, I prefer the lighter color the crust retains when using a light-colored beer.

FOR 2 (12-INCH) PIZZAS

> 3 cups unbleached flour, plus extra for dusting
>
> 1 tablespoon baking powder
>
> ½ teaspoon salt
>
> 1 (12-ounce) can or bottle beer (a cheap beer is fine)
>
> Oil for greasing or cornmeal for sprinkling

1. Combine the flour, baking powder, and salt in a large bowl and mix thoroughly. Pour in the beer and mix well; the dough will be sticky. Spread a small handful of flour on a work surface and place the dough on it. Roll the dough around to coat it with the flour and prevent it from sticking. Knead it 2 or 3 times to make it pliable. Shape the dough into a ball, then divide it in 2. 2. Grease 2 baking sheets, or if you are going to use a baking stone, sprinkle some cornmeal on a pizza peel. Use a rolling pin to roll each ball into a 12-inch circle. Place a round of dough on each baking sheet or put 1 round on the pizza peel. Proceed with your recipe.

TORTILLA PIZZA SHELLS

For a quick, easy pizza base that provides individual-size pizzas, nothing beats flour tortillas. When brushed with oil and baked until crisp, they become delicate and flaky, and will hold any topping of your choice. Remember them for your next children's party; whether the kids are 5 or 15, they'll love making their own individual pizzas.

MAKES 4 (8-INCH) PIZZA SHELLS

> **4 (8-inch) flour tortillas**
>
> **1½ tablespoons olive oil**

1. Preheat the oven to 375 degrees. **2.** Use 2 baking sheets and place 2 tortillas side by side on each sheet. With a pastry brush lightly coat each tortilla with some oil. Flip the tortillas and coat again. **3.** Bake 8–10 minutes, flipping the tortillas and alternating the placement of the baking sheets halfway through the cooking time. During the first few minutes use a knife point to pop any air bubbles that might develop. The tortillas should be golden and crisp when done. Proceed with your recipe.

TIP: The tortillas can be made up to 3 days in advance. Cool completely, seal in a plastic bag, and refrigerate until ready to use.

CLASSIC PIZZA

This pizza is classic to the United States; that is, it's the well-known pairing of tomato sauce topped with mozzarella cheese. Different regions of Italy would claim other versions as classic. However Americanized this pizza is, it is still one of my all-time favorite foods and one that I turn to when I crave a pizza that is outstanding yet familiar.

The combination of mozzarella cheese and Muenster cheese produces a creamier topping than all mozzarella; however, if you prefer to use only mozzarella cheese, you will still get great results.

MAKES 2 (12-INCH) PIZZAS
SERVES 4

> **Classic Pizza Dough (page176) or other pizza dough from this chapter**
>
> **Cornmeal for sprinkling or olive oil for greasing**
>
> **1 cup Easy Marinara Sauce (page 25)**
>
> **1½ cups grated mozzarella cheese**
>
> **1½ cups grated Muenster cheese**

1. Prepare the pizza dough according to the recipe. **2.** Preheat the oven to 450 degrees. If you are using a pizza stone, heat it at least 45 minutes before cooking the pizza on it. **3.** Lightly flour the work surface. Punch down the dough and place it on the work surface. Divide it in half. Use a rolling pin to roll 1 portion into a 12-inch circle. If the dough resists stretching, let it rest a few minutes, then roll again. If you are using a pizza stone, sprinkle some cornmeal on a pizza peel and place 1 circle of dough on the peel. Otherwise, lightly grease a baking sheet and place the dough on it. **4.** Spread half the sauce on 1 crust, then top with half of the mozzarella and Muenster cheeses. Bake 10–12 minutes if cooking directly on a baking stone; add a few minutes if cooking the pizza on a baking sheet. When done, the pizza will be golden on top and underneath. Repeat with the remaining ingredients to make another pizza.

MIXED MUSHROOM AND FONTINA PIZZA

This sensational pizza has a thin layer of sour cream as a base, is sprinkled with fontina cheese, and is topped with a mixture of exotic mushrooms.

This recipe makes three 11-inch pizzas. If you want to vary the toppings for 1 or 2 portions of the dough, just cook ⅓ or ⅔ of the mushroom topping outlined below and proceed accordingly. If you wish to make just 1 or 2 pizzas, freeze the remaining portion of the dough in a plastic bag.

MAKES 3 (11-INCH) PIZZAS
SERVES 4–6

> Semolina Pizza Dough (page 177) or other pizza dough from this chapter
>
> *The Topping:*
>
> 2 tablespoons olive oil
>
> 3 medium onions, halved and thinly sliced
>
> 1½ pounds mixed mushrooms (such as white button, shiitake, cremini, and oyster), very thinly sliced
>
> 2 sprigs fresh thyme, leaves removed and stems discarded, or ¼ teaspoon dried
>
> ½ teaspoon salt
>
> Generous seasoning freshly ground black pepper
>
> Oil or cornmeal for baking the pizzas
>
> ½ cup sour cream
>
> 4½ cups grated fontina cheese

1. Make the pizza dough as directed. **2.** While the dough is rising, make the topping. Heat the oil in a large skillet over medium heat and add the onions. Cook, stirring frequently, until the onions are golden brown all over, about 20 minutes. Mix in the mushrooms and cook until brown and juicy, about 5 minutes. Remove the pan from the heat and season with thyme, salt, and pepper. **3.** Preheat the oven to 450 degrees. If you are using a pizza stone, heat it at least 45 minutes before cooking the pizza on it. **4.** Punch down the dough and place it on a work surface. Divide it into 3. Lightly flour the work surface, then use a rolling pin to roll 1 portion of the dough into an 11-inch circle. If the dough resists stretching, let it rest a few minutes, then roll again. If you are using a pizza stone, sprinkle some cornmeal on a pizza peel and place the dough on the peel; otherwise, lightly grease a baking sheet and place the dough on it. **5.** Spread ⅓ of the sour cream all over the dough. Sprinkle on ⅓ of the fontina cheese, then scatter ⅓ of the mushroom mixture over all. If you are cooking the pizza on a baking stone, bake 8–10 minutes, or until the crust is golden brown underneath. If cooked on a baking sheet, the pizza will take a few minutes longer. Repeat with the remaining ingredients.

Grilling Pizzas

Cooking pizzas on an outdoor grill is a lot of fun, and it produces an incomparable smoky flavor and chewy crust. Roll or stretch the dough into rounds no more than 8 inches in diameter (so they are easy to handle) and brush both sides with a little olive oil. Place the dough on the grill and cook about 3 minutes on each side, or until golden. Remove and cover with your favorite toppings, then return to the grill. Close the cover and cook until the cheese has melted, about 3 minutes. Remove from the grill, cut into wedges, and serve.

FRESH MOZZARELLA, TOMATO, AND BASIL PIZZA

This is a variation of the aristocrat of all pizzas, Pizza Margherita. It seems that Queen Margherita di Savoia (Margaret of Savoy) sampled pizza in Naples that had the red (tomato), white (fresh mozzarella), and green (fresh basil) colors of the Italian flag, and she became an ardent fan. It was quickly named for her and became a great success. The toppings are vivid and fresh. In this variation I cook some garlic with the tomatoes for just a few minutes because I love the way the garlic enhances the other flavors. If you cannot find fresh mozzarella, you can substitute the packaged variety, but there will be some loss in sweetness and texture.

MAKES 2 (12-INCH) PIZZAS
SERVES 4

Classic Pizza Dough (page 176) or other pizza dough from this chapter

Cornmeal for sprinkling or olive oil for greasing

4 tablespoons olive oil, divided

6 plum tomatoes, seeded and minced

4 garlic cloves, minced

Salt to taste

Freshly ground black pepper to taste

⅔ cup (4 ounces) sliced fresh mozzarella
(quarter-size pieces)

½ cup grated or shaved Parmesan cheese

12 large basil leaves, stacked, tightly
rolled, and thinly sliced into shreds
(chiffonade)

1. Prepare the pizza dough according to the recipe. **2.** Preheat the oven to 450 degrees. If you are using a pizza stone, heat it at least 45 minutes before cooking the pizza on it. **3.** Lightly flour the work surface. Punch down the dough and divide it in half. Use a rolling pin to roll 1 portion of the dough into a 12-inch circle. If the dough resists stretching, let it rest a few minutes, then roll again. **4.** If you are using a pizza stone, sprinkle some cornmeal on a pizza peel and place 1 circle of dough on the peel; otherwise, lightly grease a baking sheet and place the dough on it. **5.** Heat 2 tablespoons oil in a medium-size skillet over medium heat. Add the tomatoes and garlic, and sauté 5 minutes, or until the tomatoes have softened. Season generously with salt and pepper and let cool. **6.** Using half of the mixture, spoon little mounds all over 1 crust. Scatter half of the mozzarella and Parmesan cheeses alongside the tomato. **7.** Bake 12 minutes, or until the crust is golden underneath. Remove the pizza from the oven, immediately drizzle 1 tablespoon oil all over the top, and sprinkle with half the shredded basil. Serve immediately. Repeat with the remaining ingredients to make another pizza.

TIP: Plum tomatoes are preferred for pizzas (and sauces) because they have dense flesh and little juice. If you use another variety of fresh tomatoes, let them drain a bit in a bowl after you seed them and then discard the accumulated juice.

PIZZA WITH POTATOES, GARLIC, AND TOMATOES

Cheese-less pizzas have recently become popular in the United States, particularly on college campuses. This version can rival traditional pizza not only with its rich, garlicky flavor but also with its wonderful contrasting texture of tender potatoes and crisp crust.

MAKES 2 (12-INCH) PIZZAS
SERVES 4

Classic Pizza Dough (page 176)

4 cups peeled and diced (½ inch) boiling
potatoes (about 4 medium potatoes)
(see Tip)

1½ cups finely diced tomatoes, fresh or
canned

3 tablespoons olive oil, plus extra for
greasing

4 garlic cloves, pressed or minced

1½ teaspoons fresh rosemary, minced, or
½ teaspoon dried, finely crumbled

½ teaspoon salt

Generous seasoning freshly ground black
pepper

1. Preheat the oven to 450 degrees. If you are using a pizza stone, heat it at least 45 minutes before cooking the pizza on it. **2.** Lightly flour the work surface. Punch down the dough and place it on the work surface. Divide it in half. Use a rolling pin to roll 1 portion of the dough into a 12-inch circle. If the dough resists stretching, let it rest a few minutes, then roll again. If you are using a pizza stone, sprinkle some cornmeal on a pizza peel and place the circle of dough on the peel; otherwise, lightly grease a baking sheet and place the dough on it. In either case, to prevent the dough from rising again, place it in the refrigerator until the topping is ready. **3.** Fill a medium-size saucepan halfway with water and bring to a boil. Add the potatoes and cook until tender, about 10 minutes. Drain thoroughly and place in a bowl. Let cool to room temperature, then stir in the tomatoes. **4.** Heat the oil in a small skillet over medium heat. Add the garlic and cook only about 15 seconds, or just enough to get rid of its raw taste. Do not let it get at all brown. Pour it over the potatoes and toss. Mix in the rosemary, salt, and pepper. **5.** Spread half of the mixture on the pizza. Bake about 12 minutes if you are baking directly on a pizza stone; add a few minutes if you are using a baking sheet. Check the bottom of the crust to make sure it is golden brown. Cut the pizza into wedges. Make another pizza with the remaining ingredients.

TIP: Be sure to use a waxy, boiling potato such as the red-skinned variety. Baking (russet or Idaho) potatoes are too mealy for this topping and will fall apart when boiled.

PIZZA BIANCO

My 13-year-old son, Daniel, is extremely fond of white food. When we had this pizza in a restaurant one day, I knew it would have to be re-created at home and join our list of family favorites. A creamy, garlic-flecked layer of ricotta cheese rests beneath melted mozzarella, a simple triumph of flavor and texture.

MAKES 2 (12-INCH) PIZZAS

SERVES 4

> **Classic Pizza Dough (page 176) or other pizza dough from this chapter**
>
> **Cornmeal for sprinkling or olive oil for greasing**
>
> **1 cup ricotta cheese**
>
> **2 garlic cloves, put through a press or minced**
>
> **¼ cup grated Parmesan cheese**
>
> **3 cups grated mozzarella cheese**

1. Prepare the pizza dough according to the recipe. **2.** Preheat the oven to 450 degrees. If you are using a pizza stone, heat it at least 45 minutes before cooking the pizza on it.

3. Lightly flour the work surface. Punch down the dough and divide it in half. Use a rolling pin to roll 1 portion of the dough into a 12-inch circle. If the dough resists stretching, let it rest a few minutes, then roll again. If you are using a pizza stone, sprinkle some cornmeal on a pizza peel and place 1 circle of dough on the peel; otherwise, lightly grease a baking sheet and place the dough on it. **4.** Combine the ricotta cheese, garlic, and Parmesan cheese in a medium-size bowl. Spread half of the mixture on the pizza crust, leaving a 1-inch border. Sprinkle half of the mozzarella cheese on top. **5.** Bake 10–12 minutes if cooking directly on a baking stone. Add a few extra minutes if using a baking sheet. When done, the pizza will be golden on top and underneath. Repeat with the remaining ingredients to make another pizza.

TIP: You can spread a thin layer of minced cooked spinach (defrosted frozen spinach that has been squeezed dry is okay) over the ricotta layer for a delicious variation.

CARAMELIZED ONION, WALNUT, AND GOAT CHEESE PIZZA WITH A BEER CRUST

The slow caramelization of onions heightens their inherent sweetness and transforms them into a rich, soft mass that is superb when used as a "sauce" on pizza. The tang of goat cheese and the earthiness of the walnuts complete a trio of flavors that are hard to surpass. This pizza will bring rave reviews.

MAKES 2 (12-INCH) PIZZAS
SERVES 4

> 2 tablespoons olive oil
>
> 3 pounds (6 large) onions, very thinly sliced
>
> Salt
>
> Freshly ground black pepper
>
> ½ cup finely chopped (not ground) walnuts
>
> Beer Pizza Dough (page 178) or other pizza dough from this chapter
>
> 1½ cups (8 ounces) crumbled soft, mild goat cheese

1. Heat the oil in a large stockpot over medium heat. Add the onions and a generous amount of salt and pepper. Toss to coat well, then cover the pot. Cook, tossing occasionally, until the onions are very soft and are caramel brown all over. After 10 minutes or so, lower the heat to prevent sticking. The onions need to be cooked slowly over low heat to caramelize properly; this will take about 45 minutes. You can use less oil if you cook them *covered*. Remove the cover from the pan and stir in the walnuts. Cook 5 minutes, tossing frequently. Remove from the heat and let cool. (You can prepare the onions to this point and refrigerate them up to 2 days in advance.) **2.** Preheat the oven to 450 degrees. If you are going to cook your pizzas on a pizza stone, heat it at least 45 minutes. **3.** To assemble the pizzas, spread half the onion mixture on each prepared crust, then sprinkle with the crumbled goat cheese. If you are cooking the pizza on a baking sheet, you can use 2 pans and cook both pizzas at once. Place the pans on 2 different oven racks and alternate the pans halfway through the cooking. Bake 12–15 minutes, or until golden brown on top and underneath. Use a spatula to peek underneath the crust to make sure it is golden and well cooked.

QUICK PESTO PIZZA

I always seem to have pesto in my freezer in the dead of winter, and I use it when I want to evoke those enticing tastes of summer associated with fresh basil. For pesto lovers this pizza is a wonderful indulgence. If you can't get fresh basil, then try Winter Pesto or purchase some ready-made pesto.

MAKES 4 (8-INCH) PIZZAS
SERVES 4

> **Quick Baking Powder Pizza Dough (page 177) or other pizza dough from this chapter**
>
> **1⅓ cups Classic Pesto (page 19) or Winter Pesto (page 21)**
>
> **4 cups grated mozzarella cheese**

> **1⅓ cups diced roasted red peppers, store-bought or freshly roasted (page 24), patted very dry**
>
> **24 black olives, pitted and halved**

1. Preheat the oven to 450 degrees. If you are going to cook your pizzas on a pizza stone, heat it at least 45 minutes. Have the rolled crusts in front of you either on a pizza peel (1 crust) or on a baking sheet (2 crusts each). **2.** Divide the topping ingredients into 4 portions. Spread 1 portion of each ingredient on each pizza. Sprinkle on ¼ of the mozzarella cheese, then top with ¼ of the roasted peppers and olives. Bake 12–15 minutes, or until richly golden on top and underneath. Use a spatula to help you peek at the underside of the crust.

TORTILLA PIZZAS WITH FETA CHEESE, TOMATOES, AND OLIVES

This Greek-style topping is teeming with flavor and zest. Because no precooking is involved, it is extremely quick. Be certain to cut the zucchini paper-thin so that it will cook easily and quickly.

MAKES 4 (8-INCH) PIZZAS
SERVES 4

Tortilla Pizza Shells (page 179)

The Topping:

   4 plum tomatoes, finely diced

   12 black olives (such as Kalamata), pitted
      and halved

   1 medium zucchini, halved lengthwise and
      sliced paper-thin

   ½ cup thin slivers red onion

   4 teaspoons finely chopped fresh oregano,
      or 2 teaspoons dried

   Generous seasoning freshly ground black
      pepper

   3 tablespoons fruity olive oil

   8 ounces (1½ cups) finely crumbled feta
      cheese

1. Preheat the oven to 375 degrees. **2.** Place 2 cooked tortillas on each of 2 baking sheets. **3.** In a large bowl combine the tomatoes, olives, zucchini, onion slivers, oregano, pepper, and oil, and toss well. Gently fold in the feta cheese. Scatter all over the 4 tortillas. **4.** Bake 12 minutes, or until the feta is sizzling and the zucchini is softened. Alternate the placement of the baking sheets halfway during the cooking time. Cut and serve immediately.

SMOKED CHEESE, POTATO, AND SPINACH CALZONES

Frozen bread dough, which is readily available in most supermarkets and contains only flour, water, and yeast, allows you to make calzones quickly and with great results. Here the smoked cheese provides a wonderful backdrop without overpowering the more delicate flavors of the potato and spinach.

MAKES 4 CALZONES

   5 cups (5 ounces) spinach, stems discarded
      and leaves torn into small pieces

   2 medium boiling potatoes, peeled and cut
      into ½-inch dice (2 cups diced)

   1 scallion, very thinly sliced

   2 tablespoons olive oil, plus extra for
      greasing

   1 cup grated smoked mozzarella or Gouda
      cheese

   Salt to taste

   Freshly ground black pepper to taste

   1 pound frozen bread dough, thawed

   Flour for dusting

1. Fill a medium-size saucepan halfway with water and bring to a boil. Drop in the spinach and cook 30 seconds, or just until it wilts. Use tongs to scoop out the spinach and place in a strainer in the sink. Press out all the liquid from the spinach with the back of a large spoon. Put in a medium-size bowl. **2.** Let the water return to a boil. Add the potatoes and cook until tender, about 15 minutes. Drain thoroughly and combine with the spinach. Let cool, then mix in the scallion, oil, cheese, salt, and pepper. **3.** Preheat the oven to 375 degrees. Lightly oil a baking sheet. **4.** Divide the dough into 4 equal pieces and roll each piece into a ball. Place a small bowl of water in front of you. Lightly dust the work surface with some flour. Use a rolling pin to roll a ball of dough into a 7-inch circle, dusting the dough with a little flour as necessary. Dip your finger in the water and moisten the edge of the circle of dough. Spoon ¼ of the potato mixture on half of the circle, then fold over the dough to form a half-moon. Pinch the edges of the dough together, stretching the bottom layer slightly over the top as you pinch. Repeat with the remaining 3 portions. **5.** Place the calzones on the baking sheet. Use your fingers or a pastry brush to lightly coat the tops of the calzones with some oil. Bake 25 minutes, or until a deep golden brown. Let cool 15 minutes before eating to avoid being burned by the inner steam.

TIP: You can assemble the calzones up to 1 hour in advance, but they must be refrigerated to prevent the dough from rising. If the calzones are cold, they will take a few more minutes to cook.

CALZONE PIE

My inventive brother-in-law, Roland Dufresne, gave me the idea for this charming, rustic vegetable pie. Here a double crust pie made with pizza dough is filled with a garlicky potato, vegetable, and cheese filling. It resembles a giant calzone but is round instead of being a turnover. Like calzone and pizza, I prefer to eat this with my hands, but you can top it with tomato sauce as Roland does and serve it with a fork and knife. A salad would go well alongside each serving.

SERVES 4

> 2 medium boiling potatoes, peeled and cut into ½-inch dice (2 cups diced)
>
> 2 tablespoons olive oil, plus extra for greasing
>
> 2 medium zucchini, cut lengthwise into quarters and thinly sliced
>
> 6 garlic cloves, minced
>
> 1 (14-ounce) can ready-diced tomatoes, well drained
>
> ½ teaspoon oregano
>
> ½ teaspoon salt
>
> Generous seasoning freshly ground pepper
>
> ¼ cup grated Parmesan cheese
>
> 1 pound frozen pizza dough, thawed and at room temperature
>
> Flour for dusting
>
> 1 cup grated mozzarella cheese

1. Fill a saucepan halfway with water and bring to a boil. Add the potatoes and boil until tender, about 10 minutes. Drain well and let cool. 2. Heat the oil in a large skillet over medium heat until hot. Add the zucchini and sauté until crisp but tender, about 5 minutes. Sprinkle on the garlic and sauté 2 minutes. Stir in the tomatoes, oregano, salt, and pepper, and cook 2 minutes more. Remove from the heat, stir in the Parmesan cheese, and let cool. 3. Preheat the oven to 400 degrees. Lightly oil a large baking sheet. 4. Divide the pizza dough into 2 equal pieces. Lightly flour a work surface and shape each piece into a perfect ball. Roll 1 ball into an 11- or 12-inch circle, dusting the top of the dough as necessary. Place the circle on the baking sheet. (If the dough resists being rolled easily, let sit a few minutes to relax the gluten, then try again.) 5. Spoon the vegetable filling all over the dough, leaving a 1-inch border. With a little water moisten the border with your fingers. Top with the mozzarella cheese. Pull the bottom edge of the dough over the top edge, pinch together, and seal the edges. Prepare the other ball of dough in the same way. 6. Brush each pie with some oil. Cut a steam vent in the center of the pie. Bake 20–25 minutes, or until golden all over. Remove from the oven and brush again with oil. Remove the pie from the baking sheet and cool on a wire rack for 10 minutes. Cut into wedges and serve.

Vegetarian Classics

TOFU AND TEMPEH

Probably no food has given a bad name to vegetarian cooking more than tofu. Jokes abound about its wobbly texture and flavorless character, and it is often implied that vegetarian cooking must be inferior to other cuisines if tofu is part of it. To that I say, "You're being cheated." It's true that tofu can be quite unappetizing if not prepared properly. But when it is roasted or fried until brown and crispy and then mixed with a flavorful assortment of ingredients, it will absorb some of those flavors and be delicious. If you are not a fan of tofu, I highly recommend that you try some recipes in this chapter and give tofu a second chance. If you already enjoy tofu, then these recipes will offer you a wide variety of dishes that highlight tofu in a special way.

Less familiar to some people but also delicious is tempeh. The texture and flavor of this Indonesian staple are completely different from tofu, although it is also made of soy. Cooking with tempeh is a great way to include high-quality protein in your meals with little effort.

Read about tempeh and tofu on pages 14–15 to familiarize yourself with these incredibly versatile foods.

See also Composed Salad Platter (page 88) and Vegetable Fried Rice (page 255).

ROASTED TOFU

There is no more delicious way to serve tofu than roasted and chilled. You can then add it to pasta salads, green salads, and Asian noodle dishes, or just eat it as is. It also becomes the ideal portable lunch when packed in a plastic container. If you have some reluctant tofu eaters at your house, this is the best way to introduce them to this much maligned food. A similar recipe is also in my previous book,

Simple Vegetarian Pleasures. Because it is so basic to the vegetarian kitchen, I thought I'd also offer it here.

SERVES 2–4

    1 pound extra-firm tofu

    1½ tablespoons tamari soy sauce

    1 tablespoon Asian sesame oil

    1 tablespoon dry sherry

1. Slice the tofu into ½-inch-thick slices. Place them on a clean cotton towel or on paper towels. Use another towel or more paper towels to pat the tofu very dry. Cut each slice in half vertically, then cut the pieces into triangles, or cut the slices into ¾-inch cubes. **2.** Combine the soy sauce, sesame oil, and sherry in a large bowl. Add the tofu and use a rubber spatula to gently toss it with the marinade. Let marinate at least 30 minutes, or cover and chill up to 24 hours. **3.** Preheat the oven to 450 degrees. **4.** Place the tofu and its marinade in a single layer in a large shallow baking dish. Bake 25–30 minutes, or until golden all over. Shake the dish after 15 minutes to prevent the tofu from sticking. You can serve the tofu warm, but it is even more delicious when cooled to room temperature and then chilled until very cold, about 2 hours.

Drying Tofu Before Cooking It

Whether tofu is sold in an open bin or in refrigerated sealed packages, it will be wet from the liquid it sits in and must be dried before it can brown properly. Wet tofu is the major cause of its not cooking properly, so you must take the time to rid it of excess moisture. There are two ways you can do this. The first method, the towel method, produces the best results. You simply slice the block of tofu into ½-inch-thick slices and lay them on one end of a cotton or linen kitchen towel. Fold the unused section over and gently press the tofu to absorb its moisture. You can also lay the tofu slices on paper towels and use some fresh, dry ones to pat the tofu dry. Repeat this a few times until the tofu seems quite dry. After you cut the tofu into the size pieces you want for your recipe, pat them again to absorb any moisture that comes to the surface.

An alternate method is to "press" tofu. Place the block of tofu on a large dinner plate, cover with a smaller plate, and position a heavy can on top of the small plate. Put a small spoon under one end of the large plate so that it tips slightly. This will allow the moisture that is released to pour into a corner. Let the tofu rest this way for about 1 hour. Discard any accumulated water, then slice the tofu into ½-inch-thick slices. Pat the slices with some paper towels to absorb any remaining moisture.

As you can see, both methods require patting with towels, but the second approach needs less towel work because much of the tofu's liquid will have drained away.

CRISPY SAUTÉED MARINATED TOFU

Here is another basic way to prepare tofu. This method uses a nonstick skillet and produces results similar to roasting. When I don't want to use my oven, this is how I make tofu with great taste and texture.

SERVES 2–4

> 1 pound extra-firm tofu
>
> 2 tablespoons tamari soy sauce
>
> 1 tablespoon Asian sesame oil
>
> 1 tablespoon canola oil

1. Slice the tofu into ½-inch-thick slices and lay them on one end of a cotton kitchen towel or on paper towels. Use the remaining half of the towel or more paper towels to pat the tofu very dry. Cut into ½-inch cubes and pat dry again. **2.** combine the soy sauce and sesame oil in a large bowl. Drop in the tofu and use a rubber spatula to gently toss it around in the marinade. Let marinate 20–30 minutes, or cover and refrigerate up to 8 hours. **3.** Heat the canola oil in a large nonstick skillet over medium-high heat. When the oil is very hot but not yet smoking, add the tofu. Cook until it is golden underneath, about 5 minutes. Shake the pan occasionally to prevent it from sticking. Use a spatula to toss the tofu around until it is golden all over, another 5–7 minutes. Place the tofu on a large plate and let cool. Serve barely warm or at room temperature, or chill until very cold. This tofu can be eaten alone, mixed into stir-fries, or tossed into salads.

CLASSIC STIR-FRIED TOFU AND VEGETABLES HOISIN

Here's a favorite stir-fry that has appeared over the years with many variations. I like broccoli and red peppers together, but carrots, snow peas, mushrooms, and green peppers are also good choices. The tofu becomes crisp and absorbs the delightfully sweet and spicy overtones of the hoisin sauce. This tasty dish is a good choice for tofu newcomers.

SERVES 4

> ¼ cup hoisin sauce (see page 10)
>
> 2 tablespoons tamari soy sauce
>
> 1 tablespoon Chinese rice wine or sherry
>
> 1 tablespoon Asian sesame oil
>
> 4 tablespoons canola oil, divided
>
> 1 pound extra-firm tofu, cut into ½-inch slices and patted very dry, then cut into ½-inch cubes and patted very dry again
>
> 5–6 cups tiny broccoli florets
>
> 1 red bell pepper, cut into 1-inch dice
>
> 3 tablespoons water

1 teaspoon minced fresh ginger

4 garlic cloves, minced

4 cups hot cooked rice (made from 1 cup
    raw rice)

1. To make the sauce combine the hoisin sauce, tamari, wine, and sesame oil, and set aside. **2.** Over medium-high heat, heat 2 tablespoons canola oil in a large nonstick skillet or wok until very hot but not smoking. Add the tofu and let sit 1 minute or so to brown. Shake the skillet a few times to prevent sticking. Toss the tofu and cook until evenly golden all over. Remove to a platter. **3.** Place the broccoli and red pepper in the skillet, toss, then add the water. Cover the pan and cook until all the water has evaporated and the broccoli is beginning to get tender yet is still quite crisp, about 3 minutes. **4.** Make a well in the center of the pan and pour in the remaining 2 tablespoons canola oil. Add the ginger and garlic, stir a few seconds, then toss with the vegetables. Add the tofu and stir-fry until hot, about 1 minute. Pour the sauce over the mixture and stir-fry 30 seconds. Serve over hot rice.

TIP: As with all stir-fried dishes, make sure you have all the ingredients laid out before you begin cooking. Have your rice completely cooked, covered, and kept warm over low heat before the stir-frying begins. Keep the skillet or wok very hot when stir-frying.

STIR-FRIED SZECHUAN TOFU, BROCCOLI, AND MUSHROOMS

Pairing tofu with a spicy sauce is a popular treatment both in the Chinese provinces of Sichuan and Hunan and in American vegetarian kitchens. Hot but not overpowering, this stir-fry gets its rich flavor from the chili paste, a condiment now found readily in the Asian section of most supermarkets.

SERVES 4

The Sauce:

2 teaspoons cornstarch

¼ cup water

1 tablespoon chili paste with garlic
    (see page 8)

¼ cup tamari soy sauce

¼ cup sherry

1 teaspoon sugar

The Vegetables:

3 tablespoons canola oil

1 pound extra-firm tofu, cut into ½-inch
    slices and patted very dry, then cut into
    ½-inch cubes and patted very dry again

3 cups (8 ounces) sliced mushrooms

5–6 cups tiny broccoli florets (from 1
    bunch broccoli)

2 carrots, very thinly sliced on the diagonal

The Season for Soy

Many Asian cultures and vegetarians all over the world have long recognized the value of soy foods. Tofu is as common in China as beef is in the United States. Tempeh has been a staple food in Indonesia for hundreds of years. For vegetarians the soybean is prized as a source of complete protein, containing all the essential amino acids. No other plant food holds this honor.

The United States produces about 75 percent of the world's soybean crop, but its use in this country has been mostly limited to feeding cattle. There are signs, however, that this is changing. Many recent studies have shown the numerous benefits of eating a diet rich in soy foods. The isoflavones present in soy products are thought to lower cholesterol, minimize menopausal symptoms in women, and perhaps help to reduce women's risk of breast cancer. Soy products such as soy cheese, soy milk, mock meats made of soy, soy nuts, tofu, and tempeh are now on the shelves in most supermarkets. Soy is slowly moving into the mainstream. No longer are these foods associated only with vegetarians, as they were in the 1960s, because they are enjoyed by many health-conscious people who want to reap the benefits of eating soy.

¼ **cup water**

**4 cups hot cooked rice (made from
   1 cup raw rice)**

1. Place the cornstarch in a small bowl and stir in the water until smooth. Stir in all the remaining sauce ingredients. Set aside. **2.** Heat the oil in a large, preferably nonstick, skillet over medium-high heat until very hot but not smoking. Add the tofu and stir-fry until deeply golden all over. Remove the tofu to a plate and set aside. **3.** Add the mushrooms to the pan and stir-fry until they begin to release their juices. Stir in the broccoli and carrots, then pour in the water. Cover the pan and cook about 5 minutes, or until the broccoli begins to get tender but is still a bright green. **4.** Return the tofu to the pan and toss. Stir the sauce once again and quickly add to the pan. Toss a few seconds until it thickens. Serve immediately over hot rice.

TIP: As with all stir-fried dishes, make sure you have all the ingredients laid out before you begin cooking. Have your rice completely cooked, covered, and kept warm over low heat before the stir-frying begins. Keep the skillet or wok very hot when stir-frying.

Tofu and Tempeh

PENNE WITH ROASTED TOFU, SPINACH, AND RED PEPPERS IN GARLIC SAUCE

The garlicky overtones saturate all the ingredients, making this a tasty dish. With the juxtaposition of chunks of roasted tofu, silken strands of fresh spinach, and slightly crisp strips of red pepper, we get a panoply of textures that, combined with the sauce, make this pasta a triumph.

SERVES 4–6

Roasted Tofu:

    1 tablespoon tamari soy sauce

    1 tablespoon Asian sesame oil

    1 pound extra-firm tofu, sliced ½ inch thick, patted very dry, then cut into ½-inch cubes

The Sauce:

    ¼ cup olive oil

    1 red bell pepper, cut into strips ½ × 2 inches

    6 large garlic cloves, minced

    ¼ teaspoon crushed red pepper flakes

    One 12-ounce package triple-washed spinach, stems discarded and leaves torn

    ½ cup vegetable stock, store-bought or homemade (page 18)

    ½ teaspoon salt

    1 pound penne

    Freshly grated Parmesan cheese

1. Preheat the oven to 450 degrees. **2.** Combine the soy sauce and oil in a medium-size bowl. Stir the dry tofu into the mixture and toss to coat. Let sit at least 20 minutes or up to 2 hours. **3.** Spread the tofu in a baking dish in 1 layer. Bake about 25 minutes, or until golden all over. Toss with a spatula halfway during the cooking time. Let the tofu cool while you prepare the pasta; it will get firmer. You can roast the tofu up to 24 hours in advance, if desired. **4.** Bring a large stockpot of water to a boil for the penne. **5.** To make the sauce, heat the oil in a large skillet over medium heat. Add the red pepper and sauté until tender yet crisp, about 5 minutes. Stir in the garlic and red pepper flakes, and toss well. Cook 2 minutes, stirring often. Mix in the spinach, stock, and salt, and cover the pan. Cook just until the spinach wilts, about 2 minutes. Remove the cover and stir in the tofu. Keep the heat low while you cook the penne. **6.** Put the penne in the boiling water and cook until al dente, about 12–15 minutes. Drain thoroughly and return to the pot. Stir in the vegetables and sauce along with a handful of Parmesan cheese. Toss well. Serve immediately with extra Parmesan cheese at the table.

PAD THAI
WITH CRISPY TOFU

This classic Thai noodle dish has become popular since Thai restaurants began to spring up all over the country. The added golden pieces of tofu absorb the sweet and spicy sauce. Traditionally pad thai is made with rice stick noodles. These clear, flat noodles can be purchased in Asian food shops and many health food stores. Although it changes the final dish in texture and appearance, I have in a pinch substituted linguine for the rice stick noodles with good results. The tasty sauce and additions are delicious with both types of noodles.

SERVES 3–4

The Sauce:

¼ cup tomato paste

⅓ cup firmly packed brown sugar

¼ cup tamari soy sauce

3 tablespoons lime juice

½ teaspoon Asian sesame oil

1 garlic clove, minced

½ teaspoon chili paste with garlic (see page 8) or ¼ teaspoon crushed red pepper flakes

8 ounces dried rice stick noodles (⅛ inch wide)

3 tablespoons canola oil

1 pound extra-firm tofu, sliced ½ inch thick, patted *very* dry, and cut into ½-inch cubes

2 large eggs, well beaten

⅓ cup chopped roasted peanuts

1 cup bean sprouts

2 scallions, cut into 2-inch lengths and shredded lengthwise

1. Mix all the sauce ingredients together in a small bowl and set aside. **2.** Bring a large stockpot of water to a boil. Drop in the rice stick noodles and toss very well with tongs to make sure they don't stick together. Cook 2–3 minutes, or until al dente. Make sure the noodles are still slightly firm because they will soften further when stir-fried. Drain thoroughly in a colander and rinse under cold running water. Drain again. **3.** Heat 1½ tablespoons oil in a large nonstick skillet over medium-high heat. When the oil is very hot, add the tofu. Stir-fry until golden all over. Place the tofu on a platter. **4.** Add a half-tablespoon oil to the pan. Pour in the eggs and quickly cook like a pancake. Remove to a plate and cut into bite-size pieces. **5.** Pour the remaining tablespoon of oil in the skillet. Add the noodles, tofu, eggs, peanuts, and bean sprouts, and mix with tongs. Pour on the sauce and toss to coat well. Cook until hot throughout, about 3 minutes. Sprinkle on the scallions, toss, and serve.

GRILLED OR ROASTED TOFU SATAY

Satay is an Indonesian shish kebab coated with a heady coconut-peanut sauce. The spiciness of curry, the sweetness of the coconut milk, and the deep, rich flavor of peanut butter commingle to create a seductive blending of flavors. You can thread the tofu onto skewers and grill it or lay the chunks in a baking dish to roast them. Either way, you'll have an electrifying dish.

SERVES 6

The Marinade:

    2 tablespoons tamari soy sauce

    2 tablespoons Asian sesame oil

    2 tablespoons sherry

    2 pounds extra-firm tofu, sliced 1 inch thick and patted very dry, then cut into 1-inch cubes and patted again

    1 red bell pepper, cut into 1-inch squares

The Sauce:

    ¾ cup canned coconut milk (see Tip)

    ½ cup natural-style peanut butter, smooth or chunky

    2 garlic cloves, minced

    1½ teaspoons curry powder

    1½ tablespoons brown sugar

    1 tablespoon lime juice

    1 tablespoon canola oil

    1½ tablespoons tamari soy sauce

    Dash cayenne pepper

1. Combine the marinade ingredients in a large bowl. Add the dry tofu and red pepper and toss gently with a rubber spatula to coat evenly. Let marinate 30 minutes or up to 8 hours. Refrigerate if longer than 1 hour. **2.** Prepare the grill or preheat the oven to 450 degrees. **3.** To make the sauce, place all the sauce ingredients in a food processor and blend until smooth. Pour into a decorative serving bowl. **4.** Remove about ⅓ cup of the sauce and drizzle it over the tofu. Use the rubber spatula to toss the tofu gently with the sauce. If you are grilling the satay, thread the tofu and red peppers on skewers. (Bamboo skewers must be soaked for 30 minutes.) If you are roasting the tofu in the oven, place it in 1 layer in a large, shallow baking dish such as a 9 × 13-inch lasagna pan. Use 2 pans if one pan isn't large enough. **5.** Cook the tofu on the hot grill at least 20 minutes, turning it occasionally, or roast in the oven for 25 minutes. The tofu is done when it is a deep golden brown. Let the tofu cool to room temperature before serving. Serve alongside the bowl of sauce for dipping.

TIP: Canned coconut milk sometimes separates so that there is a thick, pasty mass at the top of the can and thin liquid on the bottom. Also, if the can has been kept in a cool cupboard, the milk will appear solid rather than liquid. In either case, stir the coconut milk before measuring it. Once heated, the coconut milk will thin out.

Vegetarian Classics

ROASTED TOFU SALAD

Golden morsels of chewy tofu marinated in a garlicky dressing is an easy and zesty way to include tofu in your meal planning. This salad can be treated as a main couse by placing it on a bed of greens, or it can be served as a side dish to a sandwich, or it can be packed in a container and made into a portable lunch. However you serve this salad, you'll find it is as popular with tofu lovers as with newcomers.

SERVES 4

> 2 pounds extra-firm tofu
>
> 3 tablespoons tamari soy sauce
>
> 2 tablespoons Asian sesame oil
>
> Canola or olive oil for greasing pan
>
> 1 celery rib, very thinly sliced
>
> ¼ cup thin red onion slivers
>
> 1 carrot, very thinly sliced
>
> ¼ cup finely chopped fresh parsley

The Dressing:

> 2 tablespoons lemon juice
>
> 1 garlic clove, put through a press or minced
>
> ½ teaspoon Dijon-style mustard
>
> ¼ teaspoon salt
>
> Generous seasoning freshly ground pepper
>
> 2½ tablespoons olive oil

1. Pat the tofu very dry with a linen kitchen towel or paper towels. Slice it into ½-inch-thick slices and lay them on the towel(s). Pat the slices very dry, replacing the towels as necessary. Cut the tofu into ½-inch cubes and pat dry again. **2.** Combine the soy sauce and sesame oil in a large bowl. Add the tofu and toss gently with a rubber spatula, until evenly coated. Let marinate at least 30 minutes, or up to 4 hours. Refrigerate if longer than 30 minutes. **3.** Preheat the oven to 450 degrees. Very lightly grease a 17 × 11 × 2-inch baking sheet. **4.** Spread the tofu on the baking sheet in 1 layer. Bake 20–25 minutes, or until the tofu is a deep golden color all over. Halfway through the cooking time use a spatula to flip the tofu over so it browns evenly. Let the tofu cool to room temperature. **5.** Meanwhile, put the celery, onion slivers, carrot, and parsley in a large serving bowl. **6.** Place all the dressing ingredients in a jar with a tight-fitting lid and shake vigorously **7.** Mix the tofu with the vegetables, then pour on the dressing and toss. Chill at least 1 hour before serving for the flavors to blend and for the tofu to become firmer.

TIP: Blanched, chilled vegetables can be a delicious and colorful addition to this salad. Try broccoli, green beans, asparagus, or red bell peppers, and increase the dressing by half to help coat the additional vegetables.

CLASSIC TOFU "EGGLESS" SALAD

Gaining its yellow color from the addition of turmeric and its minced hard-boiled egg texture from finely chopped firm tofu, this egg salad–like sandwich filling has won over many reluctant tofu samplers. It's become a vegetarian staple over the years because it makes delicious sandwiches that transport well.

MAKES 4 SANDWICHES

> 8 ounces extra-firm tofu, patted very dry
>
> ¼ teaspoon turmeric
>
> 2 tablespoons mayonnaise
>
> 1 scallion, very thinly sliced
>
> ⅛ teaspoon celery seed
>
> ¼ teaspoon salt
>
> Freshly ground black pepper to taste

1. Place the tofu on a cotton or linen kitchen towel and gather up the corners. Twist the tofu into a ball and squeeze out all its liquid. Place the tofu in a medium-size bowl and mash with a fork until it resembles coarse crumbs the size of pine nuts. **2.** Mix in all the remaining ingredients. Cover and chill the mixture for at least 30 minutes. It will become a brighter yellow, and the flavors will meld. Serve as a sandwich spread with lettuce or sprouts on sliced bread or in pita bread.

ROASTED TOFU SANDWICHES

Thin slices of tofu roasted until golden brown and then chilled are excellent additions to sandwiches, and even more so when topped with lettuce and tomato. You can prepare the tofu early in the week so it will be readily available for sandwiches.

MAKES 4 SANDWICHES

> 1 pound extra-firm tofu
>
> 2 tablespoons tamari soy sauce
>
> 2 tablespoons Asian sesame oil
>
> ¼ cup mayonnaise
>
> 8 slices bread
>
> 8 slices tomato
>
> 4 lettuce leaves

1. Preheat the oven to 450 degrees. **2.** Slice the tofu into ½-inch-thick slices; you should get about 10 slices. Lay them on one end of a cotton kitchen towel or on paper towels and pat very dry with the remaining half of the towel or more paper towels. For a successful browning the tofu must be as dry as possible. **3.** Place the tofu slices in 1 layer in a shallow baking dish such as a 12 × 7 × 2-inch Pyrex dish. **4.** In a small cup mix the soy sauce and sesame oil together. Pour a little of the mixture on each slice of tofu and use your fingers to rub it evenly over the surface. Flip the tofu over and repeat on the other side. **5.** Bake the tofu for 10 minutes. With a spatula flip each slice over and return the dish to the oven. Bake 10 minutes more, or until golden. Let the tofu cool completely, then chill until ice cold. **6.** Spread the mayonnaise on the bread slices. Place 2½ slices of tofu on 4 slices of bread. Top with the tomato, lettuce, and remaining bread to make 4 sandwiches. Cut each sandwich in half.

Spices Versus Herbs

What should they be called, spices or herbs? Well, it depends. Spices are aromatic products that come from the seeds, bark, or stems of plants, and they are grown in the tropics. Herbs, on the other hand, are the leaves of plants, and they grow in temperate regions.

It is fascinating to contemplate how the quest for tropical spices helped shape history by stimulating world trade and exploration. Although spice trading took place as early as 1450 B.C. in Egypt with the importing of cinnamon, it was the Romans' nearly insatiable demand for exotic spices in the first century A.D. that transformed the pursuit of spices into a world-shaping force. The allure of the Asian tropics was, in fact, instrumental in the discovery of America. Christopher Columbus sought a western route to India . . . and the rest is history. All for a little black pepper.

TEMPEH RAGOUT WITH CORN, ZUCCHINI, AND TOMATOES

Simmering tempeh in an aromatic sauce tenderizes it and tones down its flavor to make it marry well with the other ingredients. Because this ragout has potatoes in it, you can serve it as a meal unto itself, as one would serve a stew, and accompany it with some crusty French bread to sop up the juices.

SERVES 4

¼ cup olive oil

4 large garlic cloves, minced

¼ teaspoon crushed red pepper flakes

1 (14-ounce) can ready-cut diced tomatoes with their juice

3 medium boiling potatoes, peeled and cut into ½-inch dice (no bigger) (4½ cups)

1 cup water

8 ounces tempeh, cut into ½-inch dice

2 medium zucchini, cut into ½-inch cubes

1½ cups frozen corn, thawed

½ teaspoon salt

¼ cup finely chopped fresh basil or ½ teaspoon dried basil and ¼ cup minced fresh parsley

1. Heat the oil in a large skillet or medium-size stockpot over medium heat. Add the garlic and crushed pepper flakes, and cook 2 minutes. Do not let the garlic get at all brown. Pour in the tomatoes and simmer 2 minutes. 2. Stir in the potatoes and water, and cover the pan. Simmer about 15 minutes, or until the potatoes are almost tender. Remove the cover and stir the mixture occasionally to prevent sticking. 3. Mix in the tempeh and zucchini, and cover the pot. Simmer the ragout until the zucchini and potatoes are tender, about 15 minutes. Check the liquid during this period. If the ragout seems dry rather than stewlike, add a bit more water. 4. Add the corn, salt, and basil, and simmer 2 minutes. Serve at once.

Tip: If you intend to make this ragout in advance, don't add the basil until just before serving.

CLASSIC TEMPEH SANDWICH SPREAD

This tempeh sandwich spread, which resembles chicken salad in flavor, has been a favorite among vegetarians for years. It is especially good when spread on white or oatmeal bread rather than a dark, whole-grain bread, and topped with lettuce and tomato.

Makes 3 sandwiches

1 tablespoon canola oil

1 (8-ounce) package tempeh, very finely chopped

¼ cup minced red onion

1 celery rib, very thinly sliced

¼ cup mayonnaise

1. Heat the oil in a medium-size, preferably nonstick, skillet over medium heat. Add the tempeh and sauté until lightly golden, about 5 minutes. Scrape it into a medium-size bowl and let cool. 2. Mix in all the remaining ingredients. Cover and chill until ready to use.

GOLDEN TEMPEH SANDWICHES

Cutlets of tempeh that have been drizzled with soy sauce and sautéed until golden make a great base for sandwiches both hot and cold. Here tempeh is matched with a tangy honey mustard dressing that enhances its nutty flavor. When I make this sandwich for lunch at home, I use yogurt in the dressing, but for a portable lunch I have found that a mayonnaise-based version holds up better and won't make the bread soggy. Both dressings are delicious.

Makes 4 sandwiches

8 ounces tempeh

2 tablespoons canola oil

2 tablespoons tamari soy sauce

The Dressing:

⅓ cup plain yogurt or mayonnaise,
   or a combination of both

1½ tablespoons Dijon-style mustard

1 tablespoon honey

8 slices bread or 4 round sandwich rolls
   cut in half

8 pieces red leaf lettuce

1. Cut the tempeh in half crosswise (vertically), then cut each piece in half horizontally to make 4 thin cutlets. **2.** Heat the oil in a large nonstick skillet over medium heat. When it is hot, fry the cutlets until golden brown on both sides, about 7 minutes. Remove the tempeh to a platter. Drizzle ½ tablespoon soy sauce on each slice and rub it in with your fingers (the tempeh will readily absorb it). Let cool to warm or room temperature. **3.** To make the dressing, mix the yogurt (or mayonnaise), mustard, and honey together in a small bowl. Spread the dressing on all the bread slices, top with the tempeh and lettuce, and close the sandwich.

TIP: Toasted bread is especially good for these sandwiches.

BARBECUED TEMPEH CUTLETS FOR SANDWICHES

Thin cutlets of tempeh that have been glazed with barbecue sauce and sautéed until deeply browned become tasty additions to sandwiches. With lettuce, tomato, and onion piled on you have a meal in a flash.

MAKES 4 SANDWICHES

Barbecue Sauce:

½ cup ketchup

2 tablespoons firmly packed brown sugar

2 teaspoons apple cider vinegar

1 tablespoon lemon juice

2 teaspoons chili powder

1 teaspoon dry mustard powder

¼ teaspoon salt

A few dashes Tabasco

8 ounces tempeh

1 tablespoon canola oil (approximately)

Sandwich additions: mayonnaise, lettuce,
   tomato, thinly sliced onion, bread

1. To make the barbecue sauce, place all the sauce ingredients in a small bowl and mix well. **2.** Slice the tempeh in half vertically. Cut each piece in half horizontally to make 4 thin cutlets. **3.** Heat the oil in a large nonstick skillet over medium heat. Brush some barbecue sauce on both sides of each tempeh piece and place in the hot skillet. Sauté on both sides until a deep golden brown, about 10 minutes total. Remove to a plate and brush some more sauce on one side of each cutlet. You'll probably have some leftover sauce. Let the tempeh cool to room temperature. **4.** To make sandwiches, lightly spread some mayonnaise on some bread. Top with the tempeh, lettuce, tomato, and onion.

PERFECT PASTAS

Pasta and vegetables are like cookies and milk; that is, they are made for each other. The revelation in the 1970s (special thanks to Marcella Hazan) that Italian pasta dishes are much more than tomato sauce and Parmesan cheese was a culinary milestone for all food lovers—in particular vegetarians. It meant that we were no longer dependent on the trick of taking traditional meat dishes and making vegetarian versions. There was now a wellspring of sophisticated meatless pasta dishes that were vegetable-based by nature. Pesto, cream sauce, olive oil, and garlic were now replacing tomato sauce as the foundation of pasta preparations, and vegetables became their natural companions.

Take a look at Pasta Tips below to learn how to cook this basic food properly. Once you get a feel for proper amounts, cooking times, and matching shapes with the right sauces, you'll find it hard to resist improvising and making your own pasta creations.

See also:

■ Lasagnas and baked pasta dishes in Casseroles, Gratins, and Lasagnas, pages 218–42.

■ Pasta Salads in Main-Course Salads, pages 75–89.

■ Penne with Roasted Tofu, Spinach, and Red Peppers in Garlic Sauce (page 194).

■ Pad Thai with Crispy Tofu (page 195).

PASTA TIPS

■ One pound of dried pasta will feed three or four people, unless you invite my husband to dinner, in which case it will feed two.

With fresh pasta you'll need 1¼ pounds to feed four people. There is moisture in fresh noodles, so they weigh more before being cooked.

To cook pasta use a large stockpot filled at least halfway with water and bring to a vigorous boil. Some people like to salt the water generously, but I have never found this necessary. Drop in the pasta and stir until it rises to the surface. If you are cooking long, thin pasta such as spaghetti, it is best to use tongs to keep the pasta from sticking. After it rises you can reduce the stirring to only occasionally. Check the package directions for the cooking time, then sample a piece of the pasta about 2 minutes before it is supposed to be done. You want the pasta to be slightly chewy in the center.

Before draining the pasta, check to see if you are supposed to remove some of the starchy water to add to your sauce. Always drain pasta in a colander before adding it to the sauce. You can return the drained pasta to the pot and pour on the hot sauce or place it in a large pasta bowl. If you do the latter, be sure you have warmed up the bowl beforehand with some very hot water so it does not cool down the pasta too quickly. Toss well with the sauce and serve immediately.

SPAGHETTI PUTTANESCA

This classic vegetarian (no anchovies) version of puttanesca sauce is robust and complex, just as it should be. The sauce derives its name from the Italian for "streetwalker" because the flavors are bold and spicy. That it is very quick might also add to its meaning. In any event, it is a great tomato sauce that works with just about any shape of pasta.

SERVES 4

¼ cup olive oil

6 garlic cloves, minced

¼ teaspoon crushed red pepper flakes, or more for an extra-spicy version

2 cups canned crushed tomatoes or tomato puree

1 teaspoon oregano

Generous seasoning freshly ground black pepper

½ cup pitted, coarsely chopped black and green olives, such as Kalamata, Niçoise, and Picholine (see Tip)

2 teaspoons drained capers

½ cup finely chopped fresh parsley

1 pound spaghetti

1. Bring a large stockpot of water to a boil for the spaghetti. 2. To make the sauce, heat the oil in a 3-quart (or larger) saucepan over medium heat. (The sauce needs a lot of room to cook because it will splatter.) Add the garlic and red pepper flakes, and cook 1 minute. Do not let the garlic get at all colored. Add the tomatoes, oregano, pepper, olives, and capers, and simmer, partially covered to prevent splattering, for 20 minutes. Stir in the parsley and keep warm while the pasta cooks. 3. Cook the spaghetti until al dente. Drain thoroughly and return to the pot. Spoon on the sauce and toss well. Serve as is; it really doesn't need any cheese.

TIP: Pit olives just the way you would crush garlic—that is, lay the flat side of a large knife on an olive and give it a thump. The flesh will release itself from the pit. Discard the pits and chop the flesh.

SPAGHETTINI WITH SPINACH IN GARLIC-CREAM SAUCE

This flavorsome treatment of pasta is so easy that it almost seems like cheating, and the excellent results conceal its quickness. A judicious amount of cream gives the dish some panache without making it too rich.

SERVES 4

1 pound spaghettini

1 (10-ounce) bag triple-washed fresh spinach, stems discarded and leaves torn, or one (10-ounce) package frozen chopped spinach

3 tablespoons olive oil

3 large garlic cloves, put through a press or minced

½ cup heavy cream

½ cup milk

Pinch nutmeg

¾ teaspoon salt

Generous seasoning freshly ground black pepper

Grated Romano or Parmesan cheese to taste

1. Bring a large stockpot of water to a boil over high heat. Drop in the spaghettini and cook until barely done—that is, with about 2 minutes more to go until al dente. 2. Add the fresh or frozen spinach to the pasta and stir until wilted (if fresh) or thawed (if frozen), about 2 minutes. Drain everything in a colander and leave undisturbed. 3. Heat the oil in the same stockpot over medium-high heat. Add the garlic and cook 1 minute. Pour in the cream and milk, then stir in the drained pasta and spinach. Sprinkle on the nutmeg, salt, and pepper. Heat everything for 1 minute. Serve with Romano or Parmesan cheese on each serving.

SPAGHETTINI WITH CRISPY BROILED EGGPLANT

The rich flavor of crispy, browned eggplant marries well with this spicy tomato sauce to make a gutsy sauce for pasta.

SERVES 4

¼ cup plus 2 tablespoons olive oil

1 medium-large (1¼ pounds) eggplant, peeled and sliced ½ inch thick

6 garlic cloves, minced

¼ teaspoon crushed red pepper flakes

2 cups canned crushed tomatoes (preferably) or tomato puree

½ teaspoon dried oregano

¼ cup minced fresh parsley

½ teaspoon salt

1 pound spaghettini

3 tablespoons grated Parmesan cheese

1. Preheat the broiler. Bring a large quantity of water to a boil in a stockpot. **2.** Lightly brush ¼ cup oil on both sides of the eggplant slices and lay them on a baking sheet. Broil until a deep golden brown, flip over, and broil again until very brown. Let cool. Cut the slices into 1-inch-wide strips. **3.** To make the sauce, heat the remaining 2 tablespoons oil in a medium-size saucepan. Gently cook the garlic and red pepper flakes until they sizzle but are not colored at all, about 1 minute. Stir in the crushed tomatoes, oregano, parsley, and salt. Simmer, partially covered to prevent splattering, for 20 minutes. **4.** Cook the spaghettini until al dente, about 8 minutes. Drain thoroughly in a colander. **5.** Stir half of the eggplant into the sauce. Return the pasta to its pot, pour on the sauce, and sprinkle on the cheese. Toss gently. Serve with the remaining eggplant mounded on each portion.

TIPS: You can broil the eggplant a few hours in advance, but keep it at room temperature so you don't top the pasta with cold eggplant.

The sauce can be made up to 24 hours in advance and refrigerated.

PASTA WITH PESTO-CREAM SAUCE AND TOASTED PINE NUTS

Pesto on pasta has long been a simple favorite among vegetarians and non-vegetarians alike, but by adding a little cream to the pesto to lighten it, you can transform it into a luxurious sauce that is hard to beat. When paired with a long, thin pasta and topped with pine nuts, you have a dish of incomparable elegance.

SERVES 4

3 tablespoons pine nuts

½ cup Classic Pesto (page 19)

½ cup light cream or ¼ cup heavy cream and ¼ cup milk

Pasta

We've all heard the story of how Marco Polo brought noodles to Italy from China, or at least the idea for making noodles. It seems, however, that this legend has lingered because of its shock value rather than its accuracy. Upon a closer reading of Marco Polo's writings, food historians have discovered that when he said he "discovered" pasta in China, he went on to say "which are like ours." So let's just say that the Chinese and Italians enjoyed pasta concurrently (and, incidentally, along with the Indians and Arabs).

Today the average Italian eats about 65 pounds of pasta a year, most of it commercial dried pasta made from only semolina and water, which is then dried in ovens and packaged. Occasional forays to the fresh pasta shop are usually to purchase filled pastas, such as ravioli and tortellini, and also fresh fettuccine and tagliatelle, which are all made with an egg-based dough.

½ teaspoon salt

Generous seasoning freshly ground black pepper

1 pound pasta, such as spaghetti, vermicelli, or linguine

1. Bring a large stockpot of water to a boil for the pasta. **2.** Place the pine nuts in a small skillet over medium heat and toast, stirring constantly, until lightly golden, about 5 minutes. Place on a small plate and let cool. **3.** In a small bowl combine the pesto, cream, salt, and pepper **4.** Cook the pasta in the boiling water until al dente. Drain in a colander and leave undisturbed. **5.** Immediately pour the pesto-cream sauce into the stockpot and heat 30 seconds. Place the pasta back in the pot and quickly toss to coat it thoroughly. Serve at once, preferably in pasta bowls, with some pine nuts sprinkled on each portion.

LINGUINE WITH SPICY MUSHROOM RAGU

A Bolognese ragu is traditionally made with generous amounts of ground beef. Here mushrooms do the trick in creating a thick, richly-flavored tomato sauce that has just a hint of rosemary in it to enliven the finished dish while still letting the intoxicating mushroom flavor shine through.

SERVES 4

3 tablespoons olive oil

4 garlic cloves, minced

¼ teaspoon crushed red pepper flakes

1 pound common white mushrooms, thinly sliced

Perfect Pastas

1½ cups canned crushed tomatoes or tomato puree

⅛ teaspoon dried rosemary, crumbled

½ teaspoon salt

1 pound linguine

Grated Parmesan cheese to taste

1. Bring a large quantity of water to a boil in a stockpot. **2.** To make the sauce, heat the olive oil in a medium-size saucepan over medium heat. Add the garlic and crushed pepper flakes, and cook 30 seconds. Stir in the mushrooms and cook until brown and juicy, about 10 minutes. Mix in the tomatoes, rosemary, and salt, and cook, stirring often, for 10 minutes. If the sauce begins to splatter during cooking, lower the heat to medium-low. Keep the sauce warm while cooking the linguine. **3.** Drop the linguine into the boiling water and cook until al dente. Taste one along the way to avoid overcooking it. Drain thoroughly in a colander and return to the pot. Pour on the sauce and toss. Serve with a light sprinkling of Parmesan cheese.

FRESH LINGUINE WITH VEGETABLES AND PINE NUTS IN A TOMATO-CREAM SAUCE

Here is an elegant pasta dish that is ideal for entertaining. A small amount of cream gives this sauce a luscious flavor and opulent touch.

SERVES 4

¼ cup pine nuts

1 tablespoon olive oil

8 ounces sliced mushrooms (3 cups)

1 medium zucchini, quartered lengthwise and thinly sliced

4 garlic cloves, minced

1 cup canned tomato puree

½ cup heavy cream

½ teaspoon salt

Generous seasoning freshly ground pepper

1¼ pounds fresh linguine or fettuccine (see Tip)

½ cup shredded fresh basil

Grated Parmesan cheese to taste

1. Bring a large quantity of water to a boil in a stockpot. **2.** Place the pine nuts in a large skillet. Toast them over medium heat, tossing continuously, until they begin to get golden. Be careful not to burn them. Drop them into a small dish and let cool. **3.** Pour the oil into the skillet. Add the mushrooms and sauté just until they begin to soften and render some of their juices. Mix in the zucchini and garlic, and sauté until the zucchini begins to get tender. Do not cook it too much at this point because it will cook more in the sauce. **4.** Stir in the tomato puree, cream, salt, and pepper, and mix thoroughly. Bring the sauce to a boil, then lower the heat to keep it warm. **5.** Drop the fresh pasta into the boiling water and cook just until al dente, about 5 minutes. Taste it a minute or so before you anticipate its being done to avoid overcooking it. Drain thoroughly in a colander and return it to the pot. **6.** Pour on the sauce, mix in the basil, and toss in a small handful of Parmesan cheese. Serve in individual pasta bowls or on large plates with some pine nuts on each serving. Pass more Parmesan cheese at the table.

T I P : Using fresh pasta makes this dish particularly special; however, you can substitute 1 pound of dried linguine and still have a wonderful creation.

VEGETABLE LO MEIN

Bits of chewy fried tofu accent this classic Chinese noodle dish, turning it into a satisfying main course. Although a wok is an excellent cooking medium for cooks who know how to take advantage of its benefits, I have never had great results maintaining a wok so that it is "seasoned" properly, and I also haven't been able to get the high heat from my stove that good wok cooking depends on. Consequently, I have tried stir-frying these noodles in a nonstick skillet and have been thrilled with the results. The noodles don't stick and break into small pieces, I can cut back on the oil used, and everything can be stir-fried quickly, the way it should be.

SERVES 3

The Sauce:

>   3 tablespoons tamari soy sauce
>   2 tablespoons Asian sesame oil
>   1 tablespoon sherry
>   ¼ cup vegetable stock, store-bought or homemade (page 18)
>   1 teaspoon sugar
>   1 teaspoon cornstarch

>   12 ounces fresh Chinese noodles or 8 ounces spaghettini
>   1 tablespoon Asian sesame oil
>   1 tablespoon canola oil
>   2 pieces gingerroot, the size of a quarter
>   2 garlic cloves, cut in half
>   8 ounces extra-firm tofu, sliced ¼ inch thick, patted very dry, and cut into small triangles
>   1 carrot, cut into matchsticks
>   2 scallions, cut into 2-inch lengths and shredded lengthwise (like matchsticks)
>   Salt to taste

1. Place the sauce ingredients in a cup and stir well to dissolve the cornstarch. **2.** Bring a large quantity of water to a boil in a stockpot. If you are using fresh noodles, cook just a few minutes, until al dente, or cook the spaghettini about 5 minutes, also until al dente. In either case be certain not to overcook the noodles. Drain them thoroughly in a colander. Pour on

Perfect Pastas

the sesame oil and toss well. Set the noodles aside. **3.** Heat the canola oil in a large nonstick skillet over medium-high heat. Add the ginger and garlic pieces, and cook 2 minutes. Remove and discard them; they are just meant to flavor the oil. Add the tofu to the skillet and cook, tossing frequently with a spatula, until golden brown all over. Stir in the carrots and cover the pan. Cook 2 minutes. **4.** Remove the cover of the pan. Use tongs to mix in the noodles, scallions, and sauce mixture. Toss well and cook until hot throughout, about 3 minutes. Season lightly with salt. Serve immediately.

TIP: The noodles should be chewy and not overcooked or they will break into tiny pieces when you toss them with tongs.

PENNE WITH GARLICKY BUTTERNUT SQUASH

The pairing of winter squash with pasta is traditional in the Emilia-Romagna region of Italy where nutmeg-spiked squash is used as a filling for cappellacci (large tortellini). Here the muskiness of sage is a delightful counterpoint to both the nutmeg and squash's inherent sweetness. Garlic and Parmesan cheese bring all these flavors together to create a sensational topping for penne.

SERVES 4

¼ **cup olive oil**

4 **cups diced (½-inch) butternut squash (from a 1½-pound squash)**

4 **large garlic cloves, minced**

¼ **cup water**

¼ **teaspoon grated nutmeg**

6 **sage leaves, minced, or ¼ teaspoon powdered sage**

¼ **cup minced fresh parsley**

½ **teaspoon salt**

Freshly ground black pepper to taste

1 **pound penne**

Grated Parmesan cheese

1. Bring a large quantity of water to a boil in a stockpot. **2.** Heat the oil in a large skillet over medium-high heat. Toss in the squash and sauté 5 minutes, or until it begins to get golden. Sprinkle in the garlic and sauté 2 minutes. Pour in the ¼ cup water and cover the pan. Cook the squash until tender, about 5 minutes more. **3.** Cook the penne until al dente, about 10 minutes. Drain thoroughly in a colander and return to the pot. Spoon on the squash mixture and toss gently. Serve with a sprinkling of Parmesan cheese and pass more at the table.

TIP: Be attentive when you cook the squash so that it becomes tender but not mushy. You want the individual pieces to remain intact when they are tossed with the pasta.

PENNE WITH RED PEPPER AND WALNUT PESTO

Red pepper and walnut pesto creates a delightful pinkish sauce when tossed on this pasta and looks particularly striking with slices of zucchini providing contrast. Although I often serve this pesto on penne, it is also good with farfalle (bow ties) and rotini.

SERVES 4

> 1 pound penne
>
> Roasted Red Pepper and Walnut Pesto (page 22)
>
> 2 small zucchini, quartered lengthwise and thinly sliced
>
> Grated Parmesan cheese (optional)

1. Bring a large quantity of water to a boil in a stockpot. Add the penne and cook until al dente, about 12 minutes. Add the zucchini and blanch for 1 minute, or just until barely tender. Remove ¼ cup of the pasta water and stir it into the pesto to thin it. **2.** Place the penne and zucchini in a colander and shake well to drain away all the liquid. Return the mixture to the pot or place in a large pasta bowl. Pour on the pesto and toss well. Serve with Parmesan cheese, if desired.

PENNE ALLA VODKA

This modern Italian dish can be found in restaurants all across the United States. It is the type of dish that is the home entertainer's dream—elegant enough for a special meal yet extremely simple to prepare. In a peculiar fashion the vodka adds a richness and complexity to the sauce without altering its flavor. For a delightful variation I sometimes mound strips of sautéed shiitake mushrooms in the center of each portion as a garnish.

SERVES 4

> 2 tablespoons olive oil
>
> 4 large garlic cloves, minced
>
> ¼ teaspoon crushed red pepper flakes
>
> 1½ cups canned crushed tomatoes or tomato puree
>
> ¼ cup vodka
>
> ½ teaspoon salt
>
> ½ cup heavy cream
>
> 2 tablespoons minced fresh parsley
>
> Freshly grated Parmesan cheese

1. Bring a large quantity of water to a boil in a stockpot. **2.** Heat the oil in a medium-size saucepan over medium heat. Add the garlic and red pepper flakes, and cook gently for 1 minute. Do not let the garlic get at all colored. Pour in the crushed tomatoes, vodka, and salt, and cook at a lively simmer for 10 minutes. Pour in the cream and keep warm while you cook the pasta. **3.** Drop the penne into the boiling water and cook until al dente, about 10 minutes. Drain thoroughly in a colander and return to the pot. Pour on the sauce, toss, and cook 1 minute. Serve sprinkled with parsley. Pass the cheese at the table.

BOW TIES WITH GREEN BEANS IN TOMATO-WINE SAUCE

Here is an easy pasta dish with just a few ingredients, yet it teems with flavor. Tender, vivid green beans and bow ties (farfalle) are coated with a modest amount of spicy tomato sauce that acts more like a glaze than a sauce, and this adds to its charm. Young, fresh green beans are essential to the success of the dish.

SERVES 4

- ¼ cup olive oil
- 4 garlic cloves, minced
- ¼ teaspoon crushed red pepper flakes
- ½ cup tomato sauce
- ¼ cup dry red wine
- ½ teaspoon salt
- 1 pound green beans, tips removed and cut in half
- 1 pound bow tie pasta (farfalle)
- Grated Parmesan cheese

1. Bring a large quantity of water to a boil in a stockpot. **2.** To make the sauce, heat the oil in a medium-size skillet over medium heat. Add the garlic and red pepper flakes, and sauté 1–2 minutes, or until the garlic softens but doesn't at all brown. Stir in the tomato sauce, wine, and salt, and boil 2 minutes. Keep warm over low heat. **3.** Drop the green beans into the boiling water and cook 5 minutes, or until tender but still bright green. Taste one to be sure. Use a strainer to scoop out the beans and place them in a bowl. Cover with a plate to keep warm. **4.** Mix the pasta into the boiling water and cook until al dente, about 12 minutes. Drain in a colander and return to the pot. Stir in the tomato sauce and green beans, and cook 1 minute. Serve with plenty of grated Parmesan cheese.

ORECCHIETTE WITH SWISS CHARD, GARLIC, AND POTATOES

Orecchiette are little ear-shaped pasta that go well with the diced potatoes, but any short, stubby pasta would pair well with this garlic-filled sauce.

SERVES 4

- 1 large boiling (waxy) potato, peeled and cut into ½-inch dice
- 1 pound orecchiette ("little ears"), farfalle, or ziti

¼ cup olive oil

6 garlic cloves, minced

¼ teaspoon crushed red pepper flakes

1 pound Swiss chard, rinsed, stems
   cut off and discarded, leaves chopped
   (see Tip)

½ teaspoon salt

Grated Parmesan cheese

1. Bring a large quantity of water to a boil in a stockpot. Drop in the potatoes and cook until tender, about 7 minutes. With a strainer scoop out the potatoes and place in a bowl. Add the orecchiette to the boiling water and cook until al dente, about 15 minutes. **2.** Meanwhile, heat the oil in a large skillet over medium heat. Add the garlic and red pepper flakes, and cook 30 seconds. Stir in the Swiss chard with the water that clings to it and toss well with the garlic. Cover and cook until wilted, about 5 minutes. **3.** Mix the potatoes into the chard along with 2 tablespoons of the pasta water. Season with salt and cook just until the potatoes are hot. **4.** Drain the orecchiette and return to the pot or place in a warm pasta bowl. Toss with the Swiss chard mixture. Serve with grated Parmesan cheese.

TIP: Other greens will work equally well here. Try broccoli rabe, kale, or escarole as alternatives and treat them as you would the Swiss chard.

GEMELLI WITH CREAMY ZUCCHINI AND BASIL SAUCE

This is an adaptation of a Marcella Hazan recipe that uses just a few flavorful ingredients to create a splendid pasta sauce. Gemelli (short braids) is a good match for this light, creamy sauce.

SERVES 4

1 pound gemelli or other twisted pasta
   such as fusilli or rotini

2 tablespoons olive oil

2 medium zucchini, quartered lengthwise
   and thinly sliced

2 garlic cloves, minced

⅓ cup finely chopped fresh basil

1 egg yolk

1 cup whole milk

½ teaspoon salt

Generous seasoning freshly ground
   black pepper

½ cup grated Parmesan cheese

1. Bring a large quantity of water to a boil in a stockpot. Drop in the gemelli and cook until al dente, about 12 minutes. **2.** To make the sauce, heat the oil in a large skillet over medium heat. Add the zucchini and sauté until it begins to get tender, about 5 minutes.

Sprinkle in the garlic and cook, stirring frequently, until the zucchini is tender yet still slightly crisp, about 5 minutes more. Sprinkle on the basil and toss. Keep over low heat. **3.** Place the yolk in a small bowl or measuring cup. Beat in the milk, salt, pepper, and Parmesan cheese until blended. **4.** Drain the pasta and return it to the pot over low heat. Stir in the zucchini, then quickly add the egg mixture. Cook, stirring continuously, until the sauce begins to thicken, about 30 seconds. You want the egg mixture to just heat through and thicken slightly, not boil or come close to a simmer. Serve at once.

RIGATONI WITH TOMATOES, WHITE BEANS, AND ZUCCHINI

A garlic-drenched sauce transports the flavors in this Tuscan-style pasta dish and is readily absorbed by the white beans, making them succulent and spicy. Choose a canned small white bean rather than cannellini, which are usually overcooked and too soft. I prefer Goya navy or Great Northern beans over most other brands of white beans.

SERVES 4

1 pound rigatoni

⅓ cup olive oil

6 garlic cloves, minced

¼ teaspoon crushed red pepper flakes

2 medium zucchini, quartered lengthwise and thinly sliced

1 (16-ounce) can ready-cut tomatoes

1 (16-ounce) can small white beans such as navy or Great Northern, rinsed well in a strainer and drained

½ teaspoon salt

¼ cup minced fresh basil or parsley

Freshly grated Parmesan cheese

1. Bring a large quantity of water to a boil in a stockpot. Drop in the rigatoni and cook until tender yet still slightly chewy, about 10 minutes. **2.** Warm the oil in a large skillet over medium heat. Add the garlic and red pepper flakes, and cook gently for 1 minute. Do not let the garlic get at all colored. Stir in the zucchini and sauté, tossing often, until almost tender yet still slightly crunchy, about 5 minutes. Add the tomatoes with their juice, white beans, and salt, and simmer about 5 minutes, or until the juices have slightly thickened. **3.** Drain the rigatoni in a colander and return it to the pot or place in a large pasta bowl. Mix in the sauce, basil, and a small handful of Parmesan cheese. Toss well. Serve immediately with some extra Parmesan cheese to pass at the table.

Vegetarian Classics

ROTINI WITH SIMPLE TOMATO SAUCE AND CRUMBLED RICOTTA

This is an especially pretty pasta dish that delivers traditional Italian charm with little effort. A topping of sweet crumbly ricotta cheese sits in visual contrast to the vivid red and green-flecked sauce and offsets its spicy overtones. You can embellish this pasta with chopped black olives or pine nuts, or leave it as is—simple yet wonderful.

SERVES 4

> ¼ cup olive oil
>
> 6 garlic cloves, minced
>
> ¼ teaspoon crushed red pepper flakes
>
> 1 (28-ounce) can ready-cut diced tomatoes
>
> ½ teaspoon salt
>
> ½ cup finely chopped fresh basil or parsley
>
> 1 pound rotini (or other short pasta such as penne, gemelli, ziti, or fusilli)
>
> ½ cup ricotta cheese (approximately)
>
> Grated Parmesan cheese (optional)

1. Bring a large quantity of water to a boil in a stockpot. **2.** To make the sauce, heat the oil in a large skillet over medium heat. Add the garlic and hot pepper flakes, and cook 1–2 minutes, or until sizzling but not at all colored. Add the tomatoes with their juice and the salt, and bring to a boil. Simmer the sauce 10 minutes, or just until it begins to thicken slightly. Use the back of a large spoon to crush some of the tomatoes slightly; this will enhance the consistency of the sauce. **3.** Cook the rotini until al dente, about 8–10 minutes. Drain thoroughly and return to the pot. Stir the basil or parsley into the sauce. Pour the sauce on the rotini and cook 1 minute. Serve in pretty pasta bowls with tiny spoonfuls of ricotta on each serving. Pass Parmesan cheese at the table, if desired.

TORTELLINI WITH SPINACH, GARLIC, AND SMOKED CHEESE

Spinach and smoked cheese are natural companions that become even more dynamic when bolstered by garlic and hot peppers. This quick sauce delivers a mountain of flavor with little effort.

SERVES 3–4

> 1 pound frozen cheese tortellini
>
> ¼ cup olive oil
>
> 4 large garlic cloves, minced
>
> ¼ teaspoon crushed red pepper flakes
>
> 1 (12-ounce) package fresh spinach, stems removed and leaves torn into small pieces
>
> Salt to taste
>
> ½ cup grated smoked Gouda

Perfect Pastas

1. Bring a large stockpot of water to a boil. Cook the tortellini according to package directions, about 5 minutes. **2.** Meanwhile, heat the oil in a large skillet over medium heat. Add the garlic and red pepper flakes, and cook 1 minute. Do not let it get at all brown. Mix in the spinach, then scoop out about ¼ cup of pasta water and add to the spinach. Cover the pan and cook the spinach about 2 minutes, or just until it wilts. Keep warm over low heat. **3.** Drain the tortellini and add it to the spinach. Season with salt. Gently toss in the smoked cheese and serve.

RAVIOLI WITH BROCCOLI AND RED PEPPERS

This dish has become a staple in our house because it is quick, tasty, and uses ingredients that are usually in the refrigerator. It is worth taking time to find a frozen ravioli that is well made and suits you because there is a lot of variation among brands. Once found, just be sure to cook it until al dente, not soft and mushy.

SERVES 4

3 tablespoons olive oil

1 red bell pepper, cut into thin 2-inch strips

3 garlic cloves, minced

1 pound frozen cheese ravioli

3 cups tiny broccoli florets

2 tablespoons shredded fresh basil, or ½ teaspoon dried

Salt to taste

Freshly ground black pepper to taste

Grated Parmesan cheese (optional)

1. Bring a large quantity of water to a boil in a stockpot. **2.** Heat 2 tablespoons oil in a medium-size skillet over medium heat. Add the red pepper and garlic, and sauté until the pepper is very soft and golden, about 10 minutes. Keep warm over low heat. **3.** Drop the ravioli into the boiling water. About 3 minutes before the ravioli is finished cooking (check the package directions for the time), drop in the broccoli. Cook together until both are tender, about 3 minutes. **4.** Drain thoroughly in a colander and return to the pot. Carefully fold in the red pepper mixture, the remaining tablespoon of oil, basil, salt, and pepper. Serve immediately with a little Parmesan cheese, if desired.

POTATO GNOCCHI WITH RED PEPPERS, YELLOW SQUASH, AND SMOKED CHEESE

You can purchase frozen gnocchi in the frozen pasta section of most supermarkets, and you'll find them a welcome alternative to the more familiar frozen pastas such as tortellini and ravioli. The smoked cheese sauce matches the heartiness of these gnocchi and complements the vegetables perfectly.

SERVES 2–3

1 tablespoon olive oil

1 red bell pepper, cut into thin 2-inch-long strips

1 yellow squash, quartered lengthwise and thinly sliced

2 garlic cloves, minced

¼ teaspoon salt

Generous seasoning freshly ground black pepper

1 pound frozen potato gnocchi

¼ cup milk

½ cup grated smoked Gouda cheese

1 tablespoon minced fresh parsley

1. Bring a large quantity of water to a boil in a stockpot. **2.** Heat the oil in a large skillet over medium heat. Add the red pepper and cook 5 minutes. Mix in the squash and cook, tossing often, until it begins to soften, about 5 minutes. Stir in the garlic, salt, and pepper, and cook 2 minutes, or until the vegetables are tender but still slightly crisp. Keep warm over low heat. **3.** Meanwhile, drop the gnocchi into the boiling water and cook until tender, about 7 minutes. **4.** Drain the gnocchi and add them to the skillet. Mix in the milk and cheese, and stir just until melted. Serve at once with parsley sprinkled on top.

CASSEROLES, GRATINS, AND LASAGNAS

Casseroles and main-course gratins are a cook's dream. These one-dish meals are hearty enough to satisfy any guest or family member. They can be made entirely in advance, ensuring a relaxed dinner for the cook. And because of the way numerous tasty ingredients are cooked together, the finished dishes teem with flavor.

Casseroles got a bad reputation after so many concoctions based on canned ingredients were thrown together in the 1950s. The baked dishes in this chapter, however, are a world apart from those creations. Here, fresh vegetables, savory cheeses, grains, and/or pastas combine to make rich mixtures that are baked to perfection and can be served as a hearty supper or as the centerpiece to a special meal. Think of these one-dish meals as versatile and appropriate for all occasions.

CLASSIC VEGETARIAN ENCHILADAS

Mexican meatless cooking became extremely popular among vegetarians in the 1960s, and it has continued to be a favorite ethnic cuisine. No only does it offer hearty, full-flavored food that novices can easily prepare, but because of its generous use of beans, cheese, and cornmeal, it ensures that it contains an ample amount of protein.

These luscious enchiladas win over even the most die-hard skeptics of vegetarian cooking. Because they are easy to assemble and can be made in advance, they are a great choice for a party or buffet. Here I use flour rather than corn tortillas because it lends a delicate touch.

SERVES 4 (2 PER PERSON)

The Filling:

> 1 tablespoon olive oil, plus extra
>   for greasing
>
> 1 large onion, very finely diced
>
> 1 medium zucchini, quartered lengthwise
>   and thinly sliced
>
> 1 cup frozen corn
>
> 1 (15-ounce) can kidney or pinto beans,
>   rinsed in a strainer
>
> 1 (4-ounce) can chopped green (mild)
>   chilies, drained
>
> 1 teaspoon dried oregano
>
> 2 tablespoons chopped cilantro
>
> Salt to taste
>
> Freshly ground black pepper to taste

The Sauce:

> 1½ cups mild or medium salsa
>
> ½ cup heavy cream
>
> ¼ cup milk
>
> 2 cups grated Monterey Jack cheese, divided
>
> 8 (8-inch) flour tortillas

1. Heat the oil in a large skillet over medium heat. Add the onion and sauté 10 minutes, or until it begins to get golden. Stir in the zucchini and sauté until tender, about 8 minutes. Mix in the corn, beans, chilies, oregano, and cilantro. Season with salt and pepper. Remove the skillet from the heat and let the filling cool. The filling can be prepared, covered, and refrigerated up to 2 days in advance. **2.** To make the sauce, combine the salsa, cream, and milk in a bowl. Lightly oil 2 shallow 2½-quart baking dishes, such as 12 × 2 × 7-inch Pyrex dishes. (You don't want to crowd the enchiladas.) Spread a thin layer of sauce on the bottom of each dish. **3.** Preheat the oven to 350 degrees. **4.** To assemble the enchiladas, mix 1 cup cheese into the cooled filling. If the tortillas look a bit dry and perhaps brittle, brush them lightly with some water to moisten them and let sit a few minutes. If they seem supple, just lay them on the counter in front of you. Spoon ⅛ of the filling along each tortilla. Roll them up and place seam side down in the baking dishes. Pour the remaining sauce over the enchiladas, then sprinkle some of the remaining cheese along each one. Cover the dishes with foil. The enchiladas can be prepared to this point and refrigerated up to 4 hours in advance. Bring to room temperature before baking. Bake 25–30 minutes, or until hot and bubbly. Serve immediately.

Casseroles, Gratins, and Lasagnas

SMOKY BLACK BEAN ENCHILADAS

In these updated enchiladas the smoky-flavored black beans get their definition from chipotle peppers (dried smoked jalapeños) and a hint of orange. This filling is so good that I find it hard to resist eating it all before the tortillas get filled. These sumptuous enchiladas are made with corn tortillas, which are the perfect match for the outstanding black bean mixture.

SERVES 6

The Filling:

> 1 chipotle pepper, preferably canned in adobo sauce, or dried (see 8)
>
> 1 tablespoon olive oil, plus extra for greasing
>
> 1 medium onion, minced
>
> 3 (15-ounce) cans black beans, rinsed in a strainer
>
> ¾ cup orange juice

The Sauce:

> 1 cup mild or medium salsa
>
> 1 cup tomato sauce
>
> 1 teaspoon dried oregano
>
> 1 teaspoon ground cumin
>
> 12 (6-inch) corn tortillas
>
> 6 ounces light cream cheese (Neufchâtel), cut into 12 slices
>
> 2 cups grated Monterey Jack cheese

1. If you are using a chipotle pepper in adobo sauce, place it on a small plate and mince it using a knife and fork. You don't want to handle it with your fingers. If you are using a dried chipotle, cover it with boiling water and soak for 10 minutes. Remove from the water and mince with a knife and fork. **2.** Heat the oil in a medium-size saucepan over medium heat. Sauté the onion and chipotle pepper until soft, about 10 minutes. Stir in the beans and orange juice, and simmer 10 minutes. Using the back of a large spoon, mash half of the beans by pressing them against the sides of the pan. Cook the beans a few more minutes, or until the texture of mashed potatoes. Let the beans cool. **3.** To make the sauce, combine the salsa, tomato sauce, oregano, and cumin in a bowl. **4.** Preheat the oven to 350 degrees. **5.** Wrap the tortillas in foil and bake 10 minutes. This will soften them and prevent them from splitting when rolled. Let cool slightly. Keep the oven on. **6.** To assemble the enchiladas, lightly oil 2 shallow 2½-quart baking dishes, such as 12 × 2 × 7-inch Pyrex dishes. (You don't want to crowd the enchiladas.) Pour a thin film of sauce on the bottom of each dish. Divide the filling in half. Lay 6 tortillas on a work surface and place 6 spoonfuls of the filling on half of each tortilla. Top with a slice of cream cheese. Roll the enchiladas and place seam side down in the baking dish. Repeat with the remaining 6 tortillas and remaining half of the filling. Pour the sauce all over the enchiladas and sprinkle on the grated cheese. Cover the dishes with foil. (The enchiladas can be prepared to this point and refrigerated up to 4 hours in advance.) Bring to room temperature before baking. **7.** Bake, covered, for 25 minutes, or just until hot throughout. Let sit 5 minutes before serving.

TIP: Because the tortillas will absorb a lot of the sauce and become very soft, it's best not to assemble the enchiladas more than 4 hours in advance. If you want to do more advance preparation, prepare all the components separately (up to 2 days in advance) and put the enchiladas together a few hours before cooking.

ENCHILADAS VERDES

I had enchiladas with green tomatillo–based salsa in Mexico recently and wanted to re-create the dish once I returned home. Tomatillos give the sauce a tangy edge, providing a nice change from the more familiar red salsas we are used to. If you cannot find fresh tomatillos or are pressed for time, you can purchase green salsa, available in many large supermarkets.

SERVES 4

The Filling:

> 2 tablespoons olive oil
>
> 1 large onion, minced
>
> 3 (15-ounce) cans pinto (pink) or kidney beans, rinsed well in a strainer

⅓ cup water

Green Salsa (page 26) or 1 (12-ounce) jar store-bought green salsa mixed with 2 tablespoons finely chopped cilantro

8 (8-inch) flour tortillas

3 cups (9 ounces) grated Monterey Jack cheese

1. To make the filling, heat the oil in a medium-size saucepan. Add the onion and sauté until very soft, about 10 minutes. Mix in the beans and water, and simmer until hot throughout, about 7 minutes. With a large spoon mash half of the beans by pressing them against the side of the pan. Set aside to cool. **2.** Use 2 medium-size baking dishes, such as 8 × 8-inch pans or 12 × 7 × 2-inch Pyrex casseroles, and spread about 2 tablespoons green salsa on the bottom of each dish. You don't want to crowd the enchiladas. **3.** Preheat the oven to 375 degrees. **4.** Spoon ⅛ of the bean mixture along the bottom of a tortilla, then roll it and place seam side down in the dish. Repeat with the remaining beans and tortillas. Spoon the salsa all over the 8 rolled tortillas, making certain to evenly moisten the tortillas with the sauce. Sprinkle on the cheese. Cover the dish with foil. **5.** Bake, covered, for 25 minutes, or just until hot and bubbly throughout. Serve at once.

TIPS: The enchiladas can be assembled and refrigerated up to 4 hours in advance. Bring to room temperature before baking.

Read about tomatillos on page 15.

TEN-MINUTE CHILAQUILES

(Layered Tortilla Casserole)

Similar to lasagna in texture and character, this Mexican casserole is so quick to prepare and so delicious to eat that it seems like cheating to create it this effortlessly. Corn chips (which are essentially pieces of fried tortillas) form the basis of this dish, with layers of sauce, beans, and cheese tying it all together. Choose good-quality corn chips that are a little on the thick side rather than paper-thin; they will give the chilaquiles the best texture.

Serves 6

The Sauce:

> 1 cup salsa (preferably medium hot)
>
> 2 cups tomato sauce
>
> ½ cup water
>
> 1 (4-ounce) can chopped green chilies, undrained
>
> 1 (14-ounce) can pinto or kidney beans, rinsed well in a strainer
>
> ½ teaspoon ground cumin
>
> ½ teaspoon dried oregano

The Fixings:

> 1 (11-ounce) bag corn chips (about 8 cups)
>
> 1 cup sour cream
>
> 2 cups grated Monterey Jack cheese
>
> 2 tablespoons minced cilantro (optional)

1. Preheat the oven to 350 degrees. **2.** Combine all the sauce ingredients in a large bowl. **3.** Pour half the sauce into a shallow 2½-quart baking dish, such as a 12 × 7 × 2-inch Pyrex dish, and top with half the corn chips. You can crumble the chips slightly to make an even layer. Drop little spoonfuls of half the sour cream all over the chips, then sprinkle on half the cheese. **4.** Top with the remaining chips, sauce, sour cream, and cheese. Bake 35 minutes, or until hot and bubbly around the edges. Sprinkle the top of the casserole with the cilantro and serve. You can cut it into squares and serve using a spatula, or use a large spoon to scoop out the chilaquiles.

TIPS: Some packaged corn chips are very salty. Look on the back of the bag for the sodium content and choose a brand that has no more than 110 milligrams of sodium per serving. These will be the most flavorful corn chips and won't be overly salty to eat or use in the casserole.

For advance preparation make the sauce up to a few hours ahead and lay out all the other ingredients. Don't assemble the chilaquiles, however, until the last minute so the corn chips retain a tiny bit of texture when baked.

TAMALE PIE

Although its name suggests this would be cooked in a circular dish and cut into wedges, tamale pie is more like a casserole—and a great one at that. Vegetarian versions contain beans instead of ground beef, and the finished dish, with its cornbread-like topping, captures the seductive charms of a full-flavored southwestern dish.

SERVES 6

2 tablespoons olive oil

1 medium onion, finely diced

2 garlic cloves, minced

1 medium green bell pepper, finely diced

1 tablespoon chili powder

2 teaspoons ground cumin

½ teaspoon cinnamon

1 cup tomato sauce, store-bought or Easy Marinara Sauce (page 25)

½ cup water

1 (4-ounce) can chopped green (mild) chilies, well drained

1 (15-ounce) can kidney beans, rinsed well and drained

2 cups frozen corn, thawed

¼ teaspoon salt

2 cups grated sharp cheddar cheese

The Topping:

1½ cups water

1 cup milk

1 cup cornmeal

1 tablespoon sugar

½ teaspoon salt

1½ teaspoons baking powder

1 large egg, beaten

1 tablespoon butter, cut into bits

1. Heat the oil in a large skillet over medium heat. Add the onion and garlic, and sauté until the onions begin to color, about 10 minutes. Mix in the green pepper and sauté, stirring often, until the pepper is soft and tender, about 10 minutes. Sprinkle in the chili powder, cumin, and cinnamon, and cook 2 minutes to "toast" the spices. **2.** Stir in the tomato sauce, water, chilies, kidney beans, corn, and salt, and bring to a boil. Scrape the mixture into a shallow 2½-quart casserole (such as a 12 × 7-inch Pyrex dish) and spread it evenly. Sprinkle with the cheese. (The casserole can be prepared to this point and refrigerated up to 48 hours in advance. Bring to room temperature before covering with the topping.) **3.** Preheat the oven to 375 degrees. **4.** To make the topping, combine the water, milk, and cornmeal in a medium-size saucepan. Bring the mixture to a boil over medium-high heat, whisking almost constantly. Cook the mixture, while continuously whisking, until very thick and it pulls away from the sides of the pan, about 7 minutes. **5.** Remove the pan from the heat and whisk in the sugar, salt, baking powder, and egg. Use a rubber spatula to spread the topping over the bean mixture. Dot with the butter bits. (When the topping cools a little, you can use your fingers to even it out.) **6.** Bake 45 minutes. Let sit 10 minutes before serving.

BAKED MEXICAN-STYLE RICE AND BEANS

The jalapeño pepper cheese gives this humble yet delicious casserole a spicy edge without overpowering it. If you prefer a milder version, you can use plain Monterey Jack cheese or a combination of both types.

SERVES 4–6

- 3 cups water
- 1 teaspoon canola oil
- 1½ cups white rice, such as converted, basmati, or long grain
- Butter for greasing
- 1 (15-ounce) can pinto or kidney beans, rinsed in a strainer
- ½ cup tomato sauce, store-bought or Easy Marinara Sauce (page 25)
- 1 (4-ounce) can chopped green (mild) chilies, drained
- 2 teaspoons chili powder
- ½ teaspon salt
- ⅔ cup sour cream
- 3 cups (9 ounces) grated Monterey Jack cheese with jalapeño peppers

1. Combine the water and oil in a medium-size saucepan and bring to a boil. Stir in the rice, cover the pot, and lower the heat to a gentle simmer. Cook the rice about 17 minutes, or until all the water is absorbed. Place in a large bowl and let cool. **2.** Preheat the oven to 350 degrees. Butter a 2½-quart shallow baking dish or oval gratin dish. **3.** Mix the beans, tomato sauce, chilies, chili powder, and salt into the rice. Spread half of the mixture into the prepared dish. Top with the sour cream and half of the cheese. Spread on the remaining rice mixture and sprinkle the remaining cheese on top. Cover with foil. (The casserole may be prepared and refrigerated up to 24 hours in advance. Bring to room temperature before baking.) Bake 30 minutes, or until piping hot throughout. Serve immediately.

BAKED PENNE WITH HEARTY MUSHROOM SAUCE

A robust red sauce spiked with red wine and ladened with mushrooms coats these penne, which are then layered with cheese and baked until bubbly. Rustic fare at its best.

SERVES 6

- 1 pound penne
- 3 tablespoons olive oil, divided
- 4 garlic cloves, minced
- ¼ teaspoon crushed red pepper flakes
- 8 ounces common white mushrooms, thinly sliced

8 ounces mixed exotic mushrooms,
such as shiitake, oyster, and cremini,
thinly sliced

½ teaspoon salt

1½ cups tomato sauce

¼ cup dry red wine

½ cup chopped fresh parsley

2 cups grated mozzarella cheese

¼ cup grated Parmesan cheese

1. Bring a large quantity of water to a boil in a stockpot. **2.** Cook the penne just until al dente, about 8 minutes; it will cook further in the oven. Drain thoroughly in a colander and return to the pot. Toss with 1 tablespoon oil and set aside. **3.** Heat the remaining 2 tablespoons oil in a large skillet over medium heat. Add the garlic and red pepper flakes, and cook about 30 seconds, or just until they sizzle a bit. Stir in the mushrooms and cook, tossing frequently, until the mushrooms are brown and juicy, about 10 minutes. At first the mushrooms will absorb the oil and be very dry, but then they will release their juices. **4.** Mix in the salt, tomato sauce, wine, and parsley. Add the sauce to the penne and mix to coat well. **5.** Preheat the oven to 375 degrees. Lightly oil a shallow 3-quart casserole such as a 13 × 9 × 2-inch baking dish. **6.** Spread half of the penne in the dish. Top with half of the mozzarella and Parmesan cheeses. Spoon on the remaining penne and sprinkle on the remaining cheeses. Cover the dish with foil. (The casserole can be prepared to this point up to 8 hours in advance. If chilled, bring to room temperature before baking.) **7.** Bake 30 minutes, or until hot and bubbly. Remove the foil and bake 5 minutes more. Let sit 10 minutes before serving.

GREEK PASTA CASSEROLE

It's hard to beat this baked pasta dish for quickness and flavor. After the pasta is cooked, all you have to do is mix in the remaining ingredients and bake the casserole until piping hot. Precede the dinner with a salad and serve this with some hot crusty bread to round out the meal.

SERVES 4

¼ cup olive oil, plus extra for greasing

4 large garlic cloves, minced

1 pound small pasta shells

1 (14-ounce) can ready-cut diced tomatoes
with their juice

1 (7-ounce) jar roasted red peppers, well
drained and diced

¼ cup pitted and roughly chopped black
olives (your favorite kind)

2 tablespoons red wine

¼ teaspoon crushed red pepper flakes

¼ cup finely chopped fresh parsley

1½ teaspoons dried oregano

1 cup (5 ounces) finely crumbled feta cheese

1. Bring a large quantity of water to a boil in a stockpot. **2.** Meanwhile, heat the oil in a small saucepan over medium-low heat. Add the garlic and cook 30 seconds; do not let it get at all colored. Remove the pan from the heat and set aside. **3.** Add the pasta to the boiling water and cook until al dente, about 15 minutes. Taste one to be sure it is cooked properly. Drain thoroughly in a colander and place in a large bowl. Pour on the garlic oil and toss well. Let cool to room temperature, tossing occasionally to prevent sticking. **4.** Preheat the oven to 375 degrees. **5.** Mix in all the remaining ingredients. Oil a shallow 3-quart casserole (such as a 13 × 9-inch Pyrex baking dish). Spoon the mixture into the dish and cover with foil. (The pasta can be assembled and refrigerated up to 24 hours in advance. Bring to room temperature before baking.) **6.** Bake, covered, for 25 minutes, or until hot and bubbly. Remove the foil the last 5 minutes of cooking to lightly brown the top of the casserole.

BAKED MACARONI AND SMOKED CHEESE

This updated version of the ultimate American comfort food gets its exquisite flavor from a touch of smoked cheese. If you have any finicky eaters who want a more traditional approach, use all cheddar cheese. It will still be delicious, just not as poetic.

SERVES 4

2 slices bread

1 tablespoon olive oil

2 tablespoons unsalted butter

2 tablespoons unbleached flour

2 cups whole or low-fat milk

⅛ teaspoon dry mustard

Dash cayenne pepper

¼ teaspoon salt

2 cups grated extra-sharp cheddar cheese

1 cup grated smoked Gouda cheese

8 ounces (2 cups) elbow macaroni

1. Bring a large quantity of water to a boil in a stockpot. **2.** Tear the bread into pieces and place in a food processor or blender to make bread crumbs. Pour the crumbs into a bowl and drizzle with the oil. Rub the oil into the crumbs with your fingertips to moisten them evenly. **3.** To make the cheese sauce, melt the butter in a medium-size saucepan over medium heat. Sprinkle in the flour and whisk until it blends with the butter. Cook this roux for 1 minute. Whisk in the milk, mustard, cayenne, and salt. Bring the mixture to a boil, whisking continuously. Lower the heat and simmer the sauce about 30 seconds. Remove from the heat and stir in the cheddar and smoked cheeses. (The sauce can be made up to 4 hours in advance. Reheat gently until warm before mixing it with the macaroni.) **4.** Drop the macaroni into the boiling water. Cook until al dente, about 7 min-

Vegetarian Classics

utes. Do not overcook it; it will cook more when it is baked. Drain thoroughly in a colander. (Toss with a bit of oil if you aren't going to bake the casserole immediately.) **5.** Preheat the oven to 400 degrees. **6.** Spoon the macaroni into a shallow 2–2½-quart casserole. Pour on the sauce and toss well. Sprinkle on the bread crumbs. **7.** Bake 15 minutes, or just until the sauce is sizzling and the crumbs begin to brown.

TIPS: The macaroni and sauce can be prepared in advance, but they should not be combined until baking time.

The white sauce can boil a few seconds, but once the cheese has been added, the sauce must not boil or else it will curdle. The same situation applies to baking; the casserole should bake only until it is hot and no more.

This recipe can be easily doubled or tripled to feed a crowd.

CLASSIC VEGETARIAN LASAGNA BÉCHAMEL

Using a thick béchamel sauce (called balsamella in Italian) instead of ricotta cheese establishes the silken character of this luscious lasagna. "Oven-ready" noodles (no precooking necessary) simplifies the assembly, making this lasagna a good choice when you want to multiply the dish for a crowd.

SERVES 6–8

Béchamel Sauce:

> **4 tablespoons unsalted butter**
>
> **6 tablespoons unbleached flour**
>
> **3 cups low-fat milk**
>
> **¼ teaspoon grated nutmeg**
>
> **¼ teaspoon salt**
>
> **½ cup grated Parmesan cheese**
>
> **3 cups Easy Marinara Sauce (page 25) or Spruced-Up Store-bought Tomato Sauce (page 25)**
>
> **¼ cup dry red wine**
>
> **Olive oil for greasing**
>
> **12 lasagna noodles from one 8-ounce package "oven-ready" (no-boil) lasagna**
>
> **2½ cups (8 ounces) grated part-skim mozzarella cheese**

1. To make the béchamel sauce: heat the butter in a medium-size saucepan over medium heat. Whisk in the flour and cook 2 minutes, whisking often. Whisk in the milk, nutmeg, and salt. Whisk until the mixture boils and thickens, then stir in the Parmesan cheese. Remove from the heat. (The sauce may be prepared and chilled up to 24 hours in advance. Warm it slightly over low heat before using.) **2.** Combine the marinara or tomato sauce with the wine (an addition to the wine already in the sauce). **3.** Preheat the oven to 375 degrees. Lightly oil a 13 × 9 × 2-inch baking dish. **4.** Spread a thin layer of tomato sauce on the bottom of the dish. Arrange 3 noodles vertically on the sauce, making sure the noodles don't touch each other; they need room for expansion. **5.** Spread about ¾ cup béchamel sauce on the noodles, then top with ¼ of the mozzarella cheese. Repeat the sequence 3 more times: tomato sauce, noodles, béchamel sauce, and mozzarella. Cover the dish with foil. (The lasagna can be assembled and refrigerated up to 8 hours in advance. Bring to room temperature before baking.) **6.** Bake 30 minutes, covered. Remove the foil and bake 15 minutes more. Let sit 15 minutes before cutting and serving.

TIP: You can add cooked mushrooms, zucchini, peppers, and/or spinach between the layers.

VEGETABLE LASAGNA WITH FRESH PASTA

When a pasta shop opened in my town, I was thrilled to discover that I could purchase sheets of pasta dough to use for lasagna. Not only do they make the assembling of lasagna easy because they require no precooking, but they also lend a special, delicate texture to the finished dish and give it an elegant quality. If you are fortunate enough to have a pasta shop in your neighborhood, take advantage of the availability of fresh pasta sheets for this spectacular dish.

SERVES 8

Béchamel Sauce:

> 6 tablespoons unsalted butter
>
> ½ cup unbleached flour
>
> 4 cups whole or low-fat milk
>
> ⅛ teaspoon nutmeg
>
> ½ teaspoon salt
>
> Freshly ground black pepper to taste
>
> ½ cup grated Parmesan cheese

The Vegetables:

> 2 tablespoons olive oil
>
> 1 medium onion, minced
>
> 4 garlic cloves, minced
>
> 12 ounces (4½ cups) thinly sliced mushrooms
>
> 1 (14-ounce) can ready-cut diced tomatoes, very well drained
>
> ¼ cup dry red wine
>
> 1 cup chopped fresh basil
>
> ¼ cup chopped fresh parsley
>
> ½ teaspoon salt
>
> Freshly ground black pepper to taste
>
> Butter for greasing
>
> 3 sheets fresh spinach or plain pasta (approximately 10 × 12 inches)
>
> 2 small to medium zucchini, thinly sliced into rounds ⅛ inch thick
>
> 1¼ cups grated fontina cheese
>
> 1¼ cups grated part-skim mozzarella cheese

Vegetarian Classics

A Lasagna Trick

I have become so enamored of no-boil lasagna noodles that I no longer use any other kind, unless, of course, I can get freshly made sheets of pasta, which also require no precooking. But a relative of mine, Gerry Curtin, whose Italian lineage is rock solid, told me about a trick that allows traditional lasagna noodles (that is, those that require precooking) to be used without cooking them first. Assemble the lasagna with the uncooked noodles, using a generous amount of sauce and a pan large enough to allow for expansion. Measure ½ cup boiling water and pour ¼ of it into each corner of the pan. Cover the pan with foil and bake about 1 hour, or until the noodles are tender. Be sure to let the lasagna sit for 15 minutes before serving it, as you should with any lasagna.

1. To make the sauce, melt the butter in a medium-size saucepan over medium heat. Whisk in the flour and cook, whisking often, for 2 minutes. Whisk in the milk, nutmeg, salt, and pepper. Raise the heat to medium-high. Bring the sauce to a boil, whisking almost constantly, then remove from the heat. Stir in the cheese and let cool. (The sauce can be prepared, covered, and chilled up to 48 hours in advance.) **2.** To make the vegetable sauce, heat the oil in a large skillet over medium heat. Add the onion and garlic, and sauté 10 minutes, or until the onion is golden. Stir in the mushrooms and sauté until they begin to brown and the juices have almost all evaporated. Mix in the tomatoes and wine, and cook until the juices thicken, about 5 minutes. There shouldn't be much liquid at this point. Remove the pan from the heat and stir in the basil, parsley, salt, and pepper. Let cool. (The sauce may be prepared, covered, and chilled up to 48 hours in advance.) **3.** Preheat the oven to 375 degrees. **4.** To assemble the lasagna, butter a 9 × 13-inch baking dish. Using scissors or a knife trim the pasta sheets to fit the bottom of the baking dish. If the white sauce has been chilled, heat it over low heat, stirring often, just until it gets warm and soft. Spread a thin layer of the sauce on the bottom of the baking dish. Top with a lasagna sheet. **5.** Cover with ⅓ of the vegetable mixture, ⅓ of the zucchini slices, ⅓ of the white sauce, then ⅓ of both the fontina and mozzarella cheeses. Repeat this layering 2 more times. Cover the dish with foil. (The lasagna can be prepared up to 24 hours in advance. Bring to room temperature before baking.) Bake, covered, for 25 minutes. Remove the foil, then bake 30 minutes more, or until bubbly and golden. Let sit 15 minutes before cutting and serving.

SPINACH LASAGNA WITH A TOMATO CREAM SAUCE

This luxurious rendition of a vegetable lasagna is as pretty to behold as it is delicious to eat. Emerald green spinach and blazing red peppers are layered between noodles, and all is encased in a salmon-colored cream sauce. The feta cheese gives the final dish a lively edge without making it overly salty or dominating its flavor.

SERVES 6–8

Tomato-cream Sauce:

6 tablespoons unsalted butter

½ cup unbleached flour

4 cups low-fat milk

¼ teaspoon nutmeg

½ teaspoon dried oregano

½ teaspoon salt

Freshly ground black pepper to taste

1 cup tomato sauce, store-bought or Easy Marinara Sauce (page 25)

Oil for greasing

15 lasagna noodles from one 8-ounce package "oven-ready" (no-boil) lasagna

1 (10-ounce) package frozen chopped spinach, thawed and squeezed dry

1 (7-ounce) jar roasted red peppers, well drained and diced

8 ounces feta cheese, very finely crumbled (1⅔ cups)

2 cups (6 ounces) grated part-skim mozzarella cheese

1. To make the cream sauce, melt the butter in a medium-size saucepan over medium heat. Add the flour and whisk until smooth. Cook 1 minute, whisking constantly. Whisk in the milk, nutmeg, oregano, salt, and pepper, and bring to a boil, whisking frequently. Boil 1 minute, whisking constantly, then remove from the heat. Whisk in the tomato sauce. (The sauce can be made, covered, and refrigerated up to 24 hours in advance. Reheat slightly or until it is smooth before assembling the lasagna.) **2.** Preheat the oven to 375 degrees. **3.** To assemble the lasagna, lightly oil a 13 × 9-inch baking dish. Spread a thin layer of sauce on the bottom of the dish. Place 3 uncooked lasagna noodles side by side, making sure they don't touch each other. Spread a thin layer of sauce on the noodles, then sprinkle on ¼ of the spinach, red peppers, and feta cheese, and ⅕ of the mozzarella cheese. Place 3 more noodles on top and repeat the sequence until all the noodles have been layered. Spread a layer of sauce on top and sprinkle on the remaining mozzarella cheese. Cover the dish with foil. (The lasagna can be made up to 8 hours in advance and refrigerated. Bring to room temperature before baking. See Tip.) **4.** Bake the lasagna, covered, for 30 minutes. Remove the foil and bake 10–15 minutes more, or until golden on top. Let the lasagna sit at least 15 minutes before serving.

TIP: If the lasagna is refrigerated for 8 hours before being baked, the noodles will soften, and only 15 minutes of covered baking will be necessary instead of 30 minutes. The uncovered baking time remains 10–15 minutes.

BAKED VEGETABLE POLENTA

Velvety smooth polenta baked with a layer of vegetables and cheese is an ideal casserole because it is so substantial and full-flavored. The fact that it can be completely assembled in advance adds to its charm. If you cannot find fennel or are not fond of it, substitute 1 large red bell pepper and get great results. This casserole is a luscious entree that can star at a dinner party or be homey fare for a rustic supper.

SERVES 4

1 tablespoon olive oil

1 medium onion, minced

1 cup thinly sliced fennel

1 small to medium zucchini, quartered lengthwise and thinly sliced

⅔ cup drained and diced canned tomatoes

1 cup frozen corn, thawed

Salt to taste

Freshly ground black pepper to taste

The Polenta:

2 cups milk

1½ cups water

1 cup cornmeal

2 garlic cloves, put through a press

¾ teaspoon salt

⅓ cup grated Parmesan cheese

1½ tablespoons finely shredded fresh basil

1½ cups grated fontina cheese

½ cup heavy cream

1. Heat the oil in a large skillet over medium heat. Add the onion and fennel, and sauté about 10 minutes, or until the fennel is crisp yet tender. **2.** Stir in the zucchini and tomatoes, and cover the pan. Cook 10 minutes, or until the fennel is very tender. Stir in the corn, salt, and pepper, and remove from the heat. **3.** Butter a 2½-quart gratin dish or other similar shallow casserole. **4.** To make the polenta, combine the milk and water in a heavy-bottomed 3-quart saucepan. Add the cornmeal, garlic, and salt, and whisk until smooth. Place over medium-high heat and bring the polenta to a boil, whisking continuously. Lower the heat and whisk until the polenta resembles soft mashed potatoes, about 10 minutes. Whisk in the Parmesan cheese and basil. **5.** Pour half of the polenta into the prepared casserole. Cover with half of the vegetables and half of the fontina cheese. Drizzle with half of the cream. Spoon on the remaining polenta and add the remaining vegetables, cheese, and cream. Let the casserole sit at least 30 minutes or up to 24 hours before baking. Cover and refrigerate if it will sit more than 1 hour. **6.** Preheat the oven to 400 degrees. Bake the polenta about 25 minutes, or until it is golden on top and bubbly. Let sit 10 minutes before serving.

BAKED CHEESE POLENTA WITH CORN AND GREEN CHILIES

Here is another delectable version of baked polenta that has a southwestern bent to it. The green chilies permeate the dish in perfect harmony with pepper jack cheese and corn. If you precede the meal with Spicy Black Bean Dip (page 35) and corn chips, you'll have a dynamic menu.

SERVES 4

Butter for greasing

1 (4-ounce) can chopped green (mild) chilies, well drained

1½ cups frozen corn, thawed

1½ cups Monterey Jack cheese with jalapeño peppers

½ cup sour cream

2 cups milk

1½ cups water

1 cup cornmeal

3 garlic cloves, put through a press (preferably) or minced

¾ teaspoon salt

Freshly ground black pepper to taste

⅓ cup grated Parmesan cheese

1. Butter a 2½-quart casserole and set aside. Place the chilies, corn, Monterey Jack cheese, and sour cream next to the casserole. **2.** In a 3-quart heavy-bottomed saucepan whisk together the milk, water, cornmeal, garlic, salt, and pepper. Bring to a boil over medium-high heat, whisking almost continuously. Cook the polenta, whisking constantly, until thickened like soft mashed potatoes, about 7 minutes. Whisk in the Parmesan cheese. **3.** Pour half of the polenta in the prepared casserole and spread evenly. Sprinkle on half of the chilies, half of the corn, and half of the Monterey Jack cheese. Spread on all of the sour cream. Quickly pour on the remaining polenta and spread evenly. Sprinkle on the remaining chilies, corn, and Monterey Jack cheese. Let the casserole sit at least 20 minutes before baking, or cover and refrigerate up to 24 hours. Bring to room temperature before baking. **4.** Preheat the oven to 400 degrees. Bake 25–30 minutes, or until the polenta is sizzling and golden on top. Let sit 10 minutes before serving.

Vegetarian Classics

BAKED ORZO WITH SPINACH, TOMATOES, AND CORN

This is an ideal casserole to make when guests are coming and you need something quick, colorful, exceptionally tasty, *and* that can be assembled in advance. The feta cheese gives a little spunk to the flavorings without dominating the finished dish, so be sure to include it.

SERVES 4–6

- 1 pound orzo (rice-shaped pasta)
- 1 (10-ounce) bag triple-washed fresh spinach, stems discarded and leaves torn in half
- 4 tablespoons olive oil
- 6 large garlic cloves, minced
- 1 (14-ounce) can ready-cut diced tomatoes
- 1 cup frozen corn, thawed
- 1 cup (4 ounces) crumbled feta cheese
- ½ teaspoon salt
- Generous seasoning freshly ground black pepper
- 1 cup grated Muenster cheese

1. Bring a large quantity of water to a boil in a stockpot. Add the orzo and cook just until it approaches the al dente stage, about 10 minutes; it will cook further in the oven. Stir in the spinach and cook 30 seconds. Drain very thoroughly in a colander. Return the mixture to the pot or place in a large mixing bowl. Pour on 1 tablespoon oil and toss to coat well. Let cool. 2. Heat the remaining 3 tablespoons oil in a medium-size skillet over medium heat. Add the garlic and cook 1 minute, or until barely colored. Stir in the tomatoes with their juice and simmer 5 minutes. 3. Mix the tomatoes into the orzo along with the corn, feta cheese, salt, and pepper. 4. Oil a shallow 3-quart casserole (such as a 9 × 13-inch baking dish). Spread half the orzo mixture into the dish. Sprinkle on the Muenster cheese. Spread the remaining orzo over the cheese. Cover the dish with foil. (The casserole can be prepared to this point up to 24 hours in advance. Chill if longer than 2 hours. Bring to room temperature before baking.) 5. Preheat the oven to 375 degrees. Bake the casserole, covered, for 30 minutes, or until piping hot throughout.

BAKED ORZO, BROCCOLI, AND CHEESE

Here's a homey casserole that's a snap to assemble and has ingredients that are often on hand. If you wish to prepare this dish in advance, shock the blanched broccoli in a bowl of cold water to stop any further cooking, pat it dry, then combine it with the other ingredients.

2–3 cups tiny broccoli florets (from 1 bunch broccoli)

1 pound orzo (rice-shaped pasta)

1 (7-ounce) jar roasted red peppers, well drained and cut into strips (¾ cup)

Butter for greasing

1 cup sour cream

¼ cup milk

¼ cup plus 2 tablespoons grated Parmesan cheese

¼ cup chopped fresh basil or parsley, or ½ teaspoon dried basil

½ teaspoon salt

Generous seasoning freshly ground black pepper

1 cup grated part-skim mozzarella cheese

1. Bring a large quantity of water to a boil in a stockpot. Drop in the broccoli and cook until almost tender (it will cook further when baked), about 5 minutes. With a strainer scoop out the broccoli and place in a large bowl. 2. Cook the orzo in the same boiling water until tender but not mushy, about 12 minutes. (Test a piece after about 9 minutes.) Drain thoroughly in a colander. If any water has accumulated in the bowl with the broccoli, drain it. Mix the orzo with the broccoli, then stir in the red peppers. Let the mixture cool at least 20 minutes or up to 4 hours. Refrigerate if longer than 1 hour, then bring to room temperature. 3. Preheat the oven to 375 degrees. Butter a 2½- to 3-quart baking dish.

4. Stir the sour cream, milk, ¼ cup Parmesan cheese, basil, salt, pepper, and mozzarella cheese into the broccoli mixture. Scrape into the baking dish and smooth over the top. Sprinkle with the remaining Parmesan cheese. 5. Bake 20–30 minutes, or just until piping hot. Do not overcook the dish or it will dry out.

BAKED VEGETABLE COUSCOUS

This dish is a spin-off of Moroccan-style couscous in which vegetables in a spicy sauce are mounded on couscous. Here everything is baked in a casserole and a thin layer of molten cheese adds a welcome cohesiveness to the finished dish. It's easy to assemble, filled with flavor, and ideal as a do-ahead dish.

SERVES 4 GENEROUSLY

1 cup couscous

¾ teaspoon salt

1½ cups boiling water

¼ cup olive oil

1 onion, very finely diced

4 garlic cloves, minced

½ teaspoon turmeric

1½ teaspoons paprika

2 teaspoons ground cumin

A few dashes cayenne pepper

2 small to medium zucchini, quartered
    lengthwise and thinly sliced

1 (14-ounce) can ready-cut diced tomatoes
    with their juice

1 (16-ounce) can chickpeas, rinsed well
    and drained

⅓ cup raisins

1 cup grated Monterey Jack cheese

1. Place the couscous and salt in a large bowl.
Pour in the boiling water and stir. Cover the bowl
with a large plate and let the couscous sit 10 minutes. Fluff with a fork and set aside, uncovered.
2. Preheat the oven to 375 degrees. **3.** Heat
the oil in a large skillet over medium heat. Stir in
the onion and garlic, and sauté until the onion
become translucent, about 5 minutes. Sprinkle
on the turmeric, paprika, cumin, and cayenne.
Toss and cook 1 minute. Mix in the zucchini and
sauté until the zucchini begins to soften but is still
crisp, about 5 minutes. Add the tomatoes, chickpeas, and raisins, and simmer 2 minutes. **4.** Stir
this mixture into the couscous and toss well.
Spread half in a shallow 2½-quart baking dish.
Sprinkle on the cheese. Top with the remaining
couscous mixture and cover with foil. (The casserole can be prepared to this point and refrigerated up to 24 hours in advance. Bring to room
temperature before baking.) Bake 45 minutes, or
until sizzling and piping hot throughout.

TIP: Although all the ingredients are essentially cooked when spooned into the baking
dish, the casserole must bake at least 45 minutes so it is hot throughout.

BAKED BARLEY
AND MUSHROOMS

Here's a wonderful way to include grains in
your diet. The rich essence of mushrooms permeates this dish, imparting a deep, lingering
flavor that matches well with mild barley. I love
to bake this casserole on a fall or winter day
because it fills the house with an aroma that is
an antidote to the harshness of cold weather.

SERVES 4

4 tablespoons unsalted butter

2 medium onions, finely diced

8 ounces (3 cups) common white
    mushrooms, coarsely chopped

4 ounces (1½ cups) assorted exotic
    mushrooms (such as shiitake, crem-
    ini, and oyster), coarsely chopped

1½ cups barley

1 carrot, minced

1 rib celery, thinly sliced

1 tablespoon sherry or marsala wine

Pinch dried thyme

½ teaspoon salt

Generous seasoning freshly ground black
    pepper

4½ cups boiling vegetable stock, store-
    bought or homemade (page 18)

1. Preheat the oven to 350 degrees. **2.** Melt
the butter in a large skillet over medium heat.

Add the onions and mushrooms, and sauté until the mushrooms render their juices and begin to brown, about 10 minutes. **3.** Stir in the barley, carrot, and celery, and cook 2 minutes. Scrape the mixture into a deep 2- to 2½-quart casserole that has a tight cover. Mix in all the remaining ingredients. **4.** Cover tightly and bake 60–75 minutes, or until all the stock has been absorbed and the barley is tender. Taste the barley. If it is still hard, pour in a ½ cup boiling stock or water and cook 10–15 minutes more. Let sit 10 minutes before serving.

TIP: Barley can easily be found in the "bean" section of the supermarket.

EGGPLANT PARMESAN

The technique for preparing the eggplant in this classic favorite has changed slightly, but the finished dish is just as good as ever. Instead of breading and deep-frying the eggplant slices, they are coated with bread crumbs and broiled for a lighter and easier touch. A long, thin pasta such a linguine or spaghetti with a light butter sauce is great alongside this casserole.

SERVES 4–6

2 medium eggplants (about 1 pound each)

¼–⅓ cup mayonnaise

¾ cup dry bread crumbs

2 cups Easy Marinara Sauce (page 25) or Spruced-up Store-bought Tomato Sauce (page 25)

½ cup finely chopped fresh parsley

½ cup grated Parmesan cheese

2 cups grated mozzarella cheese

1. Peel the eggplant and slice it into rounds about ½ inch thick—no thicker. **2.** Preheat the broiler. **3.** Place the mayonnaise in a small dish and the bread crumbs on a flat plate. Use a pastry brush to lightly coat both sides of each eggplant slice with mayonnaise. Press both sides of the slices into the bread crumbs and lay the eggplant on a baking sheet. You'll probably need 2 sheets so they can rest in 1 layer. **4.** Broil the eggplant until a deep golden brown. Turn the slices over and broil again. When done the eggplant will be very tender, not at all firm. Cool the slices. **5.** Preheat the oven to 375 degrees. **6.** Pour a thin layer of tomato sauce on the bottom of a 2½- to 3-quart shallow baking dish, such as a 11 × 7-inch or 9 × 13-inch Pyrex dish. Layer half of the eggplant slices, tomato sauce, parsley, Parmesan cheese, and mozzarella cheese. Repeat. Cover the dish with foil. (The casserole can be prepared to this point and refrigerated up to 24 hours in advance. Bring to room temperature before baking.) **7.** Bake, covered, for 15 minutes. Remove the foil and bake 15 minutes more, or until hot and bubbly. Let sit 10 minutes before serving.

TIP: You can substitute about ½ cup olive oil for the mayonnaise. Brushing oil on the egg-plant slices will make the "crust" a bit thinner but still delicious.

SWEET POTATO, WHITE BEAN, AND PEPPER TIAN

This is my favorite way to eat sweet potatoes. A tian (pronounced TEE-ahn) is an earthenware casserole as well as the name of the finished dish. Because the vegetables in a tian are coated with olive oil and slowly baked, they exude delectable juices that caramelize and develop a rich flavor. White beans enhance the protein content of the dish while adding a soft, buttery dimension. No precooking is needed before piling everything in the casserole, so you can assemble this main course in no time.

SERVES 4

> 3 medium-large sweet potatoes (preferably dark orange), peeled, quartered lengthwise, and sliced ¼ inch thick
>
> 1 (14-ounce) can small white beans, rinsed in a strainer
>
> 1 red bell pepper, cut into 1-inch chunks
>
> 1 green bell pepper, cut into 1-inch chunks
>
> 1 medium red onion, cut into 2-inch chunks and sections separated

> 2 plum tomatoes, cut into 1½-inch chunks
>
> 5 garlic cloves, thinly sliced
>
> ½ teaspoon salt
>
> Generous seasoning freshly ground black pepper
>
> ⅓ cup olive oil

The Topping:

> 3 slices homemade-style white bread
>
> 1 tablespoon olive oil

1. Preheat the oven to 375 degrees. **2.** Combine all the vegetables, garlic, salt, pepper, and oil in a large bowl and toss well. (The vegetables can be prepared to this point up to 4 hours in advance.) Pack the mixture into a 2½- or 3-quart shallow baking dish and flatten the top surface. Bake 45 minutes. **3.** To make the fresh bread crumbs, tear up the bread and make crumbs out of it in a food processor or blender. Pour the crumbs into a bowl and drizzle with the oil. Rub the oil into the crumbs with your fingertips to moisten them evenly. **4.** Remove the tian from the oven. Spread the crumbs all over the top. Return the tian to the oven and bake 15 minutes more, or until the topping is a rich golden color. Let sit 10 minutes before serving.

TIP: Although traditional tians are baked in heavy ceramic dishes, you will have good results using a more common baking dish as long as it is shallow and has 2½–3 quart capacity, such as a 12 × 2 × 7-inch Pyrex dish.

Sweet Potatoes Versus Yams

What we purchase in American supermarkets and at most greengrocers are *sweet potatoes*; some have light golden skins and yellowish or pale orange flesh, while others are darker skinned with vivid orange flesh. The latter variety of sweet potato is often erroneously called "yam." True yams are grown in Africa, can be as large as 7 feet in length, have a white or light yellow flesh, and are generally sweeter than our southern sweet potatoes. The confusion arose when African slaves were given the southern sweet potato to eat and called it *nyam* in their native tongue.

Nowadays markets often label dark orange sweet potatoes "yams" to distinguish them from paler varieties, but in fact they are both different types of sweet potatoes and are botanically unrelated to the true tropical yam.

SUMMER SQUASH CASSEROLE

For summer squash lovers here's a tasty do-ahead casserole that can be the basis of a rustic supper when accompanied by some crusty bread and a salad.

SERVES 4–6

1 cup water

½ cup white rice, preferably converted or basmati

2 tablespoons olive oil, plus extra for greasing

2 onions, finely diced

3 medium (1½ pounds) summer (yellow) squash, quartered lengthwise and thinly sliced

1 red bell pepper, cut into thin 2-inch strips

2 large eggs

½ cup milk

1½ cups grated extra-sharp cheddar cheese

½ teaspoon salt

Generous seasoning freshly ground black pepper

The Topping:

2 slices white bread

1 tablespoon olive oil

1. Bring the water to a boil in a small saucepan and add the rice. Lower the heat to a simmer and cook until all the water is absorbed, about 17 minutes. Set aside. 2. Heat the oil in a large skillet over medium-high heat. Add the onions and sauté until lightly browned. Stir in the squash and red pepper, and continue to cook at medium-high heat, stirring often, until the vegetables are tender and the juices have evaporated, about 10 minutes. Set

aside to cool. **3.** Preheat the oven to 375 degrees. Lightly oil a 2½–3-quart baking dish. **4.** Beat the eggs in a large bowl. Beat in the milk, cheese, salt, pepper, rice, and vegetables. Spread the mixture in the prepared baking dish. **5.** To make the topping, tear up the bread and place in a food processor or blender to make crumbs. Pour the crumbs into a small bowl and drizzle with oil. Rub the oil into the crumbs with your fingertips. Sprinkle the crumbs on top of the casserole. (The casserole may be prepared to this point up to 8 hours in advance. If chilled, bring to room temperature before baking.) **6.** Bake 40–45 minutes, or until a deep golden brown. The casserole must sit at least 15 minutes before serving in order for the juices to set and thicken.

STUFFED BAKED POTATOES WITH SPINACH AND FETA CHEESE

These flavor-filled potatoes can be served as a main course. Accompanied with a salad, it's a satisfying meal that's easy and casual.

SERVES 4

> 4 baking (Idaho or russet) potatoes, scrubbed well
>
> 2 tablespoons olive oil

> 2 garlic cloves, pressed or minced
>
> 4 scallions, very thinly sliced
>
> 1 (10-ounce) package frozen chopped spinach, thawed and squeezed dry
>
> 1 teaspoon minced fresh dill, or ½ teaspoon dried
>
> 2 tablespoons butter
>
> ¾ cup finely crumbled feta cheese
>
> 1 cup grated mozzarella cheese

1. Prick the potatoes with a fork or knife a few times so they don't explode in the oven when baking. Set the oven at 400 degrees and place the potatoes on the oven rack. Bake until tender when pierced with a knife, about 1 hour. **2.** Heat the oil in a medium-size skillet over medium heat. Add the garlic and scallions, and cook 2 minutes, or just until heated through and softened. Mix in the spinach and dill and remove from the heat. **3.** When the potatoes are done, slice in half lengthwise. Scoop the flesh into a bowl, leaving about ¼ inch in the shell. Mash the potatoes with a fork. Combine with the spinach mixture, butter, and feta and mozzarella cheeses. Stuff each shell with the mixture and smooth over the tops. **4.** Place the stuffed potatoes on a baking sheet and return to the oven. Bake 20 minutes, or until hot throughout and golden on top.

TIP: After stuffing the potatoes you can wait up to 2 hours before baking them again.

Casseroles, Gratins, and Lasagnas

CLASSIC MOCK MEAT LOAF

Mock meat loaves were common fare for vegetarians in the 60s and 70s, and then they went out of favor. Many deserved to be forgotten, but this walnut loaf is a gem. It has a superb flavor and texture, not at all "health foodish." If the holiday season goes by without my making this loaf for the family, they don't hesitate to tell me of their disappointment. Reminiscent of traditional meat loaf, this version also makes fabulous sandwiches when left over, especially when combined with layers of stuffing and cranberry sauce. For Thanksgiving I like to present this as a centerpiece, accompanied by mashed potatoes, gravy, cranberry sauce, stuffing, and vegetables—in other words, as one would present a traditional turkey dinner.

SERVES 6

- 9 slices (8 ounces) commercial whole wheat bread (such as Arnold or Pepperidge Farm)
- 2 cups (8 ounces) walnuts
- 3 large eggs
- 3 medium onions, diced
- 1 small green bell pepper, diced
- 1 small celery rib, minced
- 1 small bunch parsley, stems discarded and leaves chopped
- ⅔ cup canned crushed tomatoes or 1 (16-ounce) can diced tomatoes, drained very well
- 1½ tablespoons canola oil
- 1 teaspoon poultry seasoning
- 1 teaspoon salt
- Generous seasoning freshly ground black pepper

1. Toast the bread slices either in the toaster or on a baking sheet placed under the broiler. Let cool. **2.** Preheat the oven to 375 degrees. Generously butter a 9 × 5-inch loaf pan, then line the bottom with wax paper and butter the paper. **3.** Tear up the toasted bread slices and make crumbs out of them in a food processor. Place in a large bowl. **4.** Process the walnuts until finely ground and mix into the bread crumbs. Combine the eggs and onions in the processor and process until fine but not liquefied. Stir into the bread crumbs. Place the green pepper, celery, parsley, tomatoes, and oil in the processor and grind until fine but still with some texture. Stir into the loaf mixture along with the poultry seasoning, salt, and pepper. Mix this all very well until evenly moistened. (The mixture may be prepared to this point and refrigerated up to 8 hours in advance.) Scrape it into the prepared loaf pan and smooth over the top. Cover the loaf with foil. **5.** Bake 1 hour and 20 minutes, or until a knife inserted in the center of the loaf comes out dry. Let sit 5 minutes, then run a knife all along the sides of the loaf to help loosen it. Unmold the loaf onto a platter and remove the wax paper. Let the loaf cool 20 minutes or so before slicing it. It's best to serve the loaf warm and the gravy hot. Serve with Mushroom Gravy (below).

MUSHROOM GRAVY

4 tablespoons unsalted butter

2 cups (8 ounces) thinly sliced mushrooms

¼ cup unbleached flour

2½ cups vegetable stock, store-bought or homemade (page 18)

¼ cup dry red wine

2 tablespoons tamari soy sauce

Freshly ground black pepper to taste

1. Melt the butter in a medium-size saucepan over medium heat. Add the mushrooms and sauté until brown, about 7 minutes. Stir in the flour; it will become very pasty. Cook this roux for 2 minutes, stirring constantly. It will stick to the bottom of the pan a little bit; that's okay. **2.** Stir in the stock, wine, soy sauce, and pepper, and bring to a boil. Cook the sauce at a lively simmer for 5 minutes, stirring almost constantly and scraping any crusty bits that adhere to the bottom of the pan. Serve in a sauceboat.

TIPS: If you don't have a food processor, you can grind everything in a blender, but it will have to be done in many batches so the blender is not overfilled.

You can also cook the loaf a few hours in advance, then reheat slices on an oiled baking sheet in a 350-degree oven.

STUFFED BABY PUMPKIN WITH WILD RICE AND MUSHROOMS

For a striking centerpiece on the Thanksgiving table, it's hard to beat a stuffed pumpkin. I prefer to use a small pumpkin about the size of a large cantaloupe rather than a larger one because the flesh is more tender, and the pumpkin can be cut into wedges with the stuffing intact. If you are serving a large crowd, cook a few small pumpkins at once.

SERVES 4–6

1 (3½-pound) sugar or pie pumpkin

2 tablespoons unsalted butter, softened

Salt

Freshly ground pepper

¾ cup very finely diced celery

½ cup finely diced onion

1½ cups (4 ounces) sliced mushrooms

1½ cups vegetable stock, store-bought or homemade (page 18)

2 tablespoons sliced almonds

2 tablespoons Asian sesame oil

2 tablespoons sherry

¼ teaspoon salt

¼ cup wild rice

¼ cup brown rice

1. Preheat the oven to 350 degrees. 2. Slice the top off the pumpkin, reserving the lid. With a spoon scoop out and discard all the seeds and fibrous interior. (Be careful not to make any holes in the pumpkin, especially at the bottom. Leave the little "point" at the center of the bottom.) Slather 1 tablespoon butter in the interior of the pumpkin, then season with salt and pepper. Cover the pumpkin with its lid and place on a baking sheet. Bake 20 minutes. 3. Meanwhile, melt the remaining tablespoon of butter in a medium-size saucepan. Add the celery, onion, and mushrooms, and sauté 10 minutes, or until the mushrooms are juicy. Stir in the vegetable stock and bring to a boil. Add all the remaining ingredients and cook at a lively simmer for 10 minutes. 4. Remove the pumpkin from the oven. Carefully ladle in the boiling rice mixture and cover with the lid. Return to the oven and bake 1–1½ hours more, or until all the stock is absorbed and the rice is cooked. Place the pumpkin on a decorative platter and surround with some leafy greens such as kale. Let sit 10 minutes before cutting the pumpkin into wedges.

STOVETOP COOKING

I think of stovetop cooking as a last-minute affair, although you can certainly perform many of the steps in advance to cut back on your work at dinnertime. These dishes are casual, easy, and ideal for a quick supper. Their informality, however, does not make them any less delicious or satisfying. Consider the recipes in this chapter when you want to eat wholesome food that is simply prepared. You'll find that the ease with which you can put these dishes together will make you turn to them time and again.

CLASSIC VEGETABLE CURRY

A perfectly composed vegetable curry simmered in a glistening aromatic sauce is a priceless dish in a vegetarian's repertoire. Because the flavors in a well-made curry are so complex and enticing, it can be an ideal dish to serve when entertaining non-vegetarian guests who enjoy robust food. Accompany this entree with cooked basmati rice, Banana Mint Raita (page 155) or plain yogurt, Fresh Mango Chutney (page 157), and some store-bought chapatis, and you'll have a festive meal for a special occasion.

SERVES 4–6

1¾ cups dried unsweetened coconut (available at health food stores)

2½ cups very hot water

¼ cup tomato paste

3 tablespoons unsalted butter

1 large onion, minced

1 tablespoon minced fresh ginger

4 large garlic cloves, minced

2 teaspoons turmeric

1½ teaspoons ground cumin

1 tablespoon ground coriander

½ teaspoon ground cardamom

⅛ teaspoon cayenne pepper (or more to taste)

2 medium red-skinned potatoes, cut into
½-inch dice (no bigger)

4 cups very small cauliflower florets (from
1 small cauliflower)

1 carrot, thinly sliced

1½ cups frozen peas, thawed

1½ tablespoons minced cilantro

½ teaspoon salt

1. To make the coconut milk, combine the coconut and hot water in the container of a blender (preferably) or food processor and process 2 minutes. Place a strainer over a large bowl and pour in half the coconut mixture. With the back of a large spoon press the coconut to extract as much liquid as possible. Discard the pressed coconut and repeat with the remaining mixture. You should have 1⅔ cups coconut milk. **2.** Place the tomato paste in a small bowl and stir in about ½ cup coconut milk to dilute the tomato paste and make a smooth mixture. Pour this into the remaining coconut milk and set aside. **3.** Melt the butter in a stockpot over medium heat. Add the onion, ginger, and garlic, and sauté, stirring often, until the onions are golden brown, about 10 minutes. **4.** Stir in the turmeric, cumin, coriander, cardamom, and cayenne, and "toast" the spices for 2 minutes, stirring frequently. Pour in the coconut milk mixture and bring to a boil. **5.** Stir in the potatoes, tightly cover the pan, and cook 5 minutes. **6.** Carefully mix in the cauliflower and carrots, and stir to coat the vegetables evenly. Cover the pan tightly again and cook over medium heat until the potatoes are tender, about 15 minutes. Occasionally

Curry

———

The word "curry" is derived from the Indian word *kari*, meaning sauce, and also from the use of kari leaves in Indian spice blends. Curries are mixtures of vegetables and/or meat simmered in a fragrant sauce, and they are a specialty of southern India.

It is common for westerners to associate Indian cooking with commercial curry powder, a packaged mixture of spices that came into existence when the occupying British in India wanted to take the flavors of southern India home with them to try to recreate Indian dishes in their kitchens. Indian cooks, however, do not use packaged curry powder; instead they carefully combine a variety of spices when they begin cooking each dish. The resulting flavors vary and don't have the predictable homogenous flavor of commercial curry powder. Numerous spices are used to create a richly flavored curry, the most essential being turmeric, coriander, cumin, cayenne pepper, black pepper, mustard seeds, fenugreek, and kari (curry) leaves. A cook might also include cardamom, cinnamon, and cloves.

Curry powder is convenient for Western cooks to use and can add an alluring nuance to a dish, but to enjoy the fantastic range of flavors that Indian cooking offers, try blending individual spices and discover the richness and depth that this offers.

remove the cover and stir the vegetables for even cooking. (The curry can be made a few hours in advance to this point. Reheat before proceeding with step 7. If the sauce has become very thick, thin with a little water.) **7.** Stir in the peas, cilantro, and salt. Cover again and cook 1–2 minutes, or just until the peas are heated through.

TIP: To simplify the preparation of this dish I like to make the coconut milk and chop the vegetables early in the day, then cook the curry shortly before serving time.

VEGETABLE AND CASHEW CURRY

Although curry powder is rarely used in India, it can lend a tantalizing flavor that is a treat to Western palates. A spoonful of yogurt on top of this curry adds a creaminess to the sauce while providing a pleasing contrast to the spiciness.

SERVES 4

¼ cup canola oil

1 onion, finely diced

4 garlic cloves, minced

1 tablespoon minced fresh ginger

1½ tablespoons curry powder

1 teaspoon ground cumin

1 (14-ounce) can ready-cut diced tomatoes with their juice

½ teaspoon salt

2½ cups peeled and finely diced (½-inch) boiling potatoes

3 small to medium zucchini, quartered lengthwise and thinly sliced

¾ cup dry-roasted (preferably unsalted) cashews

1 tablespoon lemon juice

4 cups hot cooked basmati rice (made from 1 cup raw rice)

Plain yogurt

1. Heat the oil in a large skillet over medium heat. Add the onion, garlic, and ginger, and sauté 5 minutes. Mix in the curry powder and cumin, and cook 2 minutes to toast the spices. **2.** Add the tomatoes and 1 cup water, and bring to a boil. Stir in the potatoes and cover the pan. Cook at a gentle simmer until the potatoes are tender, about 20 minutes. Stir occasionally to prevent sticking. **3.** Remove the cover of the pan and add the zucchini and cashews. Cook, uncovered, until the zucchini are tender, about 10 minutes. Mix in the lemon juice. Serve the curry over rice with a spoonful of yogurt on top.

TIP: You can make the curry in advance and reheat it. In this case you'll have to add ¼ cup or so of water to thin the sauce while reheating.

CLASSIC POLENTA WITH WILD MUSHROOM RAGU

Vegetarians have long been clever at substituting mushrooms for meat in many traditional recipes. The use of assorted exotic mushrooms in a thick, robust tomato sauce creates a memorable ragu. When paired with polenta, a dish is created that is utterly satisfying to vegetarians and non-vegetarians alike. Although the list of ingredients is long in this recipe, it is a snap to prepare. Incidentally, if you're as wild about this sauce as I am, try it on fettuccine, tagliatelle, or penne for other great options.

SERVES 4

The Ragu:

>   3 tablespoons olive oil
>
>   4 large garlic cloves, minced
>
>   12 ounces white button mushrooms, thinly sliced
>
>   8 ounces mixed exotic mushrooms (such as shiitake, oyster, and cremini), thinly sliced
>
>   1½ cups canned crushed tomatoes or tomato puree
>
>   ¼ teaspoon sugar
>
>   ½ teaspoon salt

>   Generous seasoning freshly ground black pepper

The Polenta:

>   4 cups vegetable stock, store-bought or homemade (see page 18)
>
>   ¼ teaspoon salt
>
>   1¼ cups cornmeal
>
>   1 tablespoon unsalted butter
>
>   ⅓ cup grated Parmesan cheese

1. To make the ragu, heat the oil in a 3-quart saucepan over medium heat. Add the garlic and cook gently about 1 minute, or until very fragrant but not at all colored. Stir in the mushrooms and sauté, stirring often, until brown and juicy, about 7 minutes. Mix in all the remaining ingredients and partially cover the pan. Simmer 10 minutes, or until the sauce is thick and aromatic. **2.** To make the polenta, bring the stock and salt to a boil in a medium-size heavy-bottomed saucepan. Very slowly drizzle in the cornmeal, whisking all the while with a wire whisk. Lower the heat to a simmer and continue to whisk the polenta until it is the consistency of soft mashed potatoes, about 5 minutes. **3.** Remove the polenta from the heat. Whisk in the butter and cheese. (You can cover the polenta and keep it warm for up to 10 minutes.) On large plates or in pasta bowls serve a mound of polenta topped with the mushroom ragu.

Which Cornmeal for Polenta?

Traditionally, polenta has been made from coarse-grained cornmeal that has the germ intact, and it has a robust flavor and texture. The best way to purchase it is to get organic stone-ground cornmeal from a natural foods store or specialty shop.

Fine-grained cornmeal is another choice for making polenta. Although the germ has been removed and it is therefore a bit less nutritious, it makes delicious, creamy polenta with a smoother texture than that made from a coarser meal. Fine-grained cornmeal (Quaker Oats Cornmeal is fine) cooks a few minutes quicker than the coarser variety does.

If you purchase either coarse or fine-grained cornmeal in bulk from a natural foods store or market, it will be considerably cheaper than the small boxes labeled "polenta" or "instant polenta." Although it's all various cuts of cornmeal, once the word "polenta" is put on the package, the price goes up.

SMOKED CHEESE POLENTA WITH MIXED PEPPER TOPPING

Adding a small amount of smoked cheese and sour cream to polenta transforms it into a creamy, soft mass with a rich, seductive flavor. The spicy mixed peppers are the perfect complement to the mild smokiness. To add to this dish's charm, it's very quick to prepare.

SERVES 4

The Topping:

- 2 tablespoons olive oil
- 4 garlic cloves, minced
- ¼ teaspoon crushed red pepper flakes
- 1 large red bell pepper
- 2 large green bell peppers
- ⅔ cup canned crushed tomatoes or tomato puree
- ¼ teaspoon dried oregano
- ¼ teaspoon salt

The Polenta:

- 4 cups water
- ½ teaspoon salt
- 1¼ cups cornmeal
- ¼ cup sour cream
- ⅔ cup grated smoked Gouda cheese

1. To make the topping, heat the oil in a large skillet over medium heat. Add the garlic and crushed pepper flakes, and cook 30 seconds, or just until they sizzle a bit. Mix in the peppers and sauté 5 minutes, tossing often. Cover the pan and cook until the peppers are very soft, about 10–15 minutes. Remove the cover and mix in the crushed tomatoes, oregano, and salt. Cook about 5 minutes more, or just until the sauce thickens. Keep warm over low heat. (You can prepare the sauce up to 24 hours in advance. Reheat until hot, adding a few table-spoons of water if it has gotten too thick.) **2.** To make the polenta, combine the water and salt in a heavy-bottomed saucepan and bring to a boil over high heat. Turn the heat to medium-low, then very slowly drizzle in the cornmeal, whisking all the while with a wire whisk. Cook the polenta, whisking continuously, until it begins to tear away from the sides of the pan, about 7 minutes. Whisk in the sour cream and smoked cheese. (You can cover the pan and keep the polenta warm for up to 10 minutes.) Spoon the polenta onto each serving plate and top with a few spoonfuls of the peppers and their sauce.

Three Ways to Cook Polenta

The traditional northern Italian method of simmering polenta in a copper pot over the fire while stirring it for up to 1 hour with a wooden spoon is a rite of the past for most people. Today, with modern stoves, whisks, and fine-grained cornmeal, polenta making is a speedy affair. The quickest way to cook polenta is to bring the cooking liquid (water, milk, or stock) to a boil and then *very slowly* drizzle in the cornmeal, whisking all the while with a wire whisk. The key here is to add the cornmeal by lightly sprinkling it into the liquid bit by bit. If it is added too quickly, it will clump, and that could make your polenta lumpy.

A slower but foolproof way to produce perfectly smooth polenta is to combine the cornmeal with the cold liquid in a saucepan, then bring the mixture to a boil, again whisking all the while. It will take longer for the concoction to come to the boiling point compared to the method above, but you will have no lumps in your polenta.

The third method is a combination of the two approaches. Take half of the measured cooking liquid and mix it in a bowl with the cornmeal to create a smooth paste, then bring the remaining half of the liquid to a boil. Pour in the cornmeal paste and bring to a boil, whisking all the while. You will have perfectly smooth polenta in less time than the second method and only a bit more time than the first.

Whichever method you choose, the polenta is done when its consistency resembles soft mashed potatoes.

GORGONZOLA POLENTA TOPPED WITH BRAISED GREEN BEANS

Gorgonzola and other blue cheeses are excellent additions to polenta, contributing a deep, rich flavor and added creaminess.

SERVES 4

The Green Beans:

  1 tablespoon olive oil

  1 onion, finely diced

  1 (14-ounce) can ready-cut diced tomatoes with their juice

  1 pound green beans, cut into 1-inch lengths

  ¼ teaspoon salt

The Polenta:

  3½ cups water

  ½ teaspoon salt

  1¼ cups cornmeal

  1 tablespoon butter

  2 tablespoons grated Parmesan cheese

  4 ounces (¾ cup) diced Gorgonzola or other blue cheese

1. To make the beans, heat the oil in a medium-size saucepan over medium heat and add the onion. Sauté until it softens, about 5 minutes. Add the tomatoes, green beans, and salt, and partially cover the pan. Simmer until the green beans are very tender, about 20 minutes. **2.** To make the polenta, bring the water and salt to a boil in a medium-size heavy-bottomed saucepan. Drizzle in the cornmeal very slowly, whisking all the while with a wire whisk. When all the cornmeal has been added, turn the heat to medium-low and continue to whisk the polenta until it has thickened and is the consistency of mashed potatoes, about 7 minutes. Whisk in the butter and Parmesan and Gorgonzola cheeses. Serve immediately or remove from the heat, cover the pan, and let sit 10 minutes. Spoon onto serving plates and mound the braised green beans on top.

TIP: The green beans can be made up to 8 hours in advance and reheated, but the polenta must be made very close to serving time.

YELLOW SQUASH AND RED PEPPER SAUTÉ ON POLENTA

When red peppers are cooked until caramelized and mixed with yellow squash and garlic, as in this savory sauté, a great blending of flavors takes place. I especially love this mounded on polenta for a dynamic match.

SERVES 4

2 tablespoons olive oil

2 red bell peppers, cut into strips 2 inches
by 1 inch

2 yellow squash, halved lengthwise
and sliced ¼ inch thick

1 tomato, cored, seeded, and finely diced,
or ½ cup canned diced tomatoes

4 garlic cloves, minced

Salt to taste

Generous seasoning freshly ground
black pepper

2 tablespoons minced fresh basil,
or 1 teaspoon dried

2 tablespoons minced fresh parsley

The Polenta:

4 cups vegetable stock, store-bought
or homemade (page 18)

¼ teaspoon salt

1¼ cups cornmeal

2 tablespoons unsalted butter

⅓ cup grated Parmesan cheese

1. Heat the oil in a large skillet over medium heat until hot but not smoking. Add the red peppers and sauté 2 minutes. Cover the pan and cook until the peppers are soft and browned all over but not mushy, about 7 minutes. They should sizzle quite a bit while cooking. **2.** Remove the cover of the pan and stir in the squash, tomato, garlic, salt, and pepper. Raise the heat to medium-high and cook, uncovered, until the squash is tender, about 7 minutes more. Toss the vegetables frequently. The mix-ture will become juicy and then begin to dry. Stir in the the basil and parsley. Keep warm over low heat. **3.** To cook the polenta, bring the stock and salt to a boil in a medium-size saucepan. Drizzle in the cornmeal very slowly, whisking all the while with a wire whisk. Turn the heat to low and cook the polenta, whisking continuously, until it becomes like soft mashed potatoes, about 5 minutes. Whisk in the butter and cheese. Spoon a mound of polenta on each serving and top with some of the vegetables.

VEGETABLE TAGINE

A tagine is a North African stew traditionally served on couscous; in fact, the whole concoc-tion is often referred to simply as "couscous." Vegetable couscous is an ideal vegetarian sta-ple—quick, full-flavored, and substantial. Don't let the long list of ingredients dissuade you from preparing this dish if you are pressed for time because half of the items are spices, and the dish really is easy to assemble.

SERVES 4 GENEROUSLY

The Stew:

3 tablespoons olive oil

1 medium onion, minced

3 garlic cloves, minced

2 teaspoons ground cumin

1 teaspoon ground ginger

1½ teaspoons paprika

½ teaspoon turmeric

¼ teaspoon cinnamon

⅛ teaspoon cayenne pepper

1½ cups canned crushed tomatoes
    or tomato puree

2 cups water

⅛ teaspoon crushed saffron

1 carrot, thinly sliced

1 sweet potato, peeled and cut into
    ½-inch dice

2 cups diced green beans

¼ cup raisins

½ teaspoon salt

1 (15-ounce) can chickpeas, rinsed
    in a strainer

1 zucchini, cut lengthwise into sixths
    and diced

The Couscous:

2¼ cups water

2 tablespoons unsalted butter

½ teaspoon salt

1½ cups couscous

1. Heat the oil in a large stockpot over medium heat. Add the onion and garlic, and sauté until the onion begins to soften, about 5 minutes. Sprinkle in all the spices and sauté 2 minutes, stirring often. **2.** Mix in the tomatoes, water, saffron, carrot, sweet potato, beans, raisins, and salt. Bring the mixture to a boil. Cover the pot, lower the heat to a simmer, and cook 20 minutes, or until the sweet potatoes are tender. Stir occasionally. **3.** Mix in the chickpeas and zucchini, cover the pot, and cook 10 minutes, or until the zucchini is tender. At this point check the consistency of the sauce. If it seems too watery, cook uncovered a few minutes to thicken it. **4.** To make the couscous, combine the water, butter, and salt in a medium-size saucepan and bring to a boil. Stir in the couscous, cover the pot, and remove from the heat. Let sit 10 minutes to absorb all the liquid. Fluff with a fork before serving. Place a portion of couscous in the center of each serving plate and top with a mound of vegetables.

COUSCOUS TOPPED WITH GARLICKY ZUCCHINI, TOMATOES, AND PEPPERS

The mingling of textures and flavors is first-rate in this simple preparation. Crumbled feta cheese on top of the finished dish adds a lively edge and pleasant creaminess, so although it is an optional addition, I highly recommend it.

SERVES 4

2 tablespoons olive oil

1 medium onion, very finely diced

4 garlic cloves, minced

1 green bell pepper, cut into ½-inch dice

2 small to medium zucchini, quartered lengthwise and thinly sliced

1 (14-ounce) can ready-cut diced tomatoes

½ teaspoon dried oregano

Generous grating fresh pepper

1 cup frozen corn

1½ cups vegetable stock (store-bought or homemade, page 18), or water

1 tablespoon unsalted butter

½ teaspoon salt (or less if the stock is salty)

1 cup couscous

½ cup finely crumbled feta cheese (**optional**)

1. Heat the oil in a large skillet over medium heat. Add the onion and garlic, and sauté, stirring often, for 5 minutes. Add the green pepper and cook 5 minutes. Add the zucchini, toss well, and sauté 5 minutes. Stir the mixture often. **2.** Stir in the tomatoes with their juice, oregano, and pepper. Simmer the vegetables, uncovered, until the zucchini is tender and the juices have thickened slightly. Stir in the corn and keep warm over low heat. (You can prepare the mixture to this point up to 8 hours in advance. To reheat, add a few tablespoons of water to create a bit of sauce.) **3.** To cook the couscous, bring the stock or water to a boil in a medium-size saucepan. Add the butter and salt, stir, then mix in the couscous. Cover the pan and remove it from the heat. Let the couscous sit 5 minutes. Fluff with a fork, cover again, and let sit a few minutes more. **4.** Serve a mound of couscous on each serving plate and top with the vegetable mixture. Sprinkle some feta cheese on each serving, if desired.

BULGUR AND GREENS

This is a variation of a Greek dish that my brother-in-law, Pete Simigan, introduced me to, and I've discovered that there are similar versions of bulgur with greens all over the Mideast. The sweetness of onions, the chewy texture of bulgur, and the soft, buttery greens come together to create a peasant dish of great charm. In Greece this recipe is often made with purslane or Swiss chard; however, spinach is an equally good addition. If you use Swiss chard, add the stems to the onions when you sauté them.

SERVES 3–4 AS A MAIN COURSE

⅓ cup olive oil

2 large onions, finely diced

6 garlic cloves, minced

3 scallions, very thinly sliced, divided

¼ teaspoon crushed red pepper flakes

1¼ cups coarse bulgur

1 cup water

¼ teaspoon salt

1 pound (about 1½ bags) prewashed fresh spinach, stems removed and leaves torn into small pieces, or 1 pound Swiss chard, stems diced and leaves finely chopped (keep stems and leaves separate)

1. Heat the oil in a large (3-quart) saucepan over medium heat. Add the onions, garlic, all but 2 tablespoons scallions, and the crushed red pepper flakes (and Swiss chard stems if using) and sauté 10 minutes, or until the onions begin to soften. 2. Add the remaining ingredients (except the reserved 2 tablespoons scallions), stuffing the spinach or Swiss chard leaves on top. Cover the pot tightly, lower the heat to a simmer, and cook 30 minutes. Remove the cover occasionally and stir to distribute the greens. Remove the pot from the heat and let sit undisturbed for 10 minutes so all the liquid gets absorbed. Serve with a sprinkling of the reserved scallions on top of each serving.

TIP: Greek versions often include finely crumbled feta cheese. It is a delicious variation, adding a piquant dimension. Stir in ½–1 cup feta cheese just before serving.

BRAISED WHITE BEANS WITH TOMATOES, ZUCCHINI, AND GARLIC

This ragout is an infusion of seductive Mediterranean flavors, with white beans and bits of potato soaking up the garlicky juices. A truly delicious way to prepare beans. Serve with a chunk of Tuscan-style or French bread to dip in the sauce.

SERVES 4

¼ cup olive oil

6 garlic cloves, minced

¼ teaspoon crushed red pepper flakes

1 (14-ounce) can ready-cut diced tomatoes

¼ cup water

2 medium boiling (all-purpose) potatoes, peeled and cut into ¼-inch dice

2 small to medium zucchini, quartered lengthwise and thinly sliced

2 (14-ounce) cans small white beans, such as Great Northern or navy, rinsed well in a strainer

¼ teaspoon dried rosemary, crumbled

Salt

1. Heat the oil in a large skillet over medium heat. Stir in the garlic and red pepper flakes, and cook 1–2 minutes, or until the garlic is very tender but not at all colored. Stir in the tomatoes, water, and potatoes, and cover the pan. Cook at a lively simmer for 15 minutes, or until the potatoes are almost cooked through. 2. Mix in the zucchini, beans, rosemary, and salt. Cover the pan again and cook, stirring often, 10 minutes more, or until the zucchini and potatoes are tender. At this point check the consistency of the sauce; it should be thick and soupy,

not dry or watery. Add a bit of water if the mixture doesn't have much sauce; cook it uncovered if the juices seem watery. Serve in large pasta bowls, preferably, or on plates.

TIPS: Make sure the potatoes are cut no larger than ¼ inch so they can cook quickly.

I prefer to cook this dish just before serving because the starches from the beans and potatoes overly thicken the sauce when the dish cools. If you need to cook this dish in advance, you'll have to add some water when you reheat it. Stir gently over low heat so the beans don't split and become mushy. An alternative is to prepare the vegetables in advance (place the cut potatoes in a bowl of cold water to prevent darkening) and cook at the last minute.

BRAISED WHITE BEANS WITH ESCAROLE

Here is another favorite way to serve white beans as a main course. Escarole, garlic, and white beans are a classic combination with a gutsy marriage of flavors and textures. My stepdaughter Susanne's favorite appetizer is to mound spoonfuls of this concoction on bruschetta (grilled bread), with a glass of wine served alongside.

SERVES 3–4

¼ **cup olive oil**

6 **garlic cloves, minced**

1 **pound (1 head) escarole, well washed and torn into small pieces (see Tip)**

2 **tablespoons water**

2 **(14-ounce) cans small white beans, such as Great Northern or navy, rinsed well in a strainer**

2 **teaspoons balsamic vinegar**

Salt to taste

Generous seasoning freshly ground black pepper

1. Heat the oil in a large skillet over medium heat. Mix in the garlic and cook about 30 seconds, or until sizzling and fragrant but not at all colored. Add handfuls of the escarole, tossing it with the garlic after each addition. (Using tongs can be helpful here.) Pour in the water and cover the pan. Cook the escarole, tossing occasionally, until wilted and tender, about 5 minutes. **2.** Remove the cover and stir in the beans, vinegar, salt, and pepper. Cook, uncovered, until the escarole is very tender and the juices have thickened slightly. You want the final dish to have a sauciness but not be soupy. Check the liquid at this point; add more water if the mixture is dry, or cook a bit longer if there is too much liquid. Don't stir the beans too much, or they will break up and cause the mixture to become a bit pasty. Serve in pasta bowls with some crusty bread.

TIPS: Escarole harbors a lot of sand and must be washed carefully. Rinsing escarole in a

Vegetarian Classics

colander will not clean it sufficiently, so here's how to do it: dunk the torn-up leaves in a large bowl of cold water and let the sand fall to the bottom. Remove the leaves with your hands and pour out the water and sand. Repeat until there is no sandy residue in the bowl.

To make this dish as a topping for bruschetta, don't add water to the escarole when it cooks. The water that clings to the washed escarole should be sufficient to steam it.

RED BEANS AND RICE

This variation on the southern staple can be prepared easily with ingredients one usually has on hand. It's hearty, flavorful, and fool-proof—a good choice when you come home from work and need supper in a hurry.

SERVES 4

> 2 tablespoons olive oil
>
> 2 medium onions, finely diced
>
> 2 large garlic cloves, minced
>
> 1 green pepper, finely diced
>
> 1 tablespoon chili powder
>
> 1 teaspoon paprika
>
> 1 cup tomato sauce
>
> ¼ cup water
>
> A few dashes hot sauce (such as Tabasco)
>
> 2 (15-ounce) cans kidney beans, rinsed well in a strainer

> 4 cups hot cooked rice (from 1 cup raw rice)
>
> Sour cream (optional)

1. Heat the oil in a large skillet over medium heat. Add the onions, garlic, and green pepper, and sauté until the pepper is very tender, about 10 minutes. **2.** Sprinkle in the chili powder and paprika, and cook 30 seconds. Mix in the tomato sauce, water, hot sauce, and kidney beans, and simmer about 10 minutes, or until the mixture is hot and fragrant. Serve over rice with a small spoonful of sour cream on top, if desired.

TIP: To give the beans a smoky flavor you can add 1 small chipotle pepper in adobo sauce (see page 8). Mince it on a small plate with 2 knives before adding it to the beans. Omit the hot sauce.

VEGETABLE FRIED RICE

For a comfort food that's totally satisfying, low in fat, easy to make, and great as a leftover, you can't beat vegetable fried rice. The secret to avoiding gummy fried rice is to begin with a batch of *cold* cooked rice, so cook your rice early in the day or the night before. If you have a large nonstick skillet to cook everything in, you'll find the whole process greatly simplified.

SERVES 4 AS A MAIN COURSE

1 teaspoon plus 3 tablespoons canola oil

2 large eggs, well beaten

8 ounces extra-firm tofu, cut into ½-inch
cubes and patted very dry

1 teaspoon minced fresh ginger

2 celery ribs, thinly sliced

4 scallions, very thinly sliced

6 cups cold, cooked long-grain brown
rice (made from 2 cups raw rice and
3¾ cups water)

¼ cup tamari soy sauce

2 tablespoons Asian sesame oil

2 cups bean sprouts

1. Heat 1 teaspoon canola oil in a large, preferably nonstick, skillet over medium-high heat. Pour in the eggs and scramble a few minutes. Let the eggs set into a pancake and cook about 20 seconds, then flip over and cook a few more seconds on this side. Slide onto a large plate and cut into shreds. Set aside. **2.** Heat 2 more tablespoons canola oil in the skillet and, when hot, add the tofu. Stir-fry until golden all over. Slide onto a plate and set aside. **3.** Heat the remaining tablespoon canola oil in the skillet. Add the ginger and celery, and sauté 5 minutes. Add the scallions and cook 30 seconds. **4.** Break up the rice if it is in clumps and add to the skillet. Toss well. Drizzle on the soy sauce and sesame oil, and mix very thoroughly. **5.** Stir in the tofu, egg, and bean sprouts. Toss gently and heat through, about 5 minutes. Serve immediately or let cool and reheat.

TIP: Because fried rice reheats so well, don't hesitate to make this a few days in advance. Just sprinkle on a few tablespoons of water and reheat over low heat.

CURRIED RICE AND VEGETABLE PILAF COOKED IN COCONUT MILK

This exquisite Indian rice dish contains bits of vegetables and cashews that have been cooked in a fragrant coconut milk richly infused with spices. It is colorful, aromatic, and easy to prepare. Don't be dissuaded by the long list of ingredients; it consists mostly of spices.

SERVES 4 GENEROUSLY

3 tablespoons canola oil

1 large onion, minced

1 large boiling potato (such as red-skinned),
peeled and cut into ¼-inch dice

1½ cups basmati or other long-grain white
rice such as converted rice

2 carrots, cut into ¼-inch dice

2 garlic cloves, minced

1 tablespoon minced fresh ginger

¼ teaspoon turmeric

½ teaspoon ground cardamom

½ teaspoon ground cumin

⅛ teaspoon ground cloves

⅛ teaspoon cayenne pepper

1 (14-ounce) can coconut milk

1½ cups water (approximately)

¾ teaspoon salt

½ cup roasted cashews (salted or unsalted)

1 cup frozen peas, thawed

1 tablespoon finely chopped mint or
    cilantro (optional)

1. Heat the oil in a stockpot over medium heat. Add the onion and potato, and sauté 10 minutes, stirring often. **2.** Stir in the rice, carrots, and all the spices, and mix well. Sauté 2 minutes to toast the spices, stirring continuously. **3.** Mix the coconut milk with enough water to make 3 cups of liquid. Pour into the rice mixture and sprinkle in the salt. Cover the pot, bring the mixture to a boil, then lower the heat to a gentle simmer. Cook undisturbed until all the liquid is absorbed, about 25 minutes. **4.** Turn off the heat under the pot and gently stir in the cashews and peas. Cover the pot again and let the rice rest 10 minutes. Serve sprinkled with mint or cilantro.

TIPS: Be certain to cut the potatoes and carrots no bigger than ¼ inch so they cook by the time the rice is done.

   Because of the volume of the rice and liquid, it must be cooked in a stockpot rather than a saucepan or skillet.

   The coconut milk will probably need to be whisked once opened, so pour it into a large (4-cup) measuring cup (preferably) and whisk or stir before adding the water.

MUSHROOM AND PEPPER BURRITOS

This filling is a welcome alternative to the more common bean-based mixtures that fill vegetarian burritos. The rich flavors of the mushrooms and peppers contrast perfectly with the sour cream and cheese.

MAKES 4 LARGE BURRITOS

   4 large (10-inch) flour tortillas

   1 tablespoon olive oil

   1 red bell pepper, halved and thinly sliced

   1 green bell pepper, halved and thinly
       sliced

   1 pound (6 cups) thinly sliced mushrooms

   ¼ teaspoon dried oregano

   Salt to taste

   Freshly ground black pepper

   ⅓ cup salsa, either Cooked Tomato-
       Chipotle Salsa or store-bought

   ½ cup sour cream

   1 cup grated Monterey Jack cheese with
       jalapeño peppers

1. Heat the tortillas using one of the methods on page 258. **2.** Heat the oil in a large skillet over medium heat. Add the peppers and cover the pan. Sauté, tossing occasionally, until they become soft and begin to brown, about 10 minutes. **3.** Mix in the mushrooms, oregano, salt, and pepper, and cook, uncovered, until the

Heating Tortillas

Here are 4 methods for heating tortillas so that they are moist and supple:

1. If you have just a few tortillas, you can heat them in a toaster for a few seconds. To do so, use your hands to rub a small amount of water on each tortilla, fold them, then place in the toaster for 10 seconds or so.

2. You can stack tortillas in a terry cloth towel and place in a vegetable steamer for about 5 minutes.

3. You can lightly moisten tortillas, wrap them in foil, and heat in a 350-degree oven for 5–10 minutes.

4. This method is great when everyone is filling his own burrito, assembly-line fashion, and heats his own tortilla. Fill a medium-size saucepan with 1 inch of water. Cover the pan with foil and poke a lot of little holes all over the surface. Bring the water to a boil, then place a tortilla on the foil; the boiling water will steam it. Use tongs to flip it over after 10 seconds or so. Use the tortilla immediately.

mushrooms have released their juices and they have evaporated. When done, the mushrooms will be brown and will begin to stick to the pan. Stir in the salsa and remove the pan from the heat. Let cool a bit before filling the burritos.

4. To serve, spoon ¼ of the mushroom mixture along the center of the tortilla. Top with ¼ of the sour cream and ¼ of the cheese. Fold in the sides, then roll up the tortilla. Repeat with the remaining ingredients.

Vegetarian Classics

DESSERTS

Dessert is one of the most satisfying courses to prepare because it is so appreciated by family and guests. Almost everyone agrees that a skillfully made dessert created in the home kitchen is hard to beat.

The recipes in this chapter are not difficult to prepare. If you follow the instructions regarding pan size, measure the ingredients precisely, and make sure that your oven is accurate, you can turn out these desserts with great success.

Sometimes I encounter people who think that because I am watchful of my diet and eat healthfully, I don't prepare rich or sweet desserts. I never quite understood the connection. To me, great desserts are not something to gorge on or eat on a daily basis. Rather, they are to be eaten in small or moderate portions and only occasionally. When treated this way they are something to be savored—and savor them I do.

So make your family and guests happy by presenting them with these grand finales. If you want some guidance with selecting a dessert for a special menu, take a look at the Menus (page 282) for inspiration.

LEMON ALMOND CAKE

This superb rendition of lemon cake has a moist and captivating texture made more special by the addition of finely ground almonds. A hot lemon syrup is brushed on the finished cake, intensifying the lemon flavor and eliminating the need for any icing. For an outstanding touch serve with a demitasse of espresso.

MAKES 16 SERVINGS

> 12 tablespoons (1½ sticks) unsalted butter, very soft, plus extra for greasing
>
> 1½ cups sugar
>
> Grated zest of 2 lemons
>
> 3 large eggs, at room temperature

½ teaspoon vanilla extract

1½ cups unbleached flour

½ cup finely ground almonds (from ⅓ cup whole almonds)

1½ teaspoons baking powder

½ teaspoon salt

⅔ cup low-fat milk

Lemon Syrup:

⅓ cup lemon juice (1½ lemons)

½ cup sugar

Confectioners' sugar for dusting

1. Preheat the oven to 350 degrees. Butter and flour a 9-inch springform pan. **2.** Combine the butter, sugar, and lemon zest in a large bowl. Use an electric mixer to beat the mixture until smooth and well blended. Add the eggs and vanilla, and beat until pale and fluffy, at least 2 minutes. **3.** Thoroughly combine the flour, almonds, baking powder, and salt in a medium-size bowl. Add to the butter mixture and beat a few seconds, then pour in the milk. Beat 30 seconds or so just until well mixed. Scrape the batter into the prepared pan. **4.** Bake 55 minutes, or until a knife inserted in the center of the cake comes out clean. Cool on a wire rack for 10 minutes, then remove the outer rim of the pan. Invert the cake onto a plate, remove the bottom of the pan, then invert again, right side up, onto the rack. **5.** To make the syrup, combine the lemon juice and sugar in a small saucepan. Heat, stirring often, just until the syrup is hot and the sugar has dissolved. Don't let it boil. **6.** Using a pastry brush, brush the syrup all over the cake. It will seem as if there is a lot of syrup, but the cake will absorb it all. Slide the cake onto a decorative plate and let cool completely, at least 2 hours. Just before serving use a sieve to sprinkle some confectioners' sugar all over the top of the cake.

TIPS: If you sprinkle on the confectioners' sugar too soon, it will melt into the lemon glaze,

Zesting Lemons

Here is a trick for zesting a lemon or other citrus fruit so that most of the zest doesn't get stuck in the grater. Stretch a piece of plastic wrap around a box grater, making sure the smoothest stretch of the plastic covers the fine holes that are on the opposite side of the largest holes. Hold the lemon and grate it right on the plastic that covers the small holes. When you have grated the entire lemon, peel away the plastic wrap. Almost all of the zest will have adhered to the plastic. Scrape it off with a knife. Check inside the grater; there will probably be some accumulated zest you can scrape off and add to your pile. Don't worry. This technique for grating citrus fruit will not rip the plastic so that little pieces of plastic mix with the zest. The plastic stays intact even though it gets punctured.

Vegetarian Classics

so be certain to wait until just before serving the cake or dust again if necessary.

The cake can be made a day in advance and kept covered at room temperature.

UPSIDE-DOWN PEAR GINGERBREAD

My friend Jane Walsh made this cake for me, and I now count it among my favorite desserts. When the gingerbread is inverted, it becomes infused with caramel and pear juices and is transformed into an extra-moist and fragrant bed for the succulent pears. A spoonful of whipped cream alongside it is irresistible.

SERVES 8

The Topping:

> 4 tablespoons (½ stick) **unsalted butter**
>
> ½ **cup firmly packed light or dark brown sugar**
>
> 2 **ripe but firm pears, preferably Bosc or Anjou**

The Cake:

> 1 **cup unbleached flour**
>
> 1 **teaspoon baking soda**
>
> ¼ **teaspoon salt**
>
> 2 **teaspoons cinnamon**
>
> 1 **teaspoon ground ginger**
>
> ½ **teaspoon ground cloves**
>
> 1 **egg**

> ½ **cup firmly packed light or dark brown sugar**
>
> ⅓ **cup unsulfured molasses**
>
> ½ **cup sour milk (see Tip)**
>
> 4 **tablespoons melted butter**
>
> **Lightly sweetened whipped cream (preferably spiked with rum)**

1. Preheat the oven to 350 degrees. Butter the sides of a 9-inch round cake pan (not a springform pan). **2.** To prepare the topping, melt the butter in a small saucepan. Add the brown sugar and stir together until blended. Scrape into the cake pan and spread evenly. **3.** Peel and slice each pear into quarters; remove and discard the cores. Slice each quarter into 3 slices. Arrange the 24 slices evenly around the pan. **4.** To make the cake, in a large bowl combine the flour, baking soda, salt, cinnamon, ginger, and cloves. In a separate bowl beat together the egg, brown sugar, molasses, sour milk, and melted butter. Scrape into the flour mixture and mix until well blended. **5.** Pour the batter over the pears. Bake 30 minutes, or until a knife inserted in the center of the cake comes out clean. Cool on a wire rack for 10 minutes, then invert onto a plate. Serve slightly warm or at room temperature with the whipped cream.

TIPS: To make sour milk, combine a ½ cup milk with 1 tablespoon vinegar and let sit 5 minutes.

Although this cake is best served the day it is made, it will still be delicious if made 1 day in advance, covered, and kept at room temperature.

Comparative Cake Pan Sizes

If you don't have the pan called for in a particular recipe, check below to see if you have another pan of comparable volume or one very close in size. Adjust the cooking time accordingly by adding or subtracting 10 minutes or so if the pans aren't the exact number of square inches. For example, if a recipe calls for an 8 × 8-inch square pan and you don't have such a pan, you can substitute a 9-inch layer pan because they both measure the same volume, 64 square inches. In this case the cooking time will remain the same.

ROUND CAKE PANS:

8-inch layer	50 square inches
9-inch layer	64 square inches

SQUARE AND RECTANGULAR PANS:

8 × 8 inches	64 square inches
9 × 9 inches	81 square inches
11 × 7 × 2 inches (Pyrex)	77 square inches
13 × 9 × 2 inches (Pyrex)	117 square inches
15 × 10 × 2 inches (jelly roll)	160 square inches

UPSIDE-DOWN CARAMELIZED APPLE CAKE

Unlike many apple cakes that are dominated by spices with only a backdrop of apples, this superlative rendition has an intensely flavored caramelized apple topping that rests on a vanilla-scented, buttery cake containing just a hint of cornmeal. The result is a dessert elegant enough for entertaining and homey enough for a family treat.

SERVES 8

4 tablespoons (½ stick) unsalted butter, plus extra for greasing

½ cup firmly packed light brown sugar

¼ teaspoon cinnamon

Dash nutmeg

2½ cups thinly sliced apples, such as Cortland, MacIntosh, or Macoun (about 3 small apples)

The Cake:

> **6 tablespoons unsalted butter, very soft**
>
> **1 cup sugar**
>
> **2 eggs, at room temperature**
>
> **1 teaspoon vanilla extract**
>
> **1 cup unbleached flour**
>
> **3 tablespoons cornmeal**
>
> **1 teaspoon baking powder**
>
> **½ teaspoon salt**
>
> **½ cup milk**

1. Preheat the oven to 350 degrees. Lightly butter the sides of a 9-inch cake pan (not a springform pan). **2.** Combine the butter, sugar, cinnamon, and nutmeg in a small saucepan and boil 30 seconds. Scrape the mixture into the prepared pan and spread evenly. Sprinkle the apples all over and press them down slightly to level them. **3.** To make the cake, beat the butter and sugar with an electric mixer until creamy. Add the eggs and vanilla, and beat until very smooth and fluffy, about 2 minutes. **4.** Sprinkle in the flour, cornmeal, baking powder, and salt, and beat 10 seconds. Pour in the milk and beat just until the batter is evenly moistened, about 1 minute. Spoon the batter over the apples and smooth the top. **5.** Bake 50 minutes, or until a knife inserted in the center of the cake comes out dry. Run a knife along the outer edge of the cake to loosen it from the pan. Place a plate over the cake, then flip it over to invert the cake onto the plate. Let the cake cool completely before serving.

TIPS: Granny Smith and Golden Delicious apples are too firm for this cake.

Although this cake is best served the day it is made, it will still be delicious made 1 day in advance, covered, and kept at room temperature.

BLUEBERRY CAKE WITH ALMOND GLAZE

This is an ideal summer cake when you want something festive but with little fuss. It is also a good choice for a brunch dessert when a sweet—but not too sweet—finale is called for. Because the blueberries help keep the cake moist, it can be made a day ahead and be just as good as on the first day.

SERVES 8

> **2 cups unbleached flour**
>
> **2 teaspoons baking powder**
>
> **½ teaspoon salt**
>
> **2 cups fresh blueberries, picked over, rinsed, and patted very dry, or *unthawed* frozen blueberries (if frozen, preferably small wild berries)**
>
> **8 tablespoons (1 stick) unsalted butter, very soft**
>
> **1¼ cups sugar**
>
> **2 large eggs, at room temperature**
>
> **1 teaspoon vanilla extract**
>
> **½ teaspoon almond extract**
>
> **1⅓ cups milk, at room temperature**

Desserts

The Glaze:

> ¾ cup confectioners' sugar
>
> 3–4 teaspoons warm water
>
> ½ teaspoon almond extract

1. Preheat the oven to 350 degrees. Butter and flour a 9-inch springform pan. **2.** Whisk together the flour, baking powder, and salt in a medium-size bowl. With a spoon or rubber spatula gently fold in the blueberries to coat them evenly. **3.** Use an electric mixer in a large bowl to cream the butter and sugar until light and somewhat creamy. Add the eggs and the vanilla and almond extracts, and beat until very fluffy, at least 3 minutes. Add the milk and beat until blended. (If the milk is cold when added, it will probably cause the batter to curdle. This will not harm the cake.) **4.** Use a rubber spatula to combine the flour mixture and the wet mixture until evenly blended. Scrape the batter into the prepared pan. **5.** Bake 65 minutes, or until a knife inserted in the cake comes out clean. Cool the cake on a wire rack for 10 minutes, then remove the outside rim. Place a large plate on top of the cake and invert. Remove the bottom of the pan and invert the cake onto another plate. Let cool completely, at least 2 hours. **6.** To make the glaze, combine the confectioners' sugar, 3 teaspoons water, and the almond extract in a small bowl. Beat thoroughly with a fork until smooth. Add a bit more water if necessary to achieve the consistency of honey. Use the tines of the fork to drizzle the glaze all over the top and a little bit down the sides of the cake. Let harden before cutting the cake, at least 20 minutes. If you make the cake a day in advance, store covered at room temperature.

TIP: A spoonful of whipped cream served alongside each slice of cake adds a seductive touch, especially when the cream is flavored with a dash of Grand Marnier or Triple Sec.

CLASSIC LEMON POPPY SEED CAKE

This moist, buttery cake has a delicate crumb and distinct lemon flavor. A generous dusting of confectioners' sugar is all that's needed to finish the cake. It's ideal for a portable snack, for picnics, and for lunch boxes. Poppy seed cake and similar cakes such as pound cake always taste best to me when thinly sliced and eaten with the fingers. If you want this to be a more formal dessert, try serving it with fresh berries and/or melon chunks.

SERVES 12–16

> 2½ cups unbleached flour
>
> 1½ teaspoons baking powder
>
> 1 teaspoon baking soda
>
> ¾ teaspoon salt
>
> 3 tablespoons poppy seeds
>
> 16 tablespoons (2 sticks) unsalted butter, very soft

Keeping Cakes

You have a number of different choices for storing cakes so that they remain fresh. The ideal covering for a cake is a glass or plastic dome because it doesn't touch the surface of the cake yet keeps all air out. In a pinch you can use an inverted large bowl or stockpot and get similar results. Make sure the plate your cake rests on is large enough so the dome or bowl fits snugly where it touches the plate. This method is especially helpful when the cake has icing or a sticky surface.

Plastic wrap is also useful for covering cakes. If the cake has icing, insert a few toothpicks near the outer edge and the center of the cake, allowing them to stick out an inch or so, then cover with the plastic wrap. The toothpicks will prevent the plastic from directly touching the top of the cake.

Aluminum foil can also cover cakes; however, it won't be as airtight as plastic wrap.

Most cakes that don't have icing can be kept at room temperature for 24 hours. Beyond that they should be refrigerated. If you refrigerate the cake, bring it to room temperature before serving.

1¾ cups sugar

Zest of 2 lemons

4 large eggs

1¼ cups buttermilk, or plain yogurt
 thinned with a little milk

Confectioners' sugar

1. Preheat the oven to 350 degrees. Generously butter and flour a Bundt pan or other 10-cup tube pan. **2.** In a medium-size bowl thoroughly combine the flour, baking powder, baking soda, salt, and poppy seeds. **3.** In a large mixing bowl beat the butter with an electric mixer until soft and creamy. Add the sugar and zest, and beat until well blended and smooth, at least 2 minutes. Add the eggs and beat until very fluffy, another 2 minutes. **4.** Beat in half the flour, then half the buttermilk, then repeat, beating until the batter is smooth. Scrape down the sides of the bowl as necessary. Pour the batter into the prepared pan and give the pan a thump on the counter to remove any air pockets. **5.** Bake 45–50 minutes, or until a knife inserted in the center of the cake comes out clean. Cool 10 minutes on a wire rack, then invert the cake onto the rack and remove the pan. Let cool completely before using a sieve to cover the cake with a heavy dusting of confectioners' sugar.

TIPS: Poppy seeds are usually sold in bulk in natural foods stores and can be stored in a jar in the freezer.

This cake is best served the day it is made.

COCONUT CAKE

The natural mate to this great family cake is a glass of cold milk. This one is for coconut lovers.

SERVES 6–9

- 1½ cups unbleached flour
- 1½ teaspoons baking powder
- ¼ teaspoon salt
- 8 tablespoons (1 stick) unsalted butter, very soft, plus extra for greasing
- 1 cup sugar
- 2 large eggs
- 1½ teaspoons vanilla extract
- ¼ teaspoon almond extract
- ¾ cup milk
- 1¼ cups sweetened coconut

Coconut Buttercream Icing:

- 6 tablespoons unsalted butter, very soft
- 1 cup confectioners' sugar
- 4–5 tablespoons milk
- ¾ cup sweetened coconut, divided

1. Preheat the oven to 350 degrees. Butter an 8 × 8-inch square cake pan. **2.** Thoroughly combine the flour, baking powder, and salt in a medium-size bowl. **3.** Use an electric mixer in a large bowl to beat the butter and sugar together until very well blended. Add the egg and vanilla and almond extracts, and beat until light and fluffy. Scrape down the sides of the bowl as necessary. **4.** Sprinkle in half of the flour mixture and pour in half of the milk. Beat until blended. Repeat with the remaining flour and milk. Stir in the coconut. **5.** Scrape the batter into the prepared pan. Bake 40–45 minutes, or until a knife inserted in the center of the cake comes out clean. Cool completely on a wire rack, at least 2 hours. **6.** To make the buttercream, combine the butter and confectioners' sugar in a large bowl and beat with an electric mixer until somewhat blended; it will be crumbly. Add the milk and beat just until fluffy, about 1 minute. (The icing may look a bit curdled, but it will look fine once spread on the cake.) Stir in a ½ cup coconut. **7.** When the cake is cool, spread the icing on top. Sprinkle the remaining ¼ cup coconut all over the top.

TIPS: If you prefer to have a more formal-looking cake that can sit on a platter, make it in a 9-inch springform pan that has been buttered and floured. Spread the icing just on top of the cake.

Because of the buttercream icing, store this cake in the refrigerator and bring to room temperature before serving.

CLASSIC CHEESECAKE

A well-made cheesecake is an indulgence worth every calorie, and it is deceptively simple to make. To achieve a perfectly smooth texture be certain to have your ingredients at room temperature to avoid beating too much air into the batter. You don't want the cheesecake to rise and then deflate. Beyond that there is little you need to concern yourself with to make this luxurious crowd-pleaser.

SERVES 12–16

The Crust:

> **Butter for greasing**
>
> **6 whole graham crackers (12 halves)**
>
> **¼ teaspoon cinnamon**
>
> **3 tablespoons melted butter**

The Filling:

> **1½ pounds cream cheese (three 8-ounce packages), at room temperature**
>
> **1¼ cups sugar**
>
> **1 tablespoon vanilla extract**
>
> **3 large eggs, at room temperature**

The Topping:

> **1 (16-ounce) container sour cream**
>
> **3 tablespoons sugar**
>
> **1 teaspoon vanilla extract**

1. Preheat the oven to 350 degrees. Butter the bottom of a 9-inch springform pan. **2.** Place the graham crackers in a plastic bag and seal. Use a rolling pin to roll the crackers until they are crushed into fine crumbs. You should get just about ¾ cup crumbs. Pour the crumbs into a bowl, toss with the cinnamon, then pour on the melted butter. Mix until evenly moistened. Lightly press the crumbs onto the bottom of the springform pan. **3.** To make the filling, beat the cream cheese in the bowl of an electric mixer until smooth. Mix in the sugar and beat again until smooth. Add the vanilla and 1 egg. Beat at low speed just until incorporated. Beat in the 2 remaining eggs one by one just until combined. Pour the filling into the prepared pan and give the pan a thump on the counter to remove any air pockets. **4.** Place the pan on a baking sheet and bake 45 minutes. The cheesecake will still be somewhat jiggly in the center and lightly golden on top when removed from the oven. **5.** Mix the topping ingredients together and gently spread over the top of the cheesecake. Return the pan to the oven and bake 10 minutes more. Cool the cheesecake on a wire rack until it is room temperature, at least 4 hours. Slide a knife around the edges, then remove the sides of the pan. Loosely cover the cheesecake and refrigerate it overnight. Cut into thin wedges and serve.

TIP: This cheesecake freezes beautifully. Place on a plate and freeze until firm, about 1½ hours. Remove from the freezer, wrap in foil, and then place in a plastic bag. Return to the freezer and freeze up to 1 month.

WHITE CHOCOLATE AND RASPBERRY CHEESECAKE

The 2 sensational flavors of white chocolate and raspberry come together to create a seductive cheesecake. As in Classic Cheesecake (preceding recipe), beating as little air as possible into the batter will produce a memorable satiny creaminess.

SERVES 12–16

The Crust:

   Butter for greasing

   6 whole graham crackers (12 halves)

   ¼ teaspoon cinnamon

   3 tablespoons butter, melted

The Filling:

   6 ounces white chocolate (either morsels or finely chopped bars)

   1½ pounds cream cheese, at room temperature

   1 cup sugar

   1 tablespoon unbleached flour

   4 eggs, at room temperature

   1 teaspoon vanilla extract

   1 cup fresh or partially thawed frozen raspberries, plus extra for garnish

The Topping:

   1 (16-ounce) container sour cream

   2 tablespoons sugar

   ½ teaspoon vanilla extract

1. Preheat the oven to 350 degrees. Butter the bottom and sides of a 9-inch springform pan. **2.** Place the graham crackers in a plastic bag and seal. Use a rolling pin to roll the crackers until they are crushed into fine crumbs. You should get about ¾ cup crumbs. Pour the crumbs into a bowl, toss with the cinnamon, then pour on the melted butter. Mix until evenly moistened. Lightly press the crumbs onto the bottom of the springform pan. **3.** Place the white chocolate in a small heavy-bottomed saucepan over low heat. Stir continuously until about half melted. Remove the pan from the heat and stir until melted and smooth. Be patient and careful; white chocolate doesn't like high heat. **4.** In the bowl of an electric mixer beat the cream cheese and sugar until smooth. Add the white chocolate and flour, and beat just until incorporated. Add the eggs one by one, beating after each addition. Beat in the vanilla. **5.** Pour ⅔ of the filling into the prepared pan. Carefully place the raspberries all over the top. Gently pour on the remaining filling. **6.** Place the pan on a baking sheet and bake 50 minutes. It will still be jiggly in the center and a pale golden color on top when removed from the oven. **7.** Mix the topping ingredients together and gently spread over the top of the cheesecake. Return the pan to the oven and bake 10 minutes more. Cool the cheesecake on a wire rack until room temperature, at least 4 hours. Slide a knife around the edges, then remove the sides of the pan. Loosely cover the cheesecake and refrigerate it overnight. Cut into thin wedges and serve.

TIP: This cheesecake freezes very well. Follow the directions for Classic Cheesecake (page 266).

Rhubarb

The word "rhubarb" comes from the medieval Latin words for "barbarians beyond the Rha" (the former name of the Volga River). It presumably was considered the vegetable for certain foreigners living beyond the river. It is native to Russia and a member of the buckwheat family. Although usually used as a fruit, rhubarb is actually a vegetable.

EASY STRAWBERRY-RHUBARB TART

The delicate crust for this glorious spring dessert is pressed in the pie pan rather than rolled, and the filling requires no precooking, making this scarlet-hued tart a breeze to prepare.

SERVES 8

Walnut Crust:

   ⅔ cup walnuts

   3 tablespoons sugar

   6 tablespoons unsalted butter, very soft

   1 egg yolk

   ½ teaspoon vanilla extract

   1 cup unbleached flour

The Filling:

   1 pound rhubarb, thinly sliced (3 cups)

   1 pint strawberries, sliced

   1 cup sugar

   ¼ cup flour

   ½ teaspoon cinnamon

1. Butter the sides and bottom of a 9-inch tart pan with a removable bottom or a glass pie plate. **2.** Combine the walnuts and sugar in a food processor and process until very fine. Stop the machine and add all the remaining crust ingredients. Process just until evenly moistened and crumbly. (If you don't have a food processor, grind the nuts and sugar in a blender until fine. Pour them into a large bowl and use an electric mixer to mix in the remaining crust ingredients.) Scatter the mixture all over the pie pan and press it into the sides and bottom with your fingers. (It's easier to do the sides first.) Chill at least 30 minutes, or until very firm. **3.** Preheat the oven to 400 degrees. **4.** Combine the filling ingredients in a large bowl. Let sit for at least 20 minutes, stirring occasionally, so the juices can moisten the sugar. Scrape the mixture into the chilled crust and smooth over the top. **5.** Place the pie pan on a baking sheet and bake 45 minutes, or until the crust is golden and the filling is bubbling hot. Halfway through the cooking time use a large spoon to flatten the top of the filling; this will also moisten it for even cooking. If your tart pan has a removable rim, cool the pie 5 minutes before removing it. Cool the tart completely on a wire rack, at least 3 hours, before slicing.

STRAWBERRY AND CHOCOLATE "PIZZA"

The idea of dessert pizza has been around for a few years, but where it originated is anyone's guess. Whether you feel it is clever or silly to use the word "pizza" for a dessert, you will undoubtedly agree that this is a delicious and fun creation. A thin cookie crust is topped with layers of melted chocolate, fluffy cream cheese, and plump, juicy strawberries. Cut into wedges and eaten while held in the hands, this fruit pizza is a popular treat at a young kids' or teens' party.

SERVES 8–10

The Crust:

> 8 tablespoons (1 stick) unsalted butter, very soft
>
> 1 cup unbleached flour
>
> ½ cup very finely chopped pecans or almonds
>
> ¼ cup sugar
>
> 2 tablespoons water

The Topping:

> 1 cup semisweet chocolate chips
>
> 1 (8-ounce) package cream cheese (regular or Neufchâtel), at room temperature
>
> ½ cup confectioners' sugar
>
> 1 pint fresh strawberries, stems removed and halved

¼ cup apricot preserves, apple jelly, or red currant jelly

1 teaspoon water

1. Preheat the oven to 375 degrees. Lightly butter a 10-inch springform pan. **2.** To make the crust, place all the ingredients in a large bowl and use an electric mixer to beat them together just until blended into even, moist crumbs. Don't overbeat. Sprinkle the dough in the springform pan and press it down with your fingers to form a flat crust. Bake 15–20 minutes, or until lightly golden. **3.** Immediately scatter the chocolate chips over the hot crust. Let sit 5 minutes. Use a spatula to spread the melted chocolate all over the crust and to the outer edges. Remove the outer ring of the pan and let the crust cool completely on a wire rack, about 1 hour. If the chocolate is not hard at this point, you can chill the crust for 15 minutes or so. When cool, use a spatula to lift the crust off the pan and place it on a large, flat plate or just leave it on the base. **4.** Use an electric mixer or wire whisk to beat the cream cheese and confectioners' sugar together until blended. Spread all over the crust, leaving a 1-inch border of chocolate showing. **5.** Place the strawberry halves in concentric circles on the cream cheese. **6.** Heat the preserves or jelly with the water in a saucepan until hot, stirring all the while to blend the mixture. Use a pastry brush to dab some of the glaze on each strawberry half. Chill at least 1 hour or up to 24 hours before serving. Slide the "pizza" onto a cutting board and cut in half using a very large knife, then cut into wedges. Serve on plates and hold it in your hands to eat.

LEMON TART

This classic French tart can be found in patisseries all over Paris. This version, with a buttery almond crust, is my favorite.

SERVES 8

The Crust:

¼ cup whole almonds

1 cup unbleached flour

3 tablespoons sugar

6 tablespoons unsalted butter, cut into bits

1 tablespoon canola oil

3 tablespoons ice water

¼ teaspoon almond extract

The Filling:

6 large eggs

¾ cup sugar

Zest of 1 lemon

½ cup fresh lemon juice (about 3 lemons)

6 tablespoons unsalted butter, cut into bits

1. To make the crust, grind the almonds in a blender or food processor until very fine. Pour into a medium-size bowl and stir in the flour and sugar. Drop in the butter bits and toss to coat with the flour. Rub the butter into the flour with your fingertips until coarse crumbs form. **2.**

Combine the oil, water, and almond extract in a small bowl. Drizzle over the flour mixture and stir with a fork until moistened. Gather the mixture into a ball and knead 1 or 2 times. Form into a ball again, then flatten into a disk. Wrap in plastic and chill 20 minutes. **3.** Lightly flour a work surface. Roll the dough into an 11-inch circle and use to line a 9-inch tart pan with a removable bottom. Prick all over with a fork. Cover with plastic and chill at least 30 minutes or freeze 20 minutes. **4.** Preheat the oven to 400 degrees. **5.** Line the pastry with aluminum foil and fill with pie weights, dried beans, or rice. Bake 10 minutes. Remove the foil and beans, and bake 5 minutes more. Let cool. Lower the oven heat to 350 degrees. **6.** To make the filling, add about 1 inch of water to the bottom part of a double boiler; you don't want the water to touch the bottom of the top pan. Place over medium heat. Whisk the eggs in a large bowl until very smooth. Whisk in the sugar, lemon zest, and lemon juice. Stir in the butter. Pour into the top of the double boiler and, whisking constantly, cook until the mixture is the consistency of thick heavy cream, about 8 minutes. Do not let the mixture boil. **7.** Immediately pour the filling into the pie shell. Bake 17–20 minutes, or just until the edges are slightly set and the center is still jiggly. Cool on a wire rack until room temperature, then chill until ready to serve. The tart should be served cool or cold.

TIP: This can be made the day before you plan to serve it. Refrigerate overnight.

RHUBARB COBBLER

This crimson-colored filling, topped with a flaky biscuit crust, has that sensual blend of sweetness and tartness that is the hallmark of stewed rhubarb. A small spoonful of vanilla ice cream provides a great contrasting touch.

SERVES 6–8

The Filling:

> **8 cups diced rhubarb (2¼ pounds)**
>
> **1¼ cups sugar**
>
> **2 teaspoons cornstarch**
>
> **2 tablespoons unsalted butter**
>
> **2 tablespoons orange juice**
>
> **½ teaspoon cinnamon**
>
> **¼ teaspoon ground cloves**

The Biscuit Topping:

> **¾ cup unbleached flour**
>
> **¼ cup plus 1 tablespoon sugar**
>
> **1¼ teaspoons baking powder**
>
> **½ teaspoon salt**
>
> **3 tablespoons unsalted butter, chilled**
>
> **1 egg yolk**
>
> **¼ cup milk**
>
> **½ teaspoon vanilla extract**
>
> **¼ teaspoon almond extract**
>
> **Vanilla ice cream (optional)**

1. Preheat the oven to 375 degrees. Place an 8 × 8-inch baking pan or similar shallow 2-quart baking dish nearby. **2.** Combine all the filling ingredients in a medium-size saucepan and bring to a boil. Lower the heat to a lively simmer and cook the filling, stirring frequently, for about 10 minutes, or until the rhubarb is very tender. Pour the filling into the baking pan. **3.** To make the topping, combine the flour, ¼ cup sugar, baking powder, and salt in a medium-size bowl. Cut the butter into bits and rub it into the flour with your fingertips until little pellets form. **4.** In a small bowl stir together the egg yolk, milk, and vanilla and almond extracts. Pour into the flour mixture and stir with a fork. Scrape the dough onto a lightly floured work surface and knead once or twice. Use a rolling pin to roll the dough the same size as the top of the baking dish. Lightly flour the dough as necessary; it shouldn't be at all sticky. Drape the dough onto the rolling pin and unroll it onto the filling. Sprinkle the top with the remaining tablespoon of sugar. **5.** Bake 25 minutes, then cool on a wire rack. Serve warm with vanilla ice cream, if desired.

TIP: To get a flaky and tender biscuit topping, it is essential that you handle the dough as little as possible. The dough should be evenly moist, cohesive, and not crumbly, but you don't want to overwork it beyond that point.

BLUEBERRY CRISP

The intensity of the blueberries is electrifying in this foolproof dessert. The rich, crunchy topping is a welcome foil for the vivid, fruity filling, and it is all made more wonderful when served with a small spoonful of vanilla ice cream. Because blueberries are the ultimate hassle-free fruit, you can put this dish together in just a few minutes, making it a good choice for entertaining when time is short.

SERVES 4–6

> 1 quart fresh blueberries, picked over, washed, and well-drained, or 2 (12-ounce) packages frozen blueberries, preferably small wild ones
>
> ¼ cup firmly packed light brown sugar
>
> 1 tablespoon Grand Marnier (optional but highly recommended)
>
> 1 tablespoon unbleached flour for fresh berries or 1½ tablespoons flour for frozen berries

The Topping:
> ½ cup unbleached flour
>
> ¼ cup quick or regular oats
>
> ½ cup firmly packed light brown sugar
>
> ½ teaspoon cinnamon
>
> 4 tablespoons chilled unsalted butter, cut into bits
>
> Vanilla ice cream (optional)

1. Preheat the oven to 375 degrees. **2.** Place the blueberries in a shallow 1½-quart baking dish. Sprinkle on the sugar, Grand Marnier, and flour, and toss to coat the berries evenly. **3.** To make the topping, mix together the flour, oats, sugar, and cinnamon in a medium-size bowl. Drop in the butter bits, toss, then rub them into the flour mixture with your fingertips until a texture resembling coarse crumbs forms. Sprinkle this all over the berries. **4.** Bake 40–45 minutes for fresh berries, 45–50 minutes if using frozen berries. When done, the crisp will be golden brown on top and bubbly on the sides. Let cool on a wire rack to room temperature. Serve small portions with a scoop of vanilla ice cream, if desired.

TIP: For the juices in a crisp to thicken it is essential that they bubble (or boil) under the blanket of crumbs.

PEACH AND RASPBERRY CRISP

The summer flavors of peaches and raspberries are vibrant in this luxurious crisp, and they are enhanced by the mantle of crunchy pecan-studded crumbs. A simple, fantastic dessert.

SERVES 6 (8 IF ACCOMPANIED BY VANILLA ICE CREAM)

2½ pounds (about 9) barely ripe peaches

1 cup fresh or unthawed frozen raspberries

3 tablespoons firmly packed light brown sugar

2 tablespoons unbleached flour

The Topping:

½ cup unbleached flour

½ cup firmly packed light brown sugar

½ teaspoon cinnamon

¼ teaspoon salt

4 tablespoons (½ stick) chilled unsalted butter, cut into bits

3 tablespoons finely chopped pecans

1. Preheat the oven to 375 degrees. **2.** Bring a medium-size saucepan filled halfway with water to a boil. Drop in a few peaches and let sit 10 seconds. Remove immediately and let cool a few minutes. With a small, sharp knife peel off the skin. Repeat with the remaining peaches. Cut the peaches into small chunks and place in an 8 × 8-inch pan or other shallow 1½-quart baking dish. **3.** Sprinkle the raspberries, brown sugar, and flour over the peaches and toss lightly. **4.** To make the topping, combine the flour, brown sugar, cinnamon, and salt in a medium-size bowl. Drop in the butter bits and rub the butter into the mixture with your fingertips to form small, moist crumbs. Stir in the pecans. Sprinkle all over the peaches. **5.** Bake 40–45 minutes, or until the top is golden and the filling boils vigorously. Cool completely on a wire rack before serving.

TIPS: You want the peaches to be ripe for this dessert, but not so juicy that they'll make the filling too soupy.

Nectarines also work well here. It isn't essential that you peel them, but I highly recommend it.

GRAND MARNIER SEMOLINA PUDDING

Italian semolina pudding is a luscious, silken dessert. This version has an irresistible orange and cream flavor that reminds me of one of my favorite childhood treats—Creamsicles. The final presentation is stunning, which makes this a particularly good choice for entertaining. The pudding is chilled in a ring mold (preferably), then inverted and filled with orange sections. A Grand Marnier sauce is spooned on individual servings. Don't be reluctant to tackle this because of the lengthy directions; it is easy to prepare and well worth it.

SERVES 6–8

3 large navel oranges

2 cups milk

⅓ cup plus 3 tablespoons sugar

⅓ cup semolina or farina (see Tip)

2 egg yolks

½ teaspoon vanilla extract

Oil for greasing

1 cup heavy cream, well chilled

2 tablespoons Grand Marnier, Triple Sec,
or other orange liqueur

The Sauce:

⅔ cup orange juice (squeezed from the
above oranges)

⅓ cup sugar

1 tablespoon cornstarch

1 tablespoon unsalted butter, cut into bits

2 tablespoons Grand Marnier, Triple Sec,
or other orange liqueur

1. Grate the zest from 1 of the oranges and scrape it into a medium-size heavy-bottomed saucepan. Whisk in the milk and ⅓ cup sugar and bring to a boil, whisking often. Turn the heat to medium-low and slowly whisk in the semolina. Cook, whisking constantly, for 5 minutes, or until the mixture is like creamy mashed potatoes. Remove the pan from the heat and whisk in the egg yolks and vanilla. Scrape the semolina into a large bowl and cool 20 minutes, whisking occasionally. **2.** Meanwhile, thoroughly oil a 1-quart ring mold or other 1-quart mold, deep dish, or bowl. **3.** Whip the cream with the remaining 3 tablespoons sugar until stiff. Whisk the Grand Marnier into the semolina mixture until smooth. Carefully mix in half of the whipped cream to lighten the mixture, then use a rubber spatula to fold in the remaining cream just until no streaks show. **4.** Spoon the pudding into the mold and smooth the top. Give the mold a few thumps on the counter to make

sure there are no air pockets. Cover with plastic wrap and chill for at least 2 hours or up to 8 hours. **5.** Meanwhile, make the sauce. With a sharp paring knife cut the white pith off the orange that was grated and the entire peel off one of the remaining oranges. Over a bowl cut the sections from the oranges by slicing down on each side of every section, releasing them from the membranes. Let the sections fall into the bowl as each one is freed, then squeeze the juices from the remaining membranes into the bowl. **6.** Strain the juice into a measuring cup; you need ⅔ cup. If you don't have enough, you can squeeze the juice from *half* of the remaining orange; you will need the other half as a garnish. Set aside the orange sections. **7.** In a small saucepan thoroughly combine the sugar and cornstarch. Slowly whisk in the orange juice and cook over medium heat, stirring constantly with a rubber spatula, until the sauce is thick and clear, about 5 minutes. Do not let it boil. Remove from the heat and drop in the bits of butter. Stir until melted, then stir in the Grand Marnier. Pour into a sauceboat and chill until cold, about 1 hour. (If the sauce gets too thick to pour easily, thin with a bit of orange juice.) **8.** Run a knife around the outer and inner edges of the pudding mold, place a platter over the mold, and invert the pudding onto the platter. With a slotted spoon remove the orange sections from their bowl and fill the center of the pudding with them, or place around the outer edge of the pudding. Cut the remaining orange into thin half-moon slices and decorate the edges of the pudding. Serve the pudding cut into wedges and topped with orange sections and some sauce.

TIP: Semolina is a flour made from durum wheat, the hardest wheat there is. It is coarsely ground and resembles cornmeal in appearance. If you cannot find semolina, you can purchase "farina" in the cereal section of most supermarkets, and it will be a good substitute. Farina is also made from a hard wheat, though not as hard as durum.

PERFECT CHOCOLATE CHIP COOKIES

After much experimentation this is my version of the perfect chocolate chip cookie—thin, packed with chocolate chips, and filled with a deep, rich flavor.

MAKES 4 DOZEN

> 2 cups unbleached flour
>
> 1 teaspoon baking soda
>
> ¾ teaspoon salt
>
> 12 tablespoons (1½ sticks) unsalted butter, very soft
>
> 1 cup sugar
>
> ½ cup firmly packed light brown sugar
>
> 2 teaspoons vanilla extract
>
> 2 large eggs
>
> 3 tablespoons milk
>
> 1 (16-ounce) package (a generous 2½ cups) semisweet chocolate chips

1. Combine the flour, baking soda, and salt in a medium-size bowl. **2.** In a large bowl, using an electric mixer, beat the butter, sugar, brown sugar, and vanilla until combined. Add the eggs and milk, and beat until light and fluffy. Pour in the flour mixture and beat just until blended. Stir in the chocolate chips. Chill the dough 1 hour, or cover and chill up to 4 hours. **3.** Preheat the oven to 350 degrees. **4.** Scoop up a heaping teaspoonful of dough and roll it between the palms of your hands to form a ball. Place the balls of dough about 2 inches apart on an ungreased baking sheet and press lightly to flatten. Bake 10–12 minutes, or until lightly browned. Let sit 1 minute before transferring the cookies to a cooling rack. Cool completely before storing in a covered tin.

TIP: You can use this as a basic recipe and play around with additions, such as white chocolate chips, chocolate chunks, chopped pecans, and walnuts.

LARGE SOFT GINGER COOKIES

Filled with spices and soft and chewy in texture, these cookies are a "10," according to my son, Daniel. They match well with fresh fruit for an afternoon snack or a fun and homey dessert.

MAKES 18–20 LARGE (3½-INCH) COOKIES

Cookie Tips

— — —

■ Cookie sheets and baking sheets should be shiny silver rather than black because a dark surface causes the cookies to have dark bottoms. You can also line your baking sheets with parchment paper to prevent sticking or burned bottoms.

■ For a rich, pure flavor always use butter, not margarine, for your dough. (In fact, you should never use margarine for anything, in my opinion.)

■ Measure out the dough carefully to make the cookies all the same size. They will cook evenly as a result and look very appealing.

■ Always bake cookies on the center rack of the oven. If you are making 2 batches at the same time, place the other baking sheet on the top rack and switch the 2 batches around midway during cooking. Cookies baked on a rack placed at the bottom third of the oven will burn easily on their undersides.

■ Use large cooling racks to cool the cookies on once they are removed from their baking sheets. Cool the cookies completely before storing them.

---

2 cups unbleached flour

2 teaspoons baking soda

1 tablespoon ground ginger

1 teaspoon cinnamon

½ teaspoon ground cloves

½ teaspoon salt

12 tablespoons (1½ sticks) unsalted butter, very soft, plus extra for greasing

1 cup firmly packed light brown sugar

1 large egg

¼ cup unsulfured molasses (such as Grandma's)

¼ cup sugar (approximately) for rolling

1. In a medium-size bowl thoroughly combine the flour, baking soda, ginger, cinnamon, cloves, and salt. **2.** In a large bowl, using an electric mixer, cream the butter and sugar until smooth. Add the egg and molasses, and beat until well blended. Add the dry ingredients and beat just until combined. (I use my hands at this point to knead the dough a few times and get it evenly moistened.) Cover and chill at least 1 hour or up to 4 hours. **3.** Preheat the oven to 350 degrees. Make sure the oven rack is in the center of the oven. Lightly butter a baking sheet. Place about ¼ cup sugar on a small plate. **4.** Gather some dough and roll into a ball about 1½ inches in diameter. Roll it in the sugar to completely coat

277

Desserts

it. Continue with more dough, placing the balls about 2 inches apart on the baking sheet. You will be able to fit about 9 balls on a sheet. **5.** Bake 15–17 minutes, or until cracked on top and golden on the edges. Wait 2 minutes before removing the cookies from the sheet. Cool completely on a wire rack. Store the cookies in zippered freezer bags.

CHOCOLATE-GLAZED ALMOND COOKIES

These are the ultimate almond cookies. The crisp, buttery base is filled with ground almonds, the cookies are covered with sliced almonds, and the tops are drizzled with melted chocolate. A very special cookie indeed.

MAKES 1½ DOZEN

> 8 tablespoons (1 stick) **unsalted butter, very soft**
>
> ¾ **cup sugar**
>
> 1 **large egg**
>
> 1 **teaspoon almond extract**
>
> ½ **cup finely ground almonds (from about ⅓ cup whole almonds)**
>
> ¾ **cup unbleached flour**
>
> ½ **cup sliced almonds**
>
> ½ **cup semisweet chocolate chips**

1. Preheat the oven to 350 degrees. Make sure the oven rack is in the center of the oven. **2.** In a large bowl, using an electric mixer, beat the butter and sugar until smooth. Add the egg and almond extract, and beat until well mixed. Sprinkle in the ground almonds and flour, and beat just until combined. **3.** Set a cookie sheet in front of you. Place the sliced almonds in a small bowl. Use your hands to roll some dough into a 1½-inch ball. Press it into the sliced almonds so that one side gets coated with the nuts and flattens out somewhat. Place the cookie, nut side up, on the baking sheet. Repeat with the dough to make 12 cookies. They should be about 2 inches apart on the baking sheet. **4.** Bake 15 minutes, or until golden brown on the edges. Remove the cookies from the baking sheet and cool on a wire rack. Repeat with the remaining dough. **5.** To make the glaze: place the chocolate chips in a small zippered freezer bag. Bring a small saucepan of water to a boil. Remove the pan from the heat. Tip the bag diagonally so the chips collect in one corner. Dip that corner into the water until the chips melt, just a few minutes. Squeeze the corner occasionally to distribute the melted chips. When all the chocolate is melted, use scissors to trim off the tiniest tip on that corner. Squeeze the chocolate through the hole and drizzle it all over the tops of the cookies. I like to make "S" strokes. Let the chocolate harden before serving or storing the cookies, about 30–60 minutes, depending on the weather.

TIP: When you melt the chips in the zippered freezer bag, be careful not to overheat the chocolate because it doesn't like excessive heat. Immerse the bag in the water just enough to heat the chips through, then squeeze the bag a bit to see that they are melted.

CHOCOLATE EARTHQUAKES

These rich fudge cookies have a powdered sugar topping that creates the effect of a cracked earth peeking through a blanket of snow, hence their name. They are quick to make and freeze well.

MAKES 4–5 DOZEN

   8 tablespoons (1 stick) **unsalted butter**

   4 (1-ounce) squares **unsweetened chocolate**

   2 **large eggs**

   2 **cups sugar**

   2 teaspoons **vanilla extract**

   2 cups **unbleached flour**

   2 teaspoons **baking powder**

   ¼ teaspoon **salt**

   1 cup **confectioners' sugar**

1. Place the butter in a medium-size heavy-bottomed saucepan and begin to melt it over medium-low heat. Add the chocolate and melt it with the butter, stirring frequently. When the chocolate is about 80 percent melted, remove the pan from the heat and let the mixture continue to melt (you do not want the chocolate to get too hot). Let cool. **2.** Whisk the eggs in a large bowl. Whisk in the sugar, vanilla, and melted chocolate mixture. Add the flour, baking powder, and salt, and whisk until smooth. Chill the mixture until cold and firm, at least 2 hours or up to 24 hours. **3.** Place an oven rack in the center of the oven if you are going to bake the cookies on 1 baking sheet, or place 1 rack on the upper level and 1 in the center if you are using 2 baking sheets. Preheat the oven to 350 degrees. Lightly butter 1 or 2 baking sheets. **4.** Place the confectioners' sugar in a small bowl. Scoop up a heaping teaspoon of cookie dough and roll it between the palms of your hands to shape into a ball. Roll it in the powdered sugar and coat well. Place on the baking sheet. Make a dozen balls for each baking sheet. **5.** Bake the cookies for 12 minutes, switching the placement of the baking sheets halfway through the cooking time if you are cooking 2 batches at once. Cool slightly. Use a spatula to move the cookies from the baking sheet to a wire rack to cool. Let the cookies cool completely before storing in a covered tin with a sheet of waxed paper in between the layers.

TIP: These cookies freeze well in zippered freezer bags.

Desserts

COCONUT BARS

These scrumptuous bars are fun to make and will remind you of a Mounds candy bar, though they are not nearly as sweet. A thin, buttery crust is topped with a creamy coconut layer, then decoratively drizzled with chocolate—like a Jackson Pollock painting. If you haven't "painted" with chocolate in the manner described below, be sure to try it; it's easy and the results are eye-catching.

MAKES 18 BARS

The Crust:

> **8 tablespoons (1 stick) unsalted butter, very soft**
>
> **¼ cup sugar**
>
> **1 large egg**
>
> **1 teaspoon vanilla extract**
>
> **1 cup unbleached flour**
>
> **¼ teaspoon salt**

The Topping:

> **6 ounces Neufchâtel (light cream cheese), very soft**
>
> **3 tablespoons unsalted butter, very soft**
>
> **½ cup sugar**
>
> **1 large egg**
>
> **¼ teaspoon almond extract**
>
> **1½ tablespoons unbleached flour**
>
> **3 cups (about 12 ounces) sweetened coconut**
>
> **½ cup semisweet chocolate chips**

1. Preheat the oven to 350 degrees. Lightly butter a 9 × 13-inch Pyrex dish or baking pan. (You don't want the baking dish any smaller or the bars will be too thick.) **2.** In a large bowl, using an electric mixer, beat the butter and sugar together until blended. Beat in the egg and vanilla until smooth and creamy. Sprinkle in the flour and salt, and beat just until combined. Scrape the batter into the prepared dish and use a rubber spatula to spread it evenly on the bottom. It will be very thin. Bake 15 minutes. **3.** Meanwhile, make the topping using the same bowl and beaters (you don't have to wash them). Beat the cream cheese and butter until smooth. Add the sugar, egg, and almond extract, and beat until combined. Sprinkle in the flour and beat until blended. Stir in the coconut. **4.** When the crust is done, spoon the batter into it. Carefully spread it around to cover the crust evenly. Bake 18–20 minutes, or just until the top of the batter begins to get a tiny bit of color. Place on a wire rack to cool. **5.** While the bars are still hot, fill a medium-size saucepan halfway with water, bring to a boil, and remove the pan from the heat. Place the chocolate chips in a small zippered freezer bag and tilt the bag so the chocolate chips collect in one corner. Lower the bag into the water, keeping the chips in the corner, and let them melt, about 2 minutes. Squeeze the chips occasionally to see if they are melted. Remove the bag from the water. Keeping the bag tilted, snip off a very tiny piece of the corner. Squirt the chocolate all over the coconut surface in an abstract pattern. When everything is completely cooled, cut into small bars.

PECAN CARAMEL BARS

These outrageously delicious bars are somewhat of a cross between pralines and pecan pie, with the alluring taste of caramel.

MAKES 24 BARS

Shortbread Crust:

>   12 tablespoons (1½ sticks) unsalted butter, very soft
>
>   ½ cup confectioners' sugar
>
>   1 egg yolk
>
>   ½ teaspoon vanilla extract
>
>   1½ cups unbleached flour

Topping:

>   2 large eggs
>
>   4 tablespoons unsalted butter, melted
>
>   1 cup firmly packed light brown sugar
>
>   ½ teaspoon baking powder
>
>   ½ teaspoon vanilla extract
>
>   2 cups roughly chopped pecans

1. Preheat the oven to 350 degrees. Set out a 12 × 7 × 2-inch baking dish (such as a Pyrex glass dish) or pan. **2.** Place the butter and confectioners' sugar in the bowl of an electric mixer and beat until blended. Add the egg yolk and vanilla, and beat until smooth and incorporated. Sprinkle in the flour and beat just until mixed yet still crumbly; do not overwork the dough. **3.** Scrape the dough into the baking dish. Use your fingers or the palm of your hand to press the dough evenly into the baking dish. Bake 20 minutes, or until lightly golden around the edges. **4.** While the crust is baking, beat the eggs in a medium-size bowl. Beat in the butter, sugar, baking powder, and vanilla. Stir in the chopped pecans. **5.** When the crust comes out of the oven, immediately pour on the pecan mixture and make sure it is evenly distributed. Bake 15 minutes, or until the center is set and not jiggly when you shake the dish. Cool on a wire rack for 10 minutes, then run a knife around the edges to loosen them. Cool completely, about 2 hours. Cut into small bars.

MENUS

CASUAL MENUS

Tossed Mesclun Salad (page 62)

Baked Cheese Polenta
with Corn and Green Chilies
(page 232)

Blueberry Cake with Almond Glaze
(page 263)

■ ■ ■

Spinach Salad with Oranges,
Feta Cheese, and Olives (page 65)

Sweet Potato, White Bean,
and Pepper Tian (page 237)

Crusty bread

Upside-Down Pear Gingerbread
(page 261)

■ ■ ■

Classic Guacamole (page 36) with corn chips

Tamale Pie (page 222)

Coconut Cake (page 266)

■ ■ ■

Spinach Salad with Grapefruit
and Avocado (page 65)

Smoky Black Bean Enchiladas
(page 220)

Chocolate-Glazed Almond Cookies
(page 278)

■ ■ ■

Chopped Salad with Avocado
and Chickpeas (page 64)

Baked Orzo with Spinach,
Tomatoes, and Corn (page 233)

Chocolate Earthquakes
(page 279)

■ ■ ■

Classic Guacamole (page 36)

Ten-Minute Chilaquiles
(page 222)

Classic Lemon Poppy Seed Cake
(page 264)

■ ■ ■

Mixed Greens with Dried Cranberries
and Toasted Pecans (page 62)

Baked Macaroni and Smoked Cheese
(page 226)

French bread

Steamed green beans

Perfect Chocolate Chip Cookies
(page 276)

■ ■ ■

Tossed Mesclun Salad (page 62)

Tortellini with Spinach, Garlic,
and Smoked Cheese (page 215)

French bread

Lemon Tart (page 271)

■ ■ ■

Leafy Greens and Radicchio with Shaved
Parmesan Cheese (page 63)

Linguine with Spicy Mushroom Ragu (page 215)

French bread

Upside-Down Caramelized Apple Cake
(page 262)

■ ■ ■

Tossed Mesclun Salad (page 62)

Easy Zucchini, Tomato, and Cheese Tart
(page 163)

Egg Noodles with Garlic and Herbs
(page 149)

Blueberry Cake with Almond Glaze
(page 263)

■ ■ ■

Romaine with Apples, Walnuts,
and Blue Cheese (page 63)

Shepherd's Pie (page 170)

Pecan Caramel Bars (page 281)

■ ■ ■

Spinach Salad with Oranges,
Feta Cheese, and Olives (page 65)

Vegetable Tagine (page 250)

White Chocolate and
Raspberry Cheesecake (page 267)

■ ■ ■

Chopped Salad with Avocado
and Chickpeas (page 64)

Classic Polenta with
Wild Mushroom Ragu (page 246)

Lemon Almond Cake (page 259)

■ ■ ■

ELEGANT MENUS

Sun-Dried Tomato Pesto (page 21)
with Basic Crostini (page 39)

Tossed Mesclun Salad (page 62)

Spaghettini with Spinach
in Garlic-Cream Sauce (page 205)

Blueberry Crisp (page 273)

■ ■ ■

Classic Vegetable Curry (page 243)

Basmati rice

Banana Mint Raita (page 155) or
Cucumber and Tomato Raita (page 156)

Fresh Mango Chutney (page 157)

Papadams or Chapatis (purchased)

Masala Chai (page 134)

Classic Cheesecake (page 266)

■ ■ ■

Garlic and Oil Dipping Sauce
for Tuscan-Style Bread (page 37)

Romaine with Apples, Walnuts,
and Blue Cheese (page 63)

Vegetable Lasagna with Fresh Pasta (page 228)

Orange-Almond Biscotti (page 131)

Espresso

■ ■ ■

Spinach Salad with Grapefruit
and Avocado (page 65)

Caramelized Onion Tart (page 161)

Pesto Mashed Potatoes (page 151)
or Israeli Couscous with Tomato
and Scallions (page 150)

Steamed Green Beans

Upside-Down Caramelized Apple Cake (page 262)

■ ■ ■

White Bean and Roasted Red Pepper Spread
(page 31) with Basic Crostini (page 39) or
sliced French bread

Tossed Mesclun Salad (page 62)

Pasta with Pesto-Cream Sauce
and Toasted Pine Nuts (page 206)

Lemon Tart (page 271)

■   ■   ■

Spinach Salad with Oranges,
Feta Cheese, and Olives (page 62)

Baked Vegetable Polenta (page 231)

Lemon Almond Cake (page 259)

■   ■   ■

Portobello Mushroom Pâté
(page 32) on toast points

Mixed Greens with Dried Cranberries
and Toasted Pecans (page 62)

Penne alla Vodka (page 211)

Upside-Down Pear Gingerbread (page 261)

■   ■   ■

Classic Guacamole (page 36) with corn chips

Tossed Mesclun Salad (page 62)

Classic Vegetarian Enchiladas (page 218)

Classic Lemon Poppy Seed Cake (page 264)

■   ■   ■

Mixed Greens with Dried Cranberries
and Toasted Pecans (page 62)

Spinach Lasagna with a
Tomato Cream Sauce (page 230)

Parmesan Garlic Bread (page 132)

Lemon Almond Cake (page 259)

■   ■   ■

Beet Salad with Goat Cheese
and Walnuts (page 67)

Leek Tart (page 164)

Wasabi Mashed Potatoes (page 151)

Steamed carrots

Upside-Down Pear Gingerbread (page 261)

SUMMER MENUS

Provençal Green Bean Salad (page 68)

Spinach and Pesto Tart (page 162)

French bread

Peach and Raspberry Crisp (page 273)

■   ■   ■

Classic Tzatziki (page 36) with hot pita triangles

Curried Rice Salad with Almonds and Grapes
(page 80)

Blueberry Crisp (page 273)

■   ■   ■

Classic Summer Tomato Salad (page 67)

Rice, Red Lentil, and
Wheat Berry Salad (page 79)

French bread

White Chocolate and
Raspberry Cheesecake (page 267)

■   ■   ■

Marinated Olives (page 40)

Garlic and Oil Dipping Sauce
for Tuscan-Style Bread (page 37)

Tuscan-Style Couscous Salad (page 81)

Rhubarb Cobbler (page 272)

■   ■   ■

White Bean Spread with Lemon and Mint
(page 32) with Garlic Pita Chips (page 39)
or sliced French bread

Szechuan Noodles with Green Beans and
Cashews (page 76)

Easy Strawberry-Rhubarb Tart (page 269)

■　■　■

Classic Hummus (page 29)
with hot pita triangles

Classic Tabbouli (page 78)

Broccoli and Roasted
Red Pepper Salad (page 69)

Lemon Almond Cake (page 259)

■　■　■

Smoked Cheese and Sun-dried Tomato Spread
(page 34) with Garlic Pita Chips (page 39)
or crackers

Summer Chickpea, Tomato,
and Spinach Salad (page 85)

Tuscan-style bread or French bread

Easy Strawberry-Rhubarb Tart (page 269)

■　■　■

Composed Salad Platter (page 88)

French bread

Blueberry Crisp (page 273)

■　■　■

Spicy Black Bean Dip (page 35)
with corn chips

Marinated Penne Salad with Green Beans and
Tomatoes (page 82)

Parmesan Garlic Bread (page 132)

Strawberry and Chocolate "Pizza"
(page 270)

■　■　■

HOLIDAY MENUS

A Thanksgiving Feast

Portobello Mushroom Pâté (page 32)
on Basic Crostini (page 39)

Butternut Squash and Cider Soup (page 49)

Mixed Greens with Dried Cranberries
and Toasted Pecans (page 62)

Classic Mock Meat Loaf (page 240)

Wasabi Mashed Potatoes (page 151)
or Pesto Mashed Potatoes (page 151)

Sweet Potato, White Bean,
and Pepper Tian (page 237)

Angel Biscuits (page 100)

Upside-Down Pear Gingerbread (page 261)

A Christmas Celebration

White Bean and Roasted Red Pepper Spread
(page 31) with Garlic Pita Chips (page 39)

Leafy Greens and Radicchio with Shaved
Parmesan Cheese (page 63)

Shiitake Mushroom Tarts in Puff Pastry (page
167)

Orzo Pilaf (page 148)

Zucchini and Red Pepper Gratin (page 155)

Angel Biscuits (page 100)

White Chocolate and
Raspberry Cheesecake (page 267)

Easter Dinner

Classic Tzatziki (page 36)
with hot pita bread triangles

Roasted Asparagus with Garlic Oil, Lemon, and
Parmesan Cheese (page 66)

Fresh Linguine with Vegetables and Pine Nuts in
a Tomato-Cream Sauce (page 208)

Lemon Tart (page 271)

Index

Index

Index